Rick Steves
FOR THE LOVE OF
EUROPE

Hachette Book Group
1700 Fourth Street
Berkeley, CA 94710

Text © 2020 by Rick Steves' Europe, Inc.
All rights reserved.
Map © 2020 by Rick Steves' Europe, Inc.
All rights reserved.

Printed in China by RRD
First Edition.
Third printing December 2020.

ISBN 978-1-64171-131-9

For the latest on Rick's talks, guidebooks, tours, public television series, and public radio show, contact Rick Steves' Europe, 130 Fourth Avenue North, Edmonds, WA 98020, tel. 425/771-8303, www.ricksteves.com, rick@ricksteves.com.

RICK STEVES' EUROPE

Special Publications Manager: Risa Laib

Graphic Content Director: Sandra Hundacker

Photo Editors: Rhonda Pelikan, Rich Sorensen

Maps: David C. Hoerlein

AVALON TRAVEL

Editorial Director: Kevin McLain

Senior Editor and Series Manager: Madhu Prasher

Associate Managing Editors: Jamie Andrade, Sierra Machado

Copy Editor: Maggie Ryan

Proofreader: Elizabeth Jang

Cover Design: Gopa & Ted2, Inc.

Interior Design & Production: Gopa & Ted2, Inc.

Map: Kat Bennett

Although every effort was made to ensure that the information was correct at the time of going to press, the author and publisher do not assume and hereby disclaim any liability to any party for any loss or damage caused by errors, omissions, stinky cheese, or any potential travel disruption due to labor or financial difficulty, whether such errors or omissions result from negligence, accident, or any other cause.

Contents

Rick Steves' TV Clips Illustrate Articles

Many of the places and experiences described in this book are featured in short, broadcast-quality video clips, excerpted from my Rick Steves' Europe public television series, and free to view in my "Rick Steves Classroom Europe" program (www.classroom.ricksteves.com). It's quick, easy, and fun. To get started, see page 389.

On the road at an early age

Introduction

Falling in Love with Europe

Since I was a teenager, I've been living three or four months a year out of my backpack in Europe. An entire generation has grown up and had kids since I slept on my first train, saw my first Michelangelo, and climbed my first ruined castle.

Today, seeing young backpackers enjoying the same European thrills I did 45 years ago is one of the simple joys of my travels. Sure, things have changed a lot. But the essence of good travel—the delights of being on the road in Europe—remains wonderfully the same: exciting, eye-opening, and forever new.

Before I started writing guidebooks, I traveled purely for fun. But I still wrote. In fact, I wrote like a fiend, jamming postcards with captured memories . . . filling thick "empty books" with densely written pages. As I

Journaling enthusiastically, I was a travel writer in training.

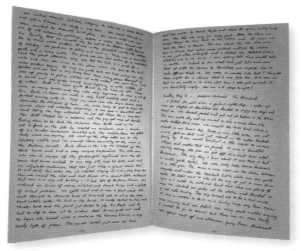
My early journals illustrated how there was plenty to write about.

ran out of pages and the travel experiences kept flowing, I had to write smaller and smaller so the entire trip would fit in one volume. Like a child might leap to net a butterfly, I needed to capture each little joy.

A young traveler recently sent me the journal of her first European adventure. While it was penned half a lifetime after my first journal, the thrills, laughs, and eurekas she shared were much the same.

While I first wrote journals for fun, now I write guidebooks for work. But with this book, I go back to my early days of writing simply out of a love for Europe. I want to share with you the places, people, and experi-

Hotel rooms make a fine office for writing guidebooks.

I'm still—and always—in love with Europe.

ences I've enjoyed over all these years—to inspire you to connect more intimately with other people and other cultures.

I've done a lot of hitting and a lot of missing in Europe over the years—that's my job. With this book, I bring home just the hits: an all-day walk on an alpine ridge, a sword-fern fantasy in a ruined castle, a friendly swing with a bell-ringer in a church spire. Together, we'll savor the quiet thrill that comes with discovering lonesome stone circles. We'll shake our shoulders dancing at a Turkish tea party. And we'll sweat with a sauna full of Finns.

I stopped collecting physical souvenirs decades ago. This book is the treasure chest of souvenirs gathered since—memories of a lifetime spent enjoying my favorite continent. I share them in hopes that the experiences that carbonated my travels will inspire a few extra bubbles in yours, too. And I share them . . . for the love of Europe.

Rick Steves

Portugal and Spain

IBERIA—the peninsula that hosts Spain and Portugal—is cut off from the rest of Europe by the Pyrenees Mountains. In fact, I remember a time when you had to change trains at the Spanish-French border, because the Iberian rail gauge was different than the European standard. In the 20th century, that geographical isolation was amped up by fascist dictators (Franco in Spain, Salazar in Portugal) who stayed in power for decades, preaching a nationalism that preferred a closed door to the rest of the world. The result was a sluggish economy and a sense of isolation.

Today, while Iberia is racing toward the future as if to make up for lost time, those historical differences have resulted in a time warp for travelers. With their glory days long gone and their once-mighty empires a distant memory, both the Spanish and the Portuguese are understandably nostalgic.

The Iberian flair for tradition is evident in Portugal's black-clad fisherwomen's blues and the salty cuisine fostered by so many of those lost fishermen. In Spain, you'll see it vividly in fiery flamenco, rooted in Roma culture and Islam. *Machismo* is still on parade in the bullring. A deep-seated Catholicism prods pilgrims to trek to Santiago and cloistered nuns to put sugar and egg whites to tasty use.

Not far across the Strait of Gibraltar, Morocco provides a tantalizing peek at how modern times also co-exist with tradition in Africa and Islam.

Toledo, the spiritual, artistic, and historic capital of Spain

Fado: The Lisbon Blues

I<small>T'S AFTER DARK</small> in Lisbon's ramshackle Alfama neighborhood. Old-timers gather in restaurants, which serve little more than grilled sardines, to hear and sing Portugal's mournful fado: traditional ballads of lament.

I grab the last chair in a tiny place, next to two bearded men hunched over their mandolins, lost in their music. A bald singer croons, looking like an old turtle without a shell. There's not a complete set of teeth in the house. A spry grandma does a little jive, balancing a wine bottle on her head. The kitchen staff peers from a steaming hole in the wall, backlit by their flaming grill. The waiter sets a plate of fish and a pitcher of cheap cask wine on my table and—like a Portuguese Ed Sullivan—proudly introduces the next singer, a woman who's been singing here for more than 50 years.

She's the star: blood-red lipstick, big hair, a mourning shawl over her black dress. Towering above me, flanked by those mandolins, she's a fusion of moods—old and young, both sad and sexy. Her revealing

Lisbon's Alfama neighborhood spills down to the sea.

Fado is sung from the heart.

neckline promises there's life after death. I can smell her breath as she drowns out the sizzle of sardines with her plush voice.

The man next to me whispers in my ear a rough English translation of the words she sings. It's a quintessential fado theme of lost sailors and sad widows: "O waves of the salty sea, where do you get your salt? From the tears shed by the women in black on the sad shores of Portugal." Suddenly it's surround-sound as the diners burst into song, joining the chorus.

Fado is the folk music of Lisbon's rustic neighborhoods: so accessible to anyone willing to be out late and stroll the back streets. Since the mid-1800s, it's been the Lisbon blues—mournfully beautiful and haunting ballads about long-gone sailors, broken hearts, and bittersweet romance. Fado means "fate"—how fate deals with Portugal's adventurers . . . and the families they leave behind. The lyrics reflect the pining for a loved one across the water, hopes for a future reunion, remembrances of a rosy past, or dreams of a better future. It's the yearning for what might have been if fate had not intervened. While generally sad, fado can be jaunty . . . in a nostalgic way.

The songs are often in a minor key. The singer (*fadista*) is accompanied by stringed instruments, including a 12-string *guitarra portuguesa*

Fado embraces life—sadness and all.

with a round body like a mandolin (or, as the man whispering in my ear said, "like a woman"). Fado singers typically crescendo into the first word of the verse, like a moan emerging from deep inside. Though the songs are often sorrowful, the singers rarely overact—they plant themselves firmly and sing stoically in the face of fate.

While fado has become one of Lisbon's favorite late-night tourist traps, I can still find funky bars—without the high prices and big-bus tour groups—that feel very local. Two districts, the Alfama and the Bairro Alto, have small, informal fado restaurants for late dinners or even later evenings of drinks and music. Handwritten "fado tonight" (*fado esta noite*) signs in Portuguese are good news, but even a restaurant filled with tourists can serve up fine fado with its sardines.

After thanking the man who'd translated the songs for me, I leave the bar late that night feeling oddly uplifted. An evening seasoned with the tears of black-clad widows reminds me that life, even salty with sadness, is worth embracing.

Seaside Traditions in Portugal's Nazaré

Settling into a grungy fishermen's bar in the beach town of Nazaré, I order a plate of barnacles. Yes, barnacles—called *percebes* here. My waiter is happy to demonstrate how to eat them: dig your thumb between the shell and the leathery skin to rip the skin off. The meat stays attached to the shell. Bite that off victoriously and wash it down with local beer. Fresh barnacles are expensive, as they cling to rocks in the turbulent waves along the coast and are difficult and dangerous to harvest. Savoring my plate of barnacles at sundown, I gaze out at the surf attacking that stark bluff. Because I know that's where they were gathered just hours ago, investing in a plate of barnacles feels like money well spent. I'm enjoying the endearing charms of unassuming Nazaré being itself.

Perched on a far corner of Europe, Nazaré is one of my favorite beach towns anywhere. It greets me with the energetic applause of the surf, widows with rooms to rent, and fishermen mending nets. This fishing-town-turned-tourist-retreat, set between cork groves and eucalyptus

Nazaré hugs its wide beach on the Atlantic.

Barnacles: Rip, bite, enjoy with beer.

trees and the open sea, is a place to relax in the sun. I join a world of
ladies in petticoats and men who still stow cigarettes and fishhooks in
their stocking caps.

Though many locals seem older than most of its buildings, the town
feels like a Portuguese Coney Island—humming with young people who
flock here for the beach. Off-season, it's almost tourist-free—the perfect
time to take in the wild surf and get a feel for a traditional way of life.

The town's layout is simple: a grid of skinny streets with sun-bleached
apartment blocks stretching away from an expansive beach. The
beach—in many places as wide as a soccer field—sweeps from the new
harbor in the south to stark cliffs in the north.

It seems that most of Nazaré's 15,000 inhabitants are in the tourist
trade. But somehow traditions survive and it's not hard to find pockets
of vivid and authentic culture. I stroll through the market and wander the back streets where people happily trade ocean views for a little
shade. Laundry flaps in the wind, kids ride plastic trikes, and fish sizzle
over tiny curbside hibachis.

Nazaré is famous for its traditionally clad women who—at least according to local lore—wear skirts with seven petticoats. Is that one for each day, or for the seven colors of the rainbow, or . . . ? Make up your own legend. While the story you'll hear may be an invention for the tourists, it contains an element of truth. In the old days, women would wait on the beach for their fishermen to sail home. To keep warm in the face of a cold sea wind, they'd wear several petticoats so they could fold layers over their heads, backs, and legs as needed. Even today, older and more traditional women wear skirts made bulky by several—but maybe not seven—petticoats. The ensemble—with boldly clashing colors—is completed with house slippers, a hand-embroidered apron, woolen cape, head scarf, and flamboyant jewelry, including chunky gold earrings (often passed down from mother to daughter).

People-watching here is like going to a living art gallery. The beach, tasty seafood, and a funicular ride are the bright lights of my lazy memories. The funicular—which leads from the beach up to the Sitio neighborhood atop the cliffs—was built in 1889, the same year as the Eiffel Tower (and was designed by a disciple of Eiffel).

Women in Nazaré traditionally layer petticoats for warmth.

Folk dancers perform on the seaside boardwalk.

Sitio, with its own church, museum, and main square, feels like a separate village. Marking a rocky viewpoint high above Nazaré, a stone memorial honors the explorer Vasco da Gama, who stopped here before leaving Europe for India. Next to that, a little chapel marks the spot where a much-venerated statue of the Black Madonna was hidden in the rocks throughout four centuries of Muslim Moorish rule before it was rediscovered during the 12th-century Christian Reconquista. (When it comes to enjoying legends like these, gullibility is a skill that serves me well.)

Back down along the beach, a local folk-music group plays and dances. This troupe—with petticoats twirling to the beat of a percussion section of bongo gourds and extra-large pinecones grating against each other—has been kicking up sand since 1934.

When these dancers were younger, the vast beach was littered with colorful fishing boats that were hauled in by oxen or teams of fishermen. But ever since a new harbor was built south of town, the working boats have been moored out of sight. Today, only a few historic vessels remain, ornamenting the sand. On the boardwalk—an artful and traditional mosaic pavement of black and white stones—squadrons of sun-dried and salted fish are stretched out on nets left under the midday sun. Locals claim they're delicious . . . but I'd rather eat barnacles.

Esperanza in Évora

Alentejo is a vast and arid land—the bleak interior of Portugal, where cork seems to be the dominant industry. The rolling hills are covered with stubby cork trees. With their bark peeled away, they remind me of St. Bartolomeo, the martyr who was skinned alive. Like him, these trees suffer in silence.

The people of Alentejo are uniformly short. They seem to look at tourists with suspicion and are the butt of jokes in this corner of Europe. Libanio, my guide, circles the words "arid" and "suspicious" in my guidebook and does his best to turn my chapter into a promo for his dusty and downtrodden region. He says, "Must you say 'arid'? Actually, in April, it is a lush countryside." Then he adds, "But I won't argue with 'suspicious.'"

Libanio says it is a mark of a people's character to laugh at themselves. He then tells me of an Alentejo man who nearly succeeded in teaching his burro to live without eating. He was so excited . . . until his burro died.

Évora's main square

Libanio asks me, "How can you tell a worker is done for the day in Alentejo?" I say, "I don't know." He says, "When he takes his hands out of his pockets." My guide continues more philosophically: "In your land, time is money. Here in Alentejo, time is time. We take things slow and enjoy ourselves."

While this corner of Portugal is humble, there's a distinct pride here. Every country has its Appalachia. I'm impressed when a region that others are inclined to insult has strong local pride, though I often wonder if it's genuine pride, or just making the best of the cards they're dealt.

For Alentejanos, quality and authenticity require the respect of tradition. The finest restaurants simply do not embellish a standard rustic dish. And they love their sweets so much that they seem to know the history of each tart.

Nuns sell sweets.

Many pastries are called "convent sweets." Portugal, with its vast empire, once had access to more sugar than any other European country. Even so, sugar was so expensive that only the aristocracy could afford to enjoy it routinely. Historically, many daughters of aristocrats who were unable to marry into suitably noble families ended up in high-class convents. Life there was comfortable, yet carefully controlled. Instead of sex, they could covet cakes and indulge in sweets. Over time, the convents became famous as keepers of wondrous secret recipes for exquisite pastries generally made from sugar and egg yolks (which were leftovers from the whites used to starch their habits). *Barrigas de Freiras* (Nuns' Tummies) and *Papos de Ango* (Angel's Breasts) are two such fancies.

Évora, the workaday capital of the region, is a fine place to taste the delights of Alentejo—both edible and historic, as well as musical and social.

Évora has barely any buildings over three stories high, but it is crowned by the granite Corinthian columns of a stately yet ruined ancient Roman temple. And just outside of town stand 92 stones three times as old as that, erected to make a Stonehenge-type celestial calendar.

I'm happy to find a romantic little restaurant that offers live fado music three nights a week. Esperanza, the woman who runs the place, explains that she likes the diners to be finished by 10 p.m. so the musicians can perform without waiters wandering around. I am impressed by her commitment to the art.

I sit in the back, enjoying the ambience. It's been a long day, so during some applause, I sneak back out and head home. When I'm half a block away, Esperanza runs out the door and charges after me. I worry that she's angry that I left without paying a cover charge, or that the door made too much noise, or that I had insulted the musicians. Like a guilty little boy, I nearly duck down an alley and run away. Then I decide to turn back and face the music.

She apologizes for not welcoming me and begs me to come back for a glass of port and to meet the musicians. The rest of the evening is a plush experience—complete with nuns' tummies and angel's breasts. Esperanza—whose name means "hope"—keeps the art of fado singing alive in Évora.

Évora's ancient Roman temple

Portugal's Sunny Salema

T<small>HE FLATBED</small> fish truck rambles into the village tooting the "1812 Overture" on its horn. Today's my beach day and I was ready to just sleep in. But it's market day in Salema and the parking lot that separates the jogging shorts from the black shawls fills up, one vehicle at a time, with horn-tooting merchants. First the fish truck rolls in, then the bakery trailer steaming with fresh bread, followed by a fruit-and-vegetable truck, and finally a five-and-dime truck for clothing and odds and ends. Groggy yet happy, I quickly get dressed and join the scene—savoring one of the last true villages on the Algarve.

Any place famous as a "last undiscovered tourist frontier" probably no longer is. But the Algarve of my dreams survives—just barely. It took me three tries to find it. West of Lagos, Luz and Burgau both offered only a corpse of a fishing village, bikini-strangled and Nivea-creamed. Then, just as darkness turned couples into peaceful silhouettes, I found Salema.

It's my kind of resort: three beachside streets, a dozen restaurants, a few hotels, time-share condos up the road, a couple of bars, English

Salema's fishermen share their beach with travelers.

Salema fisherman

and German menus, a classic beach with a paved promenade, and endless sun.

Where a small road hits the beach on Portugal's southwestern tip, Salema is an easy 15-mile bus ride from the closest train station in Lagos. Still a fishing village—but only barely—Salema has a split personality: The whitewashed old town is for residents, and the more utilitarian other half was built for tourists.

Residents and tourists pursue a policy of peaceful coexistence at the beach. Tractors pull in and push out the fishing boats, two-year-olds toddle in the waves, topless women read German fashion mags, and old men really do mend the nets. British and German connoisseurs of lethargy laze in the sun, while locals grab the shade.

While the days of black-clad widows chasing topless Nordic women off the beach are gone, nudity is still risqué. Over the rocks and beyond the view of prying eyes, Germans grin and bare it.

Unwritten tradition allocates different chunks of undersea territory to each Salema family. While the fishermen's hut on the beach no longer hosts a fish auction, it provides shade for the old-timers arm-wrestling octopi out of their traps. The pottery jars stacked everywhere are traps, which are tied about a yard apart in long lines and dropped offshore. Octopi, looking for a cozy place to set an ambush, climb inside, unaware they've made their last mistake.

The wives of fishermen serve up whatever's caught in huge pots of Portugal's beloved seafood stew *(cataplana)* in steamy hole-in-the-wall eateries, where tourists slurp it up.

Salema's tourist-based economy sits on a foundation of sand. As locals watch their sandy beach wash away each winter, they hope and pray it will return with spring.

Restaurateurs are allowed to build a temporary, summer-only

Fishing boats pulled up on Salema's beach

beachside restaurant if they provide a lifeguard and run a green/yellow/red warning-flag system for swimmers. The Atlântico Restaurant, which dominates Salema's beach, takes its responsibility seriously—providing lifeguards and flags through the summer . . . and fresh seafood by candlelight all year long.

Tourism chases the sun and quaint folksiness. And the folksiness survives only with the help of tourist dollars. Fishermen boost their income by renting spare bedrooms *(quartos)* to the ever-growing stream of tan fans from Europe's drizzly North. *Quartos* line Salema's main residential street, offering simple rooms with showers, springy beds, and glorious Atlantic views.

Salema's sleepy beauty kidnaps my momentum. At the end of the day, after enjoying a nice plate of fish, I take a glass of white wine from Atlântico and sip it with the sunset. Nearby, a withered old woman shells almonds with a railroad spike, dogs roam the beach like they own it, and a man catches short fish with a long pole. Beyond him is Cape Sagres—500 years ago, it was the edge of the world. As far as the gang sipping port and piling olive pits in the beachside bar is concerned, it still is.

Arcos de la Frontera: Pickles, Nuns, and Donkeys in the Bell Tower

I'M IN the little hill town of Arcos de la Frontera, just south of Sevilla. Today, my goal is to connect with the culture of small-town Spain.

The entertaining market is my first stop. The pickle woman encourages me to try a *banderilla,* named for the bangled spear that a matador sticks into the bull. As I gingerly slide an onion off the tiny skewer of pickled olives, onions, and carrots, she tells me to eat it all at once—the pickle equivalent of throwing down a shot of vodka. *Explosivo!* The lady in the adjacent meat stall bursts into laughter at my shock.

Like the pickle section, the meat stall—or *salchichería*—is an important part of any Spanish market. In Spain, ever since Roman times, December has been the month to slaughter pigs. After the slaughter, they salt and dry every possible bit of meat into various sausages, hams, and pork products. By late spring, that now-salty meat is cured, able to withstand the heat, and hanging in tempting market displays. Ham

Arcos, where locals "see the backs of the birds as they fly"

appreciation is big here. The word to know: *jamón*. When in Spain, I am a *jamón* aficionado.

Arcos smothers its hilltop, tumbling down all sides like the train of a wedding dress. The labyrinthine old center is a photographer's feast. I can feel the breeze funnel through the narrow streets as drivers pull in car mirrors to squeeze through.

Residents brag that only they see the backs of the birds as they fly. To see what they mean, I climb to the viewpoint at the main square, high in the old town. Bellying up to the railing—the town's suicide jumping-off point—I look down and ponder the fancy cliffside hotel's erosion concerns, orderly orange groves, flower-filled greenhouses, fine views toward Morocco . . . and the backs of the birds as they fly.

Exploring the town, I discover that a short walk from Arcos' church of Santa María to the church of San Pedro (St. Peter) is littered with subtle but fun glimpses into the town's past.

The church of Santa María faces the main square. After Arcos was reconquered from the Moors in the 13th century, the church was built—atop a mosque. In the pavement is a 15th-century magic circle: 12 red and 12 white stones—the white ones represent various constellations. When a child came to the church to be baptized, the parents would stop here first for a good Christian exorcism. The exorcist would stand inside the protective circle and cleanse the baby of any evil spirits. This was also a holy place back in Muslim times. While Christian residents no longer use it, Islamic Sufis still come here on pilgrimage every November.

Arches buttress buildings during earthquakes.

In 1699, an earthquake cracked the church's foundation. Today, arches reach over the narrow lane—added to prop the church against neighboring buildings. Thanks to these braces, the church survived the bigger earthquake of 1755. All over town, similar arches support earthquake-damaged structures.

Today, the town rumbles only when the bulls run. Señor González Oca's little barbershop is plastered with posters of bulls running Pamplona-style through the streets of Arcos during Holy Week. Locals still remember an American from the nearby Navy base at Rota, who was killed by a bull in 1994.

Walking on toward St. Peter's, Arcos' second church, I pass Roman columns stuck onto street corners—protection from reckless donkey carts. St. Peter's was, until recently, home to a resident bellman who lived in the spire. He was a basketmaker and a colorful character—famous for bringing his donkey up into the tower. The donkey grew too big to get back out. Finally, the bellman had no choice but to kill the donkey—and eat it.

The small square in front of the church—about the only flat piece of pavement around—serves as the old-town soccer field for neighborhood kids.

I step across the street from the church and into a cool dark bar filled with very short old guys. Any Spanish man over a certain age spent his growth-spurt years trying to survive the brutal Civil War (1936–39). Those who did, struggled. That generation is a head shorter than Spaniards of the next.

In the bar, the men—side-lit like a Rembrandt portrait—are fixated on the TV, watching the finale of a long series of bullfights. El Cordobés is fighting. His father, also El Cordobés, was the Babe Ruth of bullfighting. El Cordobés uses his dad's name even though his dad sued in an effort to stop him.

Marveling at the bar's cheap list of wines and hard drinks, I order a Cuba Libre for about $2. The drink comes tall and stiff, with a dish of peanuts.

Suddenly the room gasps. I can't believe the vivid scene on the screen. El Cordobés has been hooked and is flung, doing a cartwheel over the angry bull's head. The gang roars as El Cordobés lands in a heap and buries his head in his arms as the bull tramples and tries to gore him. The TV replays the scene many times, each time drawing gasps in the bar.

El Cordobés survives and—no surprise—eventually kills the bull. As he makes a victory lap, picking up bouquets tossed by adoring fans, the camera zooms in on the rip exposing his hip and a long bloody wound. The short men around me will remember and talk about this moment for years to come.

But at the convent, located piously on the next corner, no one notices. Its windows are striped with heavy bars and spikes, as if to protect the cloistered nuns from the bull bar's hedonism. Popping into the dimly lit foyer, I push the buzzer and the creaky lazy Susan spins, revealing a bag of freshly baked cookies for sale. When I spin back the cookies with a "no, *gracias*," she surprises me with a few words of English—countering, in a Monty Python-esque voice, "We have cupcakes as well." I buy a bag of cupcakes to support the mission work of the convent. I glimpse— through the not-quite one-way mirror—the not-meant-to-be-seen sister in her flowing robe and habit momentarily appear and disappear.

Saving my appetite for dinner, I dole out my cupcakes to children as I wander on. My town walk culminates at another convent—which now houses the best restaurant in town, Restaurante El Convento. María Moreno Moreno, the proud owner, explains the menu. (Spanish children take the name of both parents—who in María's case must have been distant cousins.) As church bells clang, she pours me a glass of *vino tinto con mucho cuerpo* (full-bodied red wine) from the Rioja region.

Asking for top-quality ham, I get a plate of *jamón ibérico*. María explains that, while quite expensive, it's a worthy investment. Made from acorn-fed pigs with black feet, it actually does taste better, with a bouquet of its own and a sweet aftertaste. It goes just right with my full-bodied red wine.

I tell María that the man at the next table looks like El Cordobés. One glance and she says, "El Cordobés is much more handsome." When I mention his recent drama, she nods and says, "It's been a difficult year for matadors."

Strolling Córdoba's Back Streets

WANDERING the Art Deco streets of Córdoba in southern Spain, I'm drawn to a commotion on a square. It's almost midnight and everyone's out, savoring a cool evening. The short men around me all seem to have raspy tobacco voices and big bellies they call *curvas de felicidad* (happiness curves). As the men jostle and bark, parents gather, nodding with approval, as a dozen little schoolgirls rattle a makeshift stage . . . working on their sultry. Even with a very modern young generation, flamenco culture thrives.

Córdoba is known mostly for its Mezquita, a vast mosque with a cathedral built into its middle. That Mezquita, one of the glories of Moorish Spain, is surrounded by a zone of shops and restaurants that seems designed for big tour groups. Beyond that, there are almost no crowds. And late at night there are even fewer tourists.

Avoiding tourist crowds is important these days—especially when traveling in peak season. Because I eat late and don't mind the smoke, I'm

Córdoba's back streets are a delight to explore.

surrounded only by happy locals. I've noticed that in Spain, a restaurant recommended in all the guidebooks is filled with Americans at eight or nine o'clock, but by 10 p.m., the tourists head for their hotels and the locals retake their turf. Suddenly "touristy" restaurants are filled with eager local diners. I've also noticed that some restaurateurs are pleased to have their best eating zone be the smoking zone. The intended result: a hardy local following . . . with very few tourists.

Just wandering the back streets leaves me all alone with the town. Exploring the residential back lanes of old Córdoba, I catch an evocative whiff of the old town before the recent affluence hit.

Streets are narrow—designed to provide much-appreciated shade. To keep things even cooler, walls are whitewashed and thick—providing a kind of natural air-conditioning. To counter the boring whitewash, doors and windows are colorful. Iron grilles providing security cover the windows—a reminder of the persistent gap through the ages between rich and poor. Stone bumpers on corners protect buildings from crazy drivers. As elsewhere in Andalucía, they're made from scavenged secondhand ancient Roman pillars. Lanes are made of river-stone cobbles: cheap and local. In the middle of lanes are drains, flanked by smooth stones that stay dry for pedestrians. Remnants of old towers—the stubs of lopped-off minarets—survive, built into today's structures. Muslim Córdoba peaked in the 10th century with an estimated 400,000 people . . . and lots of now-mostly-gone neighborhood mosques.

In Córdoba, patios are taken very seriously. That's especially clear

Locals proudly show off their patios.

each May, when a fiercely competitive contest is held to pick the city's most picturesque. Patios, a common feature of houses throughout Andalucía, have a long history here. The Romans used them to cool off and the Moors added lush, decorative touches. The patio functioned as a quiet outdoor living room, an oasis from the heat. Inside elaborate iron-

Conquering Christians built a cathedral in the middle of Córdoba's Mezquita (mosque).

work gates, roses, geraniums, and jasmine spill down whitewashed walls, while fountains gargle and caged birds sing. Some patios are owned by individuals, some are communal courtyards for several homes, and some grace public buildings like museums or convents.

Today, homeowners take pride in these mini paradises, and have no problem sharing them. As I stroll Córdoba's back streets, I pop my head through any wooden door that's open. The owners (who keep their inner black iron gates locked) enjoy showing off their picture-perfect patios.

Well after midnight, my cultural scavenger hunt is over and the city finally seems quiet. I climb into my bed. Just as I doze off, a noisy and multigenerational parade rumbles down the cobbled lane that I thought promised a good night's sleep. Standing in my underwear and wrapped in the drapes, I peer secretively out my window. Below, a band of guitars and castanets with a choir of those raspy tobacco voices funnels down my narrow alley. Grandmothers—guardians of a persistent culture—make sure the children pick up their Andalusian traditions. I feel like a Peeping Tom . . . until one woman looks up at me, catches my eye, and seems to nod as if satisfied that I am witnessing the persevering richness of their traditional culture.

Hair-Trigger Flamenco in Andalucía

O N A RECENT TV shoot, I was reminded that in Spain's Andalucía region, revelry and religiosity go hand in hand. The same passion and energy dedicated to partying is put into long, solemn religious processions that clog the narrow streets of its towns and cities.

We were filming a dinner at a restaurant in Córdoba with Isabel, a charming local guide who talks about food with the passion of a mother talking about her children. With the olive oil, the lighting, and her love of the cuisine all just right, every plate seemed to twinkle and shine. The meal was made to order for TV: a montage of Spanish delights, from the roasted almonds and spicy green olives that hit the table automatically, to the local *salmorejo* (like a thick, bright orange gazpacho), *boquerones* (anchovies), fried eggplant, and "Arab Salad" with cod and delicate orange sections.

The *rabo de toro* (bull-tail stew) was as dark as meat can be . . . almost inky even in flavor. The *jamón ibérico*—a gift from the restaurant—was introduced as "the best ham in Spain" and very expensive. With its fat not lining the meat but mixed in, it was glistening with flavor. Eating it

Isabel, evangelical about Andalusian cuisine, makes me a believer.

Neighbors celebrate the Festival of the Crosses.

was the culinary equivalent of pinning a boutonniere onto a tux. The wine was the kind that inspires servers to bring out the special glasses.

Feeling underdressed for the filming, I zipped back to our hotel between courses to grab my sweater. On the way, I crossed a square swarming with people partying. When I returned moments later—sweater in hand—the same street was blocked by a religious procession. One minute I was thrilled to be in the restaurant filming all that wonderful food; the next I was amazed we were missing a party in the square, and then I was enthralled by an exotic religious parade in the streets. As a TV producer, I was overwhelmed.

Seeing alcohol-fueled partying around a towering red cross—followed by a somber procession—was poignant and powerful. Everyone ran to the streets to be a part of the religious ceremony. Trumpets blared a fanfare, children carried a homemade float, and candles jostled in unison as the marchers glided in the dark of the night. While I desperately wanted my crew to be filming everything at once, we stayed focused on the meal.

Andalucía is like this. There's always something going on. Isabel explained that we happened to be in Córdoba for the Festival of the Crosses, a competition where each neighborhood parties proudly around its own towering cross made of red carnations. Church bells ring not only a call to prayer, but also a call to fiesta. Locals

The next generation learns the traditions.

enthusiastically use this special day on the church calendar as a spring-
board for a community party.

The next day, the parties were basically over. We finally found one
square in town that was still lively. It was their first year entering the
contest, their cross had won first prize, and it seemed they'd been celebrating ever since. It was a scene of exhausted, hung-over happiness—as
if they'd been eating, drinking, and dancing for 24 hours (which they
probably had). Now the cross was abandoned—missing carnations like
a bum misses his teeth—and the dancing was over. The last of the revelers gathered around the makeshift bar that seemed to provide physical
support for those determined but barely able to carry on. I needed
dancing around the cross for our TV show. Isabel said they were finished
dancing.

But with a simple request, I was able to rouse the exhausted gang
on that little plaza to dance around their tired carnation cross. Within
seconds the energy and magic of the previous night's party had reignited, and the yard was once again thriving with slinky flamenco. Sin-
uous arms, toned torsos and leggy legs, heels with attitude, flowing

For the winners, the party continues until morning.

hair . . . everything churned with a silky Andalusian soul. Like crickets rattling their wings in a mating ritual, Andalusian women—dressed in their peacock finery—fluttered their fans and clicked their castanets.

We'd been in Andalucía for a week, and I realized it's a hair-trigger flamenco society. I like hair-trigger cultures. Just as Austria is eager to waltz and Ireland is always ready for a good folk song, Andalucía is just waiting for the simplest excuse to grab castanets and dance.

With enough dancing filmed, I let the fake party die, and everyone resumed their positions—propped up by the bar. I joined them there to say thanks. They filled a bottle cap with a ritual shot of firewater and gave it to me. As a dozen onlookers watched, I downed it. With my head thrown back, knowing that the camera was rolling and all Andalusian eyes were on me, I was plunged into what seemed like a long silence. I wanted to say something really clever or meaningful. But I could only come up with a cliché. I sang, *"Olé!"* And everyone cheered.

Andalucía celebrates life with soul and with passion.

Madrid: Two Bulls is Plenty

Packed onto Madrid's subway jammed with Spaniards heading for Plaza de Toros, I'm wondering how I'll react to seeing another bullfight—my first in several years. At the last stop, everyone piles out and the escalator pumps us directly up to the looming facade of Madrid's bullring—the biggest in Spain.

It's like going to a baseball game, but rather than peanuts and cracker-jacks, it's pistachios and corn nuts. Bullfights are held on most Sunday evenings, Easter through October. Serious fights with adult matadors are called *corridas de toros*. These are most expensive and often sell out in advance. But now, in summertime, many fights are *novilladas*, with cheaper tickets, younger bulls, and teenage novices doing the killing. My ticket is just $10 because tonight's three bullfighters are *novilladas*. The man in front of me in the ticket line negotiates aggressively for a good seat. I simply say, *"Uno, por favor,"* and end up sitting right next to him.

Bullfighting comes with rituals, pageantry, and brutality.

The ramshackle band seems to be directed by the cymbal player, who claps a relentless rhythm.

It's theater in the round and there are no bad seats; paying more gets you closer to the gore. Traditionally, you could buy seats in the shade or, to save money, seats in the sun. Climate change has put an end to that tradition. This summer, with the hottest temperatures in memory, fights begin at 9 p.m . . . later than in past years, and it's all in the shade.

Bullfights are punctual. At 9:00 sharp, 500 kilos of angry, disoriented bull charges into the arena. Old men sit attentively, like season ticket holders do—ready for the routine ritual, while girls flutter their fans as if aroused by the prancing men. Many Spanish women consider bullfighting sexy, and swoon at the dashing matadors who are literally dressed to kill in the traditional tight pants (with their *partes nobles*—noble parts—usually organized to one side, or, as locals like to say, "farthest from the bull"). It's easy to tell who in the crowd is a Spaniard and who isn't. With each kill, while tourists take photos, local men croak *"Olé!"* like old goats, and Spanish women wave their white hankies.

In Spain, the standard bullfight consists of six bulls (two per matador)—that's two hours of medieval man-vs.-beast madness. Each ritual killing lasts about 20 minutes. Then another bull romps into the arena. You're not likely to see much human blood spilled. Over the last 200 years of bullfighting in Spain, only a handful of matadors have been killed. If a bull does kill a fighter, the next matador comes in to kill the bull. Historically, even the bull's mother is killed, since the evil qualities are assumed to have come from her.

On this visit, the killing—under the sword of rookies—seems to me

The matador nearly always wins.

more pathetic and cruel than ever, and the audience, though mostly Spanish, appears to include more tourists than ever. The scene just doesn't grab me. After two bulls, I leave, feeling a bit wimpy as I pass the ushers at the door. Walking from the arena back to the subway, I realize that I'm among a select little crowd—the lightest of the lightweights in the stadium—of about 20 people out of several thousand, leaving after only a third of the action. We are all tourists, including several American families. At the subway platform, I stand next to a Midwestern family—mom holding daughter's hand and dad holding son's hand. I ask, "Two bulls enough?" The parents nod. The 12-year-old boy sums it up in three words: "That was nasty."

It was nasty. The Spanish bullfight is as much a ritual as it is a sport. Not to acknowledge the importance of the bullfight is to censor a venerable part of Spanish culture. But it also makes a spectacle out of the cruel torture and killing of an animal. Should tourists boycott bullfights? I don't know. I've always been ambivalent about the spectacle, thinking that as a travel writer, I need to report on what exists, rather than judge it and support a boycott. When the event is kept alive by the patronage of tourists, I'll reconsider my reporting. In the meantime, I agree with the boy and his parents: Two bulls is plenty.

Pamplona: Feeling the Breath of the Bull on Your Pants

L IKE A COWBOY at a rodeo, I sit atop my spot on the fence. A loudspeaker declares—first in Spanish, then in English—"Do not touch
the wounded. That is the responsibility of health personnel." A line of
green-fluorescent-vested police sweeps down the street, clearing away
drunks and anyone not fit to run. Then the cleaning crew and their
street-scrubbing truck make one last pass, gathering any garbage and
clearing broken glass. The street—just an hour ago filled with throngs
of all-night revelers—is now pristine, sanitized for a televised spectacle.
It's the annual Running of the Bulls in Pamplona.

Perched on the top timber of the inner of two fences (in the prime
area reserved for press), I wait for the 8:00 rocket. I'm thinking this is
early . . . but for the mob scene craning their necks for the view behind
me, it's late. They've been up all night.

Cameras are everywhere—on remote-controlled robotic arms, vice-
gripped to windowsills, hovering overhead on cranes, and in the hands

Pamplona parties within strict parameters.

And they're off!

of nearly every spectator that makes up the wall of bodies pressed against the thick timber fence behind me.

The street fills with runners. While you can wear anything, nearly everyone is wearing the traditional white pants, white shirt, and red bandana. The scene evokes some kind of cultish clan and a ritual sacrifice. This is the Festival of San Fermín. Fermín was beheaded by the Romans 2,000 years ago, martyred for his faith. The red bandanas evoke his bloody end.

It's three minutes to eight, and the energy surges. The street is so full that if everyone suddenly ran, you'd think they'd simply trip over each other and all stack up, waiting to be minced by angry bulls. The energy continues to build. There are frat-boy runners—courage stoked by booze and by the girls they're determined to impress. And there are serious *mozos*—famous locally for their runs, who've made this scene annually for as long as people can remember. They've surveyed the photos and stats (printed in yesterday's paper) of the six bulls about to be turned loose. They know the quirks of the bulls and have chosen their favorite stretch of the half-mile run. While others are hung over, these *mozos* got a good, solid night's sleep, and are now stretching and prepping mentally.

For serious runners, this is like surfing . . . you hope to catch a good wave and ride it. A good run lasts only 15 or 20 seconds. You know you're really running with the bull when you feel its breath on your pants.

Mozos respect the bull. It represents power, life, and the great wild. Hemingway, who first came to the festival in 1923, understood. He wrote that he enjoyed watching two wild animals run together—one on two legs, the other on four.

It's 8:00 and the sound of the rocket indicates that the bulls are running. The entire scramble takes about two and a half minutes. The adrenaline surges in the crowded street. Everyone wants to run—but not too early. Suddenly, it's as if I'm standing before hundreds of red-and-white human pogo sticks. The sea of people spontaneously begins jumping up and down—trying to see the rampaging bulls to time their flight.

We've chosen to be near the end of the run—200 yards from the arena, where, later today, these bulls will meet their matador. One advantage of a spot near the end is that the bulls should be more spread out, so we can see six go by individually rather than as a herd. But today, they stay together and make the fastest run of the nine-day festival: 2 minutes and 11 seconds.

The bulls rush through, creating pandemonium—a freak wave of humanity pummels the barrier. Panicky boys—no longer macho men—

Spectators watch from fences meant to protect them from rampaging bulls.

The Running of the Bulls . . . and the People

press against my stretch of fence. It's a red-and-white cauldron of desperation: big eyes, scrambling bodies, the ground quaking, someone oozing under the bottom rail.

Then, suddenly, the bulls are gone. People pick themselves up, and it's over. Boarded-up shops reopen, and the timber fences are taken down and stacked. As is the ritual, participants drop into a bar immediately after the running, have breakfast, and together watch the rerun of the entire spectacle on TV—all 131 seconds of it.

While only 15 runners have been killed by bulls over the last century, each year, dozens of people are gored, trampled, or otherwise injured during the event. A *mozo* who falls knows to stay down—it's better to be trampled by six bulls than to be gored by one.

A bull becomes most dangerous when separated from the herd. For this reason, a few steer—castrated bulls that are calmer and slower—are released with the bulls. (There's no greater embarrassment in this

The streets of Pamplona are lively day and night during the Festival of San Fermín.

machismo culture than to think you've run with a bull, only to realize later that you actually ran with a steer.)

After the last bulls run, the rollicking festival concludes at midnight on July 14. Pamplona's townspeople congregate in front of City Hall, light candles, and sing their sad song, "Pobre de Mí": "Poor me, the Fiesta de San Fermín has ended." They tuck away their red bandanas . . . until next year on July 6.

The Camino de Santiago: A Medieval Pilgrimage in Modern Times

STANDING ON the main square of Santiago de Compostela, in front of the towering and gleaming granite facade of its cathedral, a giddy old man whose cuffs are as frayed as his walking stick lays down on the stony pavement and waves his arms and legs—as if making a snow angel. And I'm right there, sharing the joy of pilgrims who've completed the Camino de Santiago (Spanish for "Way of St. James"). With sunburned faces and tattered walking sticks, they triumphantly end their long trek by stepping on a scallop shell carved into the pavement in front of the city's magnificent cathedral.

For over a thousand years, this cathedral in the far northwest corner of Spain has been the ritualistic last stop for pilgrims who've hiked here from churches in Paris and all over Europe. And for a thousand years, pilgrims—standing before this towering cathedral—have been overcome with joy and jubilation.

St. James, Santiago's namesake and symbol, was a Christian evangelist—one of Jesus' original "fishers of men." But judging from the way he's portrayed here, his main activity was beheading Muslims with his busy sword. Propagandistic statues of James are all over town—riding in from heaven to help the Spaniards defeat the Muslim Moors.

Considering how St. James is depicted taking such joy in butchering

Muslims and the importance of Santiago for Christians, it's no wonder police guard the square. Security here has been tight ever since 9/11.

Historians figure the "discovery" of the remains of St. James in Spain was a medieval hoax. It was designed to rally Europe against the Muslim Moors, who had invaded

Spain and were threatening to continue deeper into Europe. With St. James—a.k.a. "the Moor Slayer"—buried in Iberia and that beloved tomb now in Muslim hands, all of Europe would rise up to push the Moors back into Africa . . . which, after a centuries-long "Reconquista," they finally did in 1492.

The scallop shell is the symbol of St. James.

All this commotion dates back about 1,200 years to a monk who followed a field of stars (probably the Milky Way) to this distant corner of Europe and discovered what appeared to be the long-lost tomb of St. James. Church leaders declared that St. James' relics had been found, built a church, and named the place Santiago (St. James) de Compostela (*campo de estrellas,* or "field of stars").

Walking the Way of St. James has changed little over the centuries. The gear still includes a cloak, a floppy hat, a walking stick, a gourd (for drinking from wells), and a scallop shell (symbolizing where you're going).

In recent years, the route has enjoyed a huge renaissance of interest, with nearly 100,000 pilgrims trekking to Santiago last year. Today, most take a month to walk the 450 miles from the French border town of Saint-Jean-Pied-de-Port. The walk itself is a kind of hut-hopping. At regular intervals along the route, humble government-subsidized hostels called *albergues* provide pilgrims a place to rest for the night (bunks are generally free, though a small donation is requested).

In the midst of the Camino, out on a dusty trail pilgrims have trod for a thousand years, I meet pilgrims of all types. Prepackaged groups have clean, matching T-shirts. Each hiker is issued a mass-produced walking stick with a decorative gourd tied to the top and the requisite dangling scallop shell with a brightly painted cross of St. James.

Other pilgrims are part of humbler, ragtag church groups from distant Catholic lands. Resting on a bluff, I'm passed by an otherworldly

The Camino ends at this cathedral, which holds the tomb of St. James.

group that has shuffled all the way from Lithuania to the rhythm of its raspy, amplified chant-leader. Along with their rucksacks, the group carries an old boom box, various statues, and a 10-foot-tall cross. With their intentionally monotonous chant, they trudge slowly out of sight and then out of earshot.

Later, I stop in a medieval village—like so many ghostly quiet villages pilgrims pass all along the route. Its only "shop" is a vending machine cut into a stone wall. An old woman scrubs her laundry, bent over a convenient creek-side spot as her ancestors have for centuries. She ignores a shepherd herding his gangly flock over a narrow bridge.

In this idyllic corner, pilgrims are eager to share their experiences. I meet a New Yorker who has just hiked for days across the vast Spanish plain and learned nothing about life or himself. He is, in his words, "a little pissed off with it all." Then comes a bouncy flower child from Berlin—a 20-year-old girl hiking alone, singing to herself, and radiant with appreciation for this personal journey. She speaks to me as if she were a real saint come to Earth. Talking with her, I feel I've entered a Botticelli painting (and don't want to leave).

An Englishman I meet is doing the trail in three successive years because he can't get enough time away from his 9-to-5 job to do it in one 30-day stretch. While he walks, he reflects on simplicity. Everyone

I meet (except for the one pissed-off guy) is having a richly rewarding time. I keep thinking how a standard RV vacation—with its clever abundance of comforts—couldn't be more different than this chance to be away from the modern world with all that it entails.

Because the last overnight stop on the Camino is just two miles away from the city of Santiago, most pilgrims arrive at the cathedral late in the morning, in time for the midday Mass.

Like a kid follows a parade, I follow the pilgrims as they approach the cathedral. I try to imagine the mindset of a medieval pilgrim, so exhausted yet so triumphant. You've just walked from Paris—about a thousand miles—to reach this holy spot. Your goal: to request the help of St. James in recovering from an illness. Or maybe you've come to honor the wish of a dying relative . . . or to be forgiven for your sins. Whatever the reason, you know the pope promised that any person who walked to Santiago in a Holy Year, confessed their sins, and took communion here would be forgiven.

After weeks of hiking, the spires of the cathedral come into view and jubilation quickens your tired pace. Finally, you stand upon that shell in the pavement to gaze up at the awe-inspiring cathedral. Stepping inside, you squint down the nave and see the statue of St. James that marks his tomb.

Kneeling at the silver tomb, you pray and make your request. Then you climb the stairs behind the altar up to the saint's much-venerated statue—gilded and caked with precious gems. Embracing him from behind while gazing thankfully out over the cathedral, you have completed the Camino de Santiago.

Reaching his goal, a pilgrim is overcome with joy.

Whether you hike the entire route or just the last stretch, it's an experience that will stay with you forever. And, if you need an excuse to be thankful, consider that—unlike your medieval counterpart—you don't need to hike back to Paris.

Tantalizing Tangier

As I STAND on the bow of my ferry, the Rock of Gibraltar disappears in the mist behind me, while the fabled Pillars of Hercules marking Africa appear ahead of me. I enjoy the thought that you encounter more cultural change by taking this hour-long ride from Spain to Morocco than you do by flying all the way from the US to Spain.

For years, when I sailed from Tarifa across the Strait of Gibraltar to Tangier, I braced myself for a city known as the armpit of Morocco. Tangier was long neglected. It was an "international city"—favored by the West and therefore disdained by the previous king of Morocco, who made a point of diverting national investment *away* from Morocco's fourth city.

Hopping off my ferry, I'm eager to get up to date with the city. I've heard that everything changed when the current king, Mohammed VI, took the throne. He believes Tangier should be a great city once again. As a symbolic show of support, the first city he visited after his coronation was Tangier.

A gate in Tangier's old town

Walking out of the port, I see the king's grand-scale restorations—the beach has been painstakingly cleaned, pedestrian promenades have popped up everywhere, and gardens bloom with lush, new greenery. The difference is breathtaking. The city, long exotic, is now likeably exotic.

I hike up to the venerable Hotel Continental, where I stay when visiting. As I check in, flamboyant Jimmy, who's always around and runs the shop adjacent to the lobby, greets me as an old friend. He famously knows every telephone area code in the US. On a visit several years ago, when he asked where I lived, I told him Seattle. He answered "206." This time, knowing we have new area codes, I test him. He asks. I say "Seattle." And Jimmy nails it, saying, "206, 360, and 425."

Hotel Continental takes me back to Bogart days. Gramophones gather dust on dressers under dingy lights. Day after day, a serene woman paints a figure-eight on the loose tiles with her mop.

In the morning, roosters and the call to prayer work together to wake me, along with the rest of this world. When the sun gets high enough to send a rainbow plunging into the harbor amid ferries busily coming and going, I stand on my balcony and survey Tangier kicking into gear.

Tangier's main square, the Grand Socco

Women in colorful flowing robes walk to sweat shops adjacent to the port—happy to earn $15 a day sewing for big-name European clothing lines.

It's a fascinating time for Morocco. The king is modernizing. His queen was a commoner. Moroccans say she's the first queen to be seen in public. They never saw the king's mother. (They don't even know what she looked like.)

Moroccans don't seem to emulate or even care about the United States. Al Jazeera blares on teahouse TVs—with ugly images of American military activities in Islamic countries. But people seem numb to the propaganda. I feel not a hint of animosity toward me as an American—something I had been concerned about.

Ruled by Spain in the 19th century and France in the 20th, Tangier is a rare place where signs are in three languages . . . and English doesn't make the cut (it's Arabic, French, and Spanish). In this Muslim city, you'll find a synagogue, Catholic and Anglican churches, and the town's largest mosque—all within a block of each other.

For little more than the cost of taking a standard tour you can hire a private guide. With the luxury of my own guide, I venture into the old town. He leads me directly into the market. The scene is a wonderland, with everything on sale—except for pork, forbidden to Muslims. Mountains of brilliant olives, a full palette of spices, children with knives happy to perform for my camera. Each animal is slaughtered in accordance with halal: in the name of Allah, with a sharp blade, its head pointed to Mecca, ritually drained of its blood.

Most tourists I see on the streets are with large groups day-tripping over from Spain. A typical day-trip tour includes the round-trip ferry crossing and a guide who meets you at the port. All offer the same five-hour experience: a city bus tour, the famous ride-a-camel stop, a drive through the ritzy palace neighborhood, a walk through the market, a quick bit of snake charming, a visit to a sales-starved carpet shop, and lunch.

With my private guide, I walk essentially the same route and catch the same colorful glimpses of traditional folk culture. But I'm free to skip the tiresome photo ops, the kickback-oriented shopping stops, and the tourist-trap lunch spot. I visit places that can't handle large groups. And I enjoy the services of a knowledgeable and English-speaking local friend all to myself. He swats away hustlers and other guides.

While the tangled lanes of old Tangier are a cauldron of activity, roof-top teahouses let you enjoy a privileged tranquility while eavesdropping on all the commotion. Perched like a sultan, I sip chai—my chipped antique glass filled with tea leaves, steaming water, and lots of sugar, as locals like it. Below us a tour group passes, walking in a tight single-file. Clutching their purses and day bags nervously to their bellies like paranoid kangaroos, they trundle past one last gauntlet of street merchants hoping only to get safely back onto their ferry and "home" to Europe. I'm so comfortable, and they are so nervous and embattled. The scene seems pathetic, reminding me of some kind of self-inflicted hostage crisis.

Do yourself a favor: Visit Tangier . . . but not as part of a tour group.

France

FRANCE is a laboratory for high culture: art, fashion, cuisine, wine. It's no wonder that my favorite French memories feature Europe's ultimate window shopping, its most venerable pipe organ, and tales of bountiful markets and gourmet meals. A dozen garlic-roasted snails, the tasty liver of a force-fed goose, a trio of lovingly wrapped macarons to go—France can be a spa for the traveler's taste buds.

The country is also marinated in history: Its people rioted over the price of a baguette—and wound up inventing modern democracy. What was once a divine monarch's carriageway is now a people's shopping boulevard.

France is a land that praises a struggling grape vine producing sweeter fruit. It's a land that exalts a well-designed cheese course capping the perfect meal. France is much more than a collection of sights—it's a celebration of sensory experiences.

Fireworks at the Eiffel Tower on Bastille Day

Fine Living at a Paris Market

I GREW UP THINKING cheese was no big deal. It was orange and the shape of the bread: *slap, fwomp* . . . cheese sandwich. Even though I'm still far from a gourmet eater, my time in Paris—specifically shopping at the Rue Cler street market with my restaurateur friend Marie—has substantially bumped up my appreciation of good cuisine.

In the skinny shadow of the Eiffel Tower, Rue Cler still feels like village Paris. Lined with shops that spill out into the street, it's also bustling with shoppers. Marie explains that Parisians shop almost daily for three good reasons: their tiny kitchens have tiny refrigerators, fresh produce makes for a good meal, and they like shopping. It's an important social event: a chance to hear about the butcher's vacation, see photos of the florist's new grandchild, relax over *un café*, and kiss the cheeks of friends. Demonstrating back and forth on my cheeks, Marie says, "The Parisian standard is twice for acquaintances (kiss, kiss) and three times for friends you haven't seen in a while—like you (kiss, kiss, kiss)."

Rue Cler's stores make picnic-shopping fun in Paris.

Observing Parisian shoppers, I quickly recognize the cardinal rule: Whenever popping in and out of French shops, it's polite to greet the proprietor *("Bonjour, Madame")* and say *"Merci"* and *"Au revoir"* as you leave. This simple practice can make the difference between being treated as an ignorant tourist and being treated as a temporary local.

The neighborhood produce shop wraps around the corner with an enticing rainbow of fruits and vegetables on display. Marie, using it as a classroom in smart grocery shopping, explains, "We Parisians demand the freshest fruits and vegetables and we shop with our noses." As if to demonstrate how exacting she is when shopping for her restaurant, Marie flips into gear: "Smell the cheap foreign strawberries. Then smell the torpedo-shaped French ones *(gariguettes)*. Find the herbs. Is today's delivery in? Look at the price of those melons! What's the country of origin? It must be posted. If they're out of season, they come from Guadeloupe. Many Parisians buy only French products and don't compromise on flavor because they eat with the season."

Next door, the fishmonger sells the freshest fish, which is brought in daily from ports on the English Channel, 100 miles away. In fact, seafood in Paris is likely fresher than in many towns closer to the coast because Paris is a commerce hub and from here it's shipped out to outlying towns. Anything wiggling?

At the *boucherie*, Marie shows me things I might have otherwise avoided on her menu: *rognons* (kidneys), *foie* (liver), *coeur de boeuf* (heart of beef). She hoists a duck to check the feet; they should be rough and calloused, an indication that they weren't stuck in an industrial kennel but ran free on a farm. She explains, "While Americans prefer beef, pork, and chicken, we French eat just as much rabbit *(lapin)*, quail *(caille)*, lamb *(agneau)*, and duck *(canard)*. The head of a calf is a delight for its many tasty bits." The meat is seasonal. In the winter, game swings from the ceiling.

Farther down Rue Cler, the picnic-friendly *charcuterie* (or *traiteur*) sells mouthwatering deli food to go. Because apartment kitchens are so small, these handy gourmet delis make it easy for Parisians to supplement their dinners in style.

At the *cave à vin* (wine shop), the clerk is a counselor who works with

The *boulangerie* gives bread the respect it deserves.

customers' needs and budgets. He will even uncork a bottle for picnickers. While drinking wine outdoors is taboo in the US, it's *pas de problème* in France.

The smell of cheese heralds the *fromagerie*. It's a festival of mold, with wedges, cylinders, balls, and miniature hockey pucks all powdered white, gray, and burnt marshmallow. Browsing with me through a world of different types of cheese, Marie explains, "*Ooh la la* means you're impressed. If you like cheese, show greater excitement with more *las. Ooh la la la la.*"

She leads me to the goat-cheese corner, holds the stinkiest glob close to her nose, takes a deep, orgasmic breath, and exhales, saying, "Yes, this smells like zee feet of angels."

The white-smocked cheesemonger knows Marie well. Sensing I'm impressed by his shop, he points out the old photo on the wall from when his father ran the shop. It was labeled BOF for *beurre, oeuf, fromage.*

The *fromagerie* offers an exotic array of cheeses.

What to choose for dessert?

For generations, this has been the place where people go for butter, eggs, and cheese. As if I'm about to become a convert to the church of stinky cheese, he takes us into the back room for a peek at *les meules*—the big, 170-pound wheels (250 gallons of milk go into each). Explaining that the "hard" cheeses are cut from these, he warns me, "Don't eat the skin of these big ones . . . they roll them on the floor. But the skin on most smaller cheeses—the Brie, the Camembert—that is part of the taste." Marie chimes in, "It completes the package."

And what's cheese without bread? The bakery is our final stop. Locals debate the merits of rival *boulangeries*. It's said that a baker cannot be good at both bread and pastry. At cooking school, they major in one or the other. But here on Rue Cler, the baker bucks the trend. Marie explains that this baker makes good bread (I get a baguette for my sandwich) and delicious pastries. *Voilà*, dessert!

By now, I've assembled the ingredients for the perfect picnic. Marie heads off to her restaurant, while I head for a park bench with a view of the Eiffel Tower, settle in, and enjoy my Rue Cler feast. A passerby smiles and wishes me a cheery *"Bon appétit!"*

Champs-Elysées: The Parisian Promenade

I HAVE A RITUAL when in Paris. I ask my cabbie to take me around the Arc de Triomphe two times, then drop me off to stroll down the city's grand boulevard, the Champs-Elysées.

We plunge into the grand traffic circle where a dozen venerable boulevards converge on this mightiest of triumphal arches. Like referees at gladiator camp, traffic cops are stationed at each entrance to this traffic circus, letting in bursts of eager cars.

In the mid-19th century, Baron Haussmann set out to make Paris the grandest city in Europe. The 12 arterials that radiate from the Arc de Triomphe were part of his master plan: the creation of a series of major boulevards, intersecting at diagonals, with monuments (such as the Arc de Triomphe) as centerpieces. As we careen around the chaotic circle, I wonder what Haussmann would think of the scene today.

Each visit here reminds me of the greatness of France. As the marble

The Arc de Triomphe stands proudly at the top of the Champs-Elysées.

Cafés offer colorful macarons.

relief of Lady Liberty scrambles up the arch Napoleon ordered built, heroically thrusting her sword and shrieking at the traffic, all of Paris seems drawn into this whirlpool. Being immersed in this scene with my cabbie so in control always makes me laugh out loud.

The commotion of cars fights to get to the arch at the center as if to pay homage to the national spirit of France. Cars entering the circle have the right-of-way; those already in the circle must yield. Parisian drivers navigate the circle like roller derby queens. Tippy little Citroën 2CVs, their rooftops cranked open like sardine lids, bring lumbering buses to a sudden, cussing halt. It's a game of fender-bender chicken.

On this visit, after barely avoiding an accident, my cabbie calms me, saying, "In Paris, a good driver gets only scratches, not dents." Groping for the lost end of my seatbelt, I say, "There must be an accident here every few minutes." He explains, "In the case of an accident here, each driver is considered equally at fault. This is the only place in Paris where the accidents are not judged. No matter what the circumstances, insurance companies split the costs 50-50." While we're momentarily stalled on the inside lane, I pay and hop out.

I'm ready for my stroll on the Champs-Elysées. I like to say it out loud: *shahn-zay-lee-zay*. This grandest of boulevards is Paris at its most Parisian: sprawling sidewalks, stylish octogenarians caked in makeup, concept cars glimmering in showroom windows, and pastel macarons in grand cafés.

Paris' characteristic love of strolling (a stately paced triathlon of walking, window-shopping, and high-profile sipping) dates from the booming 19th century, with its abundance of upper-class leisure time and cash. Donning an aristocratic air, I amble gently downhill to the immense and historic square called the Place de la Concorde.

Even small-town French kids who haven't traveled beyond a TV screen know that this boulevard is their country's ultimate parade ground, where major events unfold: the Tour de France finale, Bastille Day parades, and New Year's festivities.

In 1667, Louis XIV opened the first stretch of the Champs-Elysées: a short extension of the Tuileries Gardens leading to the palace at Versailles. Many consider this moment to be the birth of Paris as a grand city. The Champs-Elysées soon became *the* place to cruise in your carriage. It still is today—traffic can be jammed up even at midnight.

A century after Louis XIV, the café scene arrived. Cafés were ideal for both Parisian pleasure-seekers and thinkers, conspiring to share ideas and plot revolutions. That coffee-sipping ambience survives today, amid pop-clothing outlets and music megastores. Two cafés, Le Fouquet's and Ladurée, are among the most venerable in Paris.

Le Fouquet's started as a coachman's bistro. Then it gained fame as the hangout of French biplane pilots during World War I, when Paris was just a few nervous miles from the Western Front. Today, it's pretty stuffy—unless you're a film star. The golden plaques at the entrance honor winners of France's version of our Oscars, the Césars. While I find the interior intimidating, the people-watching from the sidewalk tables makes the most expensive espresso I've found in Paris a good value.

You're more likely to see me hanging out at Ladurée, working delicately through an Oreo-sized macaron with fine silverware. This classic 19th-century tea salon and pastry shop has an interior right out of the 1860s. The bakery makes traditional macarons with a pastel palette of flavors, ranging from lavender and raspberry to rose. Get a frilly little gift box to go, or pay the ransom and sit down and enjoy the Champs-Elysées show in sweet style.

Until the 1960s, the boulevard was pure Parisian elegance, lined with top-end hotels, cafés, and residences. Locals actually dressed up to stroll here. Then, in 1963, the government, wanting to pump up the neighborhood's commercial metabolism, brought in the Métro to connect the Champs-Elysées with the suburbs. Suddenly, the working class had easy access. And *bam*—there goes the neighborhood.

The arrival of McDonald's was another shock. At first it was allowed only white arches painted on the window. Today, the hamburger joint spills out onto the sidewalk with café-quality chairs and stylish flower boxes.

As fast food and pop culture invaded and grand old buildings began to fall, Paris realized what it was losing. In 1985, a law prohibited the demolition of the classy facades that once gave this boulevard a uniform grace. Consequently, many of today's modern businesses hide behind 19th-century facades.

The wide sidewalks of the Champs-Elysées invite strolling.

The *nouvelle* Champs-Elysées, revitalized in 1994, has new street benches, lamps, and an army of green-suited workers armed with high-tech pooper scoopers. Two lanes of traffic were traded away to make broader sidewalks. And plane trees (a kind of sycamore that thrives despite big-city pollution) provide a leafy ambience.

As I stroll, I notice the French appetite for a good time. The foyer of the famous Lido, Paris' largest cabaret, comes with leggy photos and a perky R-rated promo video.

The nearby Club Med building is a reminder of the French commitment to vacation. Since 1936, France's employees, by law, have enjoyed one month of paid vacation. The French, who now have five weeks of paid vacation, make sure they have plenty of time for leisure.

On the Champs-Elysées, the shopping ends and the park begins at a big traffic circle called Rond-Point. From here, it's a straight shot down the last stretch of the boulevard to the sprawling square called the Place de la Concorde. Its centerpiece was once the bloody guillotine but is now the 3,300-year-old Obelisk of Luxor. It was shipped here from Egypt in the 1830s, a gift to the French king.

I stand in the shadow of that obelisk with my back to the Louvre, once Europe's grandest palace, and now its grandest museum. Looking up this ultimate boulevard to the Arc de Triomphe, I can't help but think of the sweep of French history . . . and the taste of those delightful macarons.

St. Sulpice: The Grand Organ of Paris

ON SUNDAY MORNING in Paris, I'm enjoying Mass in a church with perhaps Europe's finest pipe organ. St. Sulpice has only 40 or 50 worshippers this morning. I grab a pew.

Going to church anywhere south of the Rhine generally means going to Mass. Catholics claim that since Mass is the same everywhere, there's no language barrier. Maybe it's just the Lutheran in me, but I miss the alpha, the omega, and, except for Communion, nearly everything in between.

When I do make it to church in Europe, I'm surrounded by towering vaults, statues of weary saints, and small congregations, but it's the music that sends me. The spiritual sails of St. Sulpice have been filled for two centuries by its 6,600-pipe organ. Organists from around the world come to Paris just to hear this organ.

As the first Mass of the morning finishes, half the crowd remains seated as the organist runs a musical victory lap. I happen to sit next to Lokrum, a young organist from Switzerland. He never comes to Paris without visiting St. Sulpice. When the organ stops, he whispers, "Follow me. You see nothing like this in America."

I follow Lokrum to the back of the church. A small church-mouse

Mass at St. Sulpice

of a man opens a little, unmarked door and we scamper like sixteenth notes up a spiral staircase into the organ loft of our wildest dreams. Here, organists are intimate with an obscure world few have entered. They speak of masters from 200 years ago as if they have just heard them in concert.

Lokrum stops me at a yellowed document. Dragging his finger down the glass frame, he says reverently, "The 12 St. Sulpice organists. Most of them are famous in the evolution of pipe-organ music. They have made wonderful music in this church for over 200 years, with no break."

Like presidents or kings, the lineage is charted on the wall. Charles-Marie Widor played from 1870 to 1933. Marcel Dupré from 1934 to 1971. "Dupré started a tradition at St. Sulpice," Lokrum says. "For generations people who love the organ have been welcomed here in the loft every Sunday." (Note that recently, this practice was discontinued.)

And now, the organist is Daniel Roth. I join a select group of aficionados who gather around this slight, unassuming man, who looks like an organist should. He pushes back his flowing hair with graceful fingers. He knows he sits on a bench that organists the world over dream of warming. Maintaining Dupré's tradition of loft hospitality, Roth is friendly in four languages.

History is thumbtacked all around: dusty charts of the pipes, master organ builders, busts of previous organists, and a photo of Albert Schweitzer with Dupré. And watching over it all is a bust of the idol of organists, Johann Sebastian Bach.

Lokrum pulls me behind the organ into a dark room filled with what looks like 18th-century Stairmasters. "Before electricity, it took five men to power these bellows. And these bellows powered the organ."

Suddenly, the music begins, signaling the start of the next Mass. Back

Daniel Roth at the
St. Sulpice organ,
powering worship
with music

at the organ, a commotion of music lovers crowds around a tower of
keyboards in a forest of pipes. In the middle of it all, under a dangling
heat lamp, sits Monsieur Roth. With boyish enthusiasm, he sinks his
fingers into the organ.

Flanked by an assistant on either side of the long bench, his arms
and legs stretched out like an angry cat, Roth plays all five keyboards.
Supremely confident, he ignores the offbeat camera flashes of his adoring fellow organ lovers, follows the progress of the Mass via a tiny mirror,
and makes glorious music.

The keyboards are stacked tall, surrounded by 110 stops—wooden
knobs that turn the pipes off and on—in a multitude of tonal packages.
His assistants push and pull the stops after each musical phrase. They
act quickly but as carefully as though God were listening.

Lokrum motions me to a chair with a commanding perch to oversee the musical action. On a well-worn wooden keyboard of foot pedals spreading below the bench, Roth's feet march with his fingers. A
groupie turns on his recorder to catch the music as Roth cranes his neck
to find the priest in his mirror.

I peer down at the busy keyboards and Roth's marching feet. Then,
turning around, I peek through the pipes and down on a small congregation. Just as priests celebrate Mass in a church whether worshippers
are present or not, this organ must make music. I marvel at how the high
culture of Europe persists. I'm thankful to experience it so intimately.

Alsace and Colmar:
France and Germany Mix It Up

Biking down a newly paved but skinny one-lane service road through lush vineyards, I notice how the hills seem to be blanketed in green corduroy.

My Alsatian friend hollers at me, "Germany believes the correct border is the mountains behind us. And we French believe the Rhine—you can almost see it ahead—is the proper border. That's why Alsace changes sides with each war. That's why we are a mix of France and Germany."

I yell back, "And that's why you are called Jean-Claude Schumacher."

The French province of Alsace is a region of Hansel-and-Gretel villages, ambitious vineyards, and vibrant cities. It stands like a flower-child referee between France and Germany, bound by the Rhine River on the east and the well-worn Vosges Mountains on the west. It has changed hands between the two countries several times because of its location, natural wealth, and naked vulnerability. Centuries as a political pawn have given Alsace a hybrid culture. Natives (with names like Jacques Schmidt or Dietrich Le Beau) who curse do so bilingually. Half-timbered restaurants serve sauerkraut and escargot.

Jean-Claude and I are exploring Alsace's Wine Road. This Route du

The famed vineyards of Alsace yield fine wines.

Vin is an asphalt ribbon tying 90 miles of vineyards, villages, and feudal fortresses into an understandably popular tourist package. The dry, sunny climate has produced good wine and happy travels since Roman days.

All along the road, *dégustation* signs invite us into wine *caves*. We drop by several. In each case, the vintner serves sips of all seven Alsatian wines from dry to sweet, with educational commentary.

There's more to Alsace than meets the palate. Centuries of successful wine production built prosperous, colorful villages. Alsatian towns are historic mosaics of gables, fountains, medieval bell towers, ancient ramparts, churches, and cheery old inns.

Colmar, my favorite city in Alsace, offers heavyweight sights in a warm, small-town setting. This well-pickled town of 70,000 sees relatively few American tourists but is popular with the French and Germans.

Historic beauty was usually a poor excuse to be spared the ravages of World War II, but it worked for Colmar. Thankfully, American and British military were careful not to bomb the half-timbered old burghers' houses, characteristic red- and green-tiled roofs, and cobbled lanes of the most beautiful city in Alsace.

Today, Colmar is alive with colorful buildings, impressive art treasures, and enthralled visitors. Schoolgirls park their rickety horse carriages in front of City Hall, ready to give visitors a clip-clop tour of the old town. Antique shops welcome browsers, and hoteliers hurry down the sleepy streets to pick up fresh croissants in time for breakfast.

Colmar, a French town with German flair

By the end of the Middle Ages, the walled town was a bustling trade center filled with the fine homes of wealthy merchants. The wonderfully restored tanners' quarter is a quiver of tall, narrow, half-

Grünewald's Isenheim Altarpiece: *Crucifixion*

The altarpiece has many panels, culminating with the *Resurrection*.

Schongauer's *Madonna in the Rose Garden*

timbered buildings. Its confused rooftops struggle erratically to get enough sun to dry their animal skins. Nearby, "La Petite Venise" comes complete with canals and gondola rides.

Colmar combines its abundance of art with a knack for showing it off. The artistic geniuses Grünewald, Schongauer, and Bartholdi all called Colmar home. Frédéric-Auguste Bartholdi, who created our Statue of Liberty a century and a half ago, adorned his hometown with many fine, if smaller, statues. The little Bartholdi Museum offers a good look at the artist's life and some fun Statue of Liberty trivia.

Four hundred years earlier, Martin Schongauer was the leading local artist. His *Madonna in the Rose Garden* is sublime. Looking fresh and crisp, it's set magnificently in a Gothic Dominican church. I sit with a dozen people, silently, as if at a symphony, as Schongauer's *Madonna* performs solo on center stage. Lit by 14th-century stained glass, its richness and tenderness cradles me in a Gothic sweetness that no textbook can explain.

The Unterlinden Museum, housed in a 750-year-old convent, holds the highlight of the city—Matthias Grünewald's gripping Isenheim altarpiece. It's actually a series of paintings on hinges that pivot like shutters. Designed to help people in a hospital suffer through their horrible skin diseases (long before the age of painkillers), the main panel—the Crucifixion—is one of the most powerful paintings ever. I stand petrified in front of it and let the vivid agony and suffering drag its fingers down my face. Just as I'm ready to sob with those in the painting, I turn to the happy ending: a psychedelic explosion of Resurrection joy. We know very little about Grünewald except that his work has played tetherball with human emotions for 500 years.

A hard-fought land on the conflicted border of Europe's two leading powers, Alsace is also a powerful example of the high culture, cuisine, and art that results when two great nations mix it up.

Well-Fed Geese in the Dordogne

Elbows on a rustic windowsill at a farm in the Dordogne region, I lose track of time watching Denis grab one goose at a time from an endless line. In a kind of peaceful, mesmerizing trance, he fills each one with corn. Like his father and his father's father before him, Denis force-feeds geese for a living. He spends five hours a day, every day, all year long sitting in a barn on a rolling stool with a machine that looks like a giant vacuum cleaner, surrounded by geese.

Denis rhythmically grabs a goose by the neck, pulls him under his leg and stretches him up, slides the tube down to the belly, and fills it with corn. He pulls the trigger to squirt the corn, slowly slides the tube up the throat and out, holds the beak shut for a few seconds, lets that goose go, and grabs the next.

When I tell friends I've witnessed geese being force-fed—the traditional way their livers are fattened to make foie gras, the prized delicacy in the Dordogne—many express disgust. There are people who want to boycott French foie gras for what they consider inhumane treatment of the geese. That's why I'm on Denis' farm: to learn more about *la gavage* (as the force-feeding process is called) with a firsthand visit.

Elevage du Bouyssou, a big homey goose farm a short drive from Sarlat, is run by Denis and Nathalie Mazet. Their geese are filled with corn three times a day for the last months of their lives. They have expandable livers and no gag reflex, so the corn stays there, gradually settling as it's digested and making room for the next visit from Denis and his corn gun. Watching Denis work, I wonder what his life is like . . . spending so much time with an endless cycle of geese. Do geese populate his dreams?

Denis at work, feeding his geese

Nathalie explains that happy geese produce top-quality foie gras.

How does it affect his relations with his wife?

While Denis squirts corn, Nathalie meets tourists—mostly French families—who show up each evening at 6 p.m. to see how their beloved foie gras is made. The groups stroll the idyllic farm as Nathalie explains how they raise a thousand geese a year. She emphasizes that the all-important key to top-quality foie gras is happy geese raised on quality food in an unstressed environment. They need quality corn and the same feeder. To his geese, Denis is calm and no threat.

I join the group as we scatter seed for the baby geese. We stroll into the grassy back lot where the older geese run free. Backlit by the low early-evening sun, they glow in rich colors.

Two geese are humping. I can't help but notice the gander yanking feathers off the back of the female goose's head as he (I suppose) enjoys his orgasm. Nathalie says she can tell which girls are getting action by the bald spots on the backs of their heads. About half the birds in the yard sport the souvenir—the fowl equivalent of love-bites.

The Mazets sell every part of the goose except the head and feet. The down feathers net less than a euro per goose. The serious money is in the livers. A normal liver weighs a quarter-pound. After the force-feeding process is finished, the liver weighs about two pounds. With a thousand geese, they produce a ton of foie gras annually. "Barely enough to support one family," Nathalie says.

These mature geese actually have a special shape, like they're waddling around with a full diaper under their feathers. This fattened goose silhouette has become a sales icon in shops throughout the Dordogne.

Just the sight of it is enough to make English travelers salivate. They come here in droves for the foie gras.

Why the Dordogne? This region in southwest France is on the goose migratory path south. Ages ago, locals caught geese on their migration, livers voluntarily enlarged in anticipation of the long journey. As the French are inclined to do, they ate the innards, found them extra tasty, and decided to produce their own. Those first French foie gras farmers didn't know it, but they didn't invent the technique of keeping geese

In the Dordogne, foie gras is on nearly every menu.

and enlarging the livers for human consumption. *Le gavage* goes back to ancient Egyptian times.

When I tell Nathalie that some of my American readers will say I've been duped, she reminds me that their geese are calm, in no pain, and designed to take in food in this manner, while American farm animals are typically kept in little cages and fed chemicals and hormones to get fat. Most battery chickens in the US live less than two months and are plumped with hormones. Nathalie's free-range geese live six months.

Dordogne geese live their lives at least as comfy as the other farm animals that many people (so upset with the foie gras process) have no problem eating. They are slaughtered as humanely as any non-human can expect in this food-chain existence.

After a few days in the Dordogne, where markets are filled with zealous farmers passing out little goose-liver sandwiches and where every meal seems to start with foie gras, I always leave with a strong need for a foie gras detox . . . and a strong desire to return soon.

Escargot and the Beauty of *Terroir*

WALKING THROUGH France's finest vineyards in the fabled Côte d'Or (or "Gold Coast") of Burgundy, the proud vintner guiding me becomes evangelical.

Pointing to the ground, she says, "A good grape must suffer. Look at this soil—it is horrible . . . it is only rocks. That is why these grapes have character. The roots of these struggling vines are thin as hairs. Searching as much as 30 meters down, they reach, reach, reach for moisture. The vines in the flat fields"—she motions, almost disdainfully, to fields just a kilometer away—"have it too easy . . . a silver spoon in their mouths. It's like people. Kim Kardashian, she is not interesting. The fine wines of humanity, they are the ones who have suffered."

"Like Tina Turner?" I ask.

"Exactly!" she says.

"The best vintners don't force their style on the grape. They play to the wine's strength, respecting the natural character of the sun, soil, and vine . . . the *terroir*. They play the wine like a great musician plays classical music. You don't want to recognize the musician. You want to hear the Beethoven."

That afternoon, I bike through these revered vineyards, where road signs read like a list of fine wines. Wines here are named not for the grape, but for the place of their origin. The more specific the place name, the higher the quality. A wine called simply "Burgundy" for the region would be a basic table wine. A wine labeled by the village (for instance, "Pommard") would be better. Those named for the vineyard (such as "Clos de Pommard") would be excellent and for a certain patch of land within that vineyard *(cru* or *grand cru)* the very best.

I head to a restaurant set in a vineyard that I remember from a previous visit, a place called Le Relais de la Diligence. Two years ago, the vines were lapping at its tables. Today, it's in a wheat field. I'm told that with the whole world making good wines, the French are cutting back on quantity, using marginal land for other crops, and working to build the quality.

Vintners appreciate how fine wine owes its character to the *terroir*—its unique mix of sun, soil, and vine.

Despite the view of wheat instead of grape vines, the food is delightful, as is the wine. I'm struck by the sophistication of the presentation and service as well as the casual atmosphere, with families and even dogs enjoying the scene. (There is a doggy meal printed on the menu.)

Feeling adventurous, I order the escargot, a classic French dish that's sourced a little differently these days. Good escargot must grow wild. The great French snail was once so common that early-19th-century train companies hired women and children to clean them off the tracks so the trains could get a grip. Today, the French snail has gone the way of the great American buffalo. As effective chemicals have successfully killed off weeds and undesirable insects, they have also decimated the slug and snail populations. Much of the escargot in France is farmed. Locals know the farmed gray snails are mediocre at best. The top-quality free-range snails most likely last slithered in Poland.

Through my meal, I ponder, not for the first time, whether there is something pseudo-sophisticated about all this finicky French food culture. While buying wine, if you ask what would be good with escargot, the wine merchant will need to know how you plan to cook the snails. "Oh, you're cooking it *that* way? Then you need something flinty—a Chablis." Too bad if you were hoping for a good Chardonnay.

Then I think of the way an American who pooh-poohs the French

A dozen snails and a glass of fine wine? Yes!

passion for fine points in cuisine might celebrate the nuances of baseball. Take a Frenchman to the ballpark. All the stuff that matters to me—how far the runner is leading off first base, who's on deck and how he does against left-handed pitchers, how deep the bullpen is, put in a pinch runner!— is nonsense to him.

The next time I put a little ketchup on my meat and my French friend is aghast, I'll accept it with no judgment. I'll just remember that with two outs and a full count, he'll have no idea how I know the runner's off with the pitch.

Escargot—a hit with the French

The French Restaurant:
A Spa for Your Taste Buds

BECAUSE I come from backpacker travel heritage where a good picnic is the answer to a prayer, it's taken me decades to recognize the value of a fine meal. Now I can enthusiastically embrace a long, drawn-out dinner splurge as a wonderful investment of both time and money. Nowhere is this truer than in France.

My friend and co-author Steve Smith and I head to a fine restaurant in Amboise, in the midst of France's château-rich Loire Valley. Some Americans are intimidated when they go to a fine French restaurant, but they needn't be. Many waiters speak English and are used to tourists. It's helpful to know what to expect.

In France, you can order off the menu, which is called *la carte,* or you can order a multi-course, fixed-price meal, which, confusingly, is called *le menu.* Steve orders a basic *menu* and I go top end, ordering off *la carte.*

French service is polished and polite, but not chummy. Waiters are

Steve and I enjoy an unforgettable cheese course, with the guidance of our server.

professionals who see it as their job to help you order properly for the best possible dining experience. If you get a cranky waiter . . . you're not alone. Even the French love to complain about grouchy service.

Aurore, our waitress, is no grouch. She smiles as I order escargot for my first course. Getting a full dozen escargot rather than the typical six snails doubles the joy. Eating six, you're aware that the supply is very limited. Eating 12, it seems for the first eight like there's no end to your snail fun. For the full experience, match your snails with a good white wine.

With my crust of bread, I lap up the homemade garlic-and-herb sauce while asking Aurore how it could be so good. With a sassy chuckle she says, "Other restaurateurs come here to find the answer to your question." Then she adds, "It's done with love." While I've heard that line many times, here I believe it.

In France, slow service is good service. After a pleasant pause, my main course arrives: tender beef with beans wrapped in bacon. Slicing through a pack of beans in their quiver of bacon, I let the fat do its dirty deed. A sip of wine, after a bite of beef, seems like an incoming tide washing the flavor farther ashore.

My crust of bread, a veteran from the escargot course, is called into action for a swipe of sauce. Italians brag about all the ingredients they use. But France is proudly the land of sauces. If the sauce is the medicine, the bread is the syringe. Thanks to the bread, I enjoy one last saucy encore, a tasty echo of the meat and vegetables I've just savored.

Shifting my chair to stretch out my legs, I prepare for the next course: a selection of fine cheeses. It sounds like a lot of food but portions are smaller in France. What we typically cram onto one large plate they spread out over several courses.

Aurore brings out her cheese platter, a cancan of moldy temptations on a rustic board, the mellow colors promising a vibrant array of flavors. With the cheeses is a special extra item: raisins soaked in Armagnac brandy. The lovingly sliced selection of cheeses arriving on my plate makes me want to sing—but in consideration for other diners, I just mime my joy silently.

Then comes dessert. Mine is a tender crêpe papoose of cinnamon-flavored baked apple with butterscotch ice cream, garnished with a

To explore both the country and the barn, think of the cheese course as a tour of France.

tender slice of kiwi. That doesn't keep me from reaching over for a snippet of Steve's lemon tart with raspberry sauce.

Even though we've finished our dessert, Aurore doesn't rush us. In France your server will not bring your bill until you ask for it. When I'm in a rush, here's my strategy: When I'm done with dessert, and the waiter asks if I'd like some coffee, I use it as the perfect opening to ask for the bill.

Our entire meal costs us about $60 each. I consider it $20 for nourishment and $40 for three hours of bliss . . . a spa for my taste buds. I can't imagine a richer travel experience, one that brings together an unforgettable ensemble of local ingredients, culture, pride, and people.

Britain and Ireland

GREAT BRITAIN is a celebration of pomp and tradition—of heritage and history. And while so much of Britain is indeed great, it's at its best in small, intimate slices of life: beachcombing on the Thames, being gobsmacked by English slang, and taking "quaint" to new heights in the Cotswold villages.

England is a whirlpool of vivid impressions: an iron helmet bent from some medieval battle, a thatcher hard at work on a cottage rooftop, the poetry of rustling leaves that frame lakeside vistas. Hikers find dog-friendly pubs, kissing gates, and lonely stone circles ever so English. Grail searchers ponder Camelot and ley lines at Glastonbury while "candy floss" makes grannies giddy in Blackpool.

One island over, Ireland's far west coast is the edge of Europe—where, as the Irish say, "The next parish over is Boston."

London's Millennium Bridge leads across the Thames to St. Paul's Cathedral.

London: Beachcombing Through History

I'VE SPENT more time in London than in any other European city. Its people, its traditions, and its history keep drawing me back.

In England, history means museums, churches, and castles. But my favorite ways to learn history don't always require entry through a turnstile.

Strolling with a good local guide is like beachcombing. I pick up obscure shards of a neighborhood's distant past, unlocking unexpected stories. On a bright, brisk January morning, I join David Tucker, who runs a tour company called London Walks.

From London Bridge, David points downriver past the Tower of London and says, "During the Second World War, Nazi bombers used the Thames as a guide on their nightly raids. When moonlit, they called it a 'silver ribbon of tin foil.' It led from the English Channel right to our mighty dockyards. Even with all the city lights carefully blacked out, those bombers easily found their targets. Neighborhoods on both banks

The silvery Thames River in London

of the river went up in flames. After the war, the business district on the North Bank was rebuilt, but the South Bank . . . it was long neglected."

Turning his back to St. Paul's Cathedral, David points to a vast complex of new buildings showing off the restored, trendy South Bank, and continues, "Only recently has the bombed-out South Bank been properly rebuilt. There's a real buzz in London about our South Bank."

Then we walk down to the beach and do some actual beachcombing. The Thames is a tidal river. At low tide, it's literally littered with history. Even today, London's beaches are red with clay tiles from 500-year-old roofs. Picking up a chunky piece of tile worn oval by the centuries, with its telltale peg hole still clearly visible, David explains that these tiles were heavy, requiring large timbers for support. In the 16th century, when large timbers were required for shipbuilding for the Royal Navy, lighter slate tiles became the preferred roofing material. Over time, the heavy, red-clay tiles migrated from the rooftops to the riverbank . . . and into the pockets of beachcombers like us.

Like kids on a scavenger hunt, we study the pebbles. David picks up a chalky white tube. It's the fragile stem of an 18th-century clay pipe. Back then, tobacco was sold with disposable one-use pipes, so used pipes were routinely tossed into the river. David lets it fall from his fingers.

Beachcombing on London's riverbank

A pub on the South Bank

Thinking, "King George may have sucked on this," I pick it up.

Climbing back to street level, we prowl through some fascinating relics of the South Bank neighborhood that survived both German bombs and urban renewal. Scaling steep stairs, we visit the Operating Theatre Museum, a crude surgical theater where amputations were performed in the early 1800s as medical students watched and learned. Down the street, we wander through the still-bustling Borough Market to see farmers doing business with city shopkeepers.

Walking through this area puts us in a time warp. David leads us into a quiet courtyard, where we look up at three sets of balconies climbing the front of an inn. He explains, "Coaching-inn courtyards like this provided struggling theater troupes—like young William Shakespeare's—with a captive audience."

A typical day in London can be spent at the Tower of London, Westminster Abbey, or the British Museum. But it can also be spent sifting through the tides of history.

A cheery Borough Market vendor

Westminster Abbey:
The National Soul of England

WEARING a red robe and a warm smile, Eddie works as a verger at London's Westminster Abbey. As a church official, he keeps order in this space—which is both very touristy and very sacred.

I tell him I'm working on a Rick Steves guidebook, and he says, "I'd like a word with that Rick Steves. He implies in his guidebook that you can pop in to worship or pay respects to the Unknown Soldier in order to get a free visit to the abbey."

Showing him my photo on the back cover, I say, "Well, I am Rick Steves."

I'm really charmed by Eddie, who explains that it's his responsibility to sort out believers (who get in free to pray), tourists (who must pay the entrance fee), and scammers who fold their hands reverently, hoping to avoid paying. Together, we agree on a new tactic: Rather than promote deception for the sake of free entry, I'll encourage my readers to attend a free worship service. The musical evensong service is a glorious experience that occurs several times a week. Everyone is welcome, free of charge.

Proving it helps to have friends in holy places, Eddie takes me into a room where no tourist goes: the Jerusalem Chamber, where scholars met

British pageantry in a Gothic jewel box

Friendly vergers welcome guests.

from 1604 to 1611 to oversee the translation of the Bible from ancient Greek and Hebrew into English, creating the King James Version.

Appreciating the danger of translating the word of God from dead ancient languages into the people's language and the importance of these heroic efforts in the 16th and 17th centuries, I get goose bumps. When visiting Germany's Wartburg Castle, I felt goose bumps when stepping into the room where Martin Luther translated the Bible for the German-speaking world. And I enjoyed a little goose-bump déjà vu here when Eddie let me slip into the Jerusalem Chamber.

Eddie then escorts me to the abbey and I quickly become immersed in the history that permeates it. This is where every English coronation since 1066 has taken place. At a coronation, the Archbishop of Canterbury stands at the high altar. The coronation chair is placed before the altar on the round, brown pavement stone, which represents the Earth. After a church service, the new king or queen sits in the chair, is anointed with holy oil, and then receives a ceremonial sword, ring, and cup. The royal scepter is placed in the new ruler's hands, and— *dut-dutta-dah*—the archbishop lowers the crown onto the royal head.

Westminster Abbey, filled with the tombs of the people who made Britain great

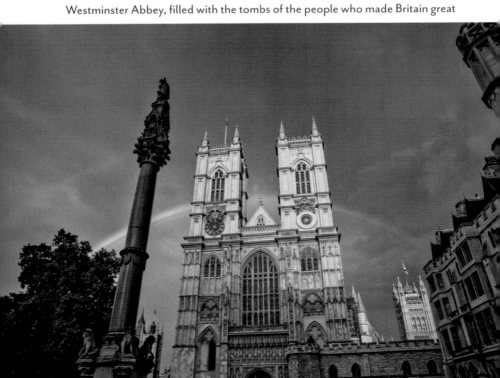

As I walk, I listen to the audio tour narrated by actor Jeremy Irons. With his soothing voice in my ear, I enjoy some private time with remarkable artifacts. The marble effigy of Queen Elizabeth I was made from her death mask in 1603 and is considered her most realistic likeness. The graves of literary greats of England are gathered, as if for a posthumous storytelling session, around the tomb of Geoffrey Chaucer (Mr. *Canterbury Tales*). Poppies line the tomb of Britain's Unknown Soldier, with the US Medal of Honor (presented by General John J. Pershing in 1921) hanging from a neighboring column. More recently, the statue of Martin Luther King, Jr. has been added as an honorary member of this heavenly English host.

My favorite stained-glass window features saints in robes and halos mingling with pilots in parachutes and bomber jackets. It's in the Royal Air Force Chapel, a tribute to WWII flyers who "earned their angel wings" in the 1940 Battle of Britain. Hitler's air force seemed to rule the skies in the early days of the war, bombing at will and threatening to snuff Britain out. While determined Londoners hunkered down, British pilots in their Spitfires and Hurricanes took advantage of newly invented radar systems to get the jump on the more powerful Luftwaffe. These were the fighters about whom Churchill said, "Never . . . was so much owed by so many to so few." The book of remembrances lists the names of each of the 1,497 pilots and crew members who died.

Grabbing a pew to ponder this grand space, I look down the long and narrow center aisle of the church. It's lined with Gothic arches, providing a parade of praying hands and glowing with colored light from the windows. It's clear that this is more than a museum. With saints in stained glass overhead, heroes in carved stone all around, and the bodies of England's greatest citizens under the floor, Westminster Abbey is more than the religious heart of England—it's the national soul as well.

The Queen's English

OSCAR WILDE famously said that the English "have really everything in common with America nowadays—except, of course, language." It's still true. A trip to Britain comes with plenty of linguistic surprises.

I'll never forget checking into a small-town B&B as a teenager on my first solo European adventure. The landlady cheerily asked me, "And what time would you like to be knocked up in the morning?"

I looked over at her husband, who winked, "Would a fry at half-eight be suitable?" The next morning I got a rap on the door at 8 a.m. and a huge British breakfast a half-hour later.

Britain can be an adventure in accents and idioms . . .

Every day you'll see babies in prams and pushchairs, sucking dummies as mothers change wet nappies. Soon the kids can trade in their nappies for smalls and spend a penny on their own. "Spend a penny" is British for a visit to the loo (bathroom). Older British kids enjoy candy floss (cotton candy), naughts and crosses (tic-tac-toe), big dippers (roller coasters), and iced lollies (popsicles). Kids are constantly in need of an Elastoplast or sticking plaster (Band-Aid), which their parents buy at the chemist's (pharmacy).

In a stationery store, you can get sticky tape or Sellotape (adhesive tape), rubbers (erasers), and scribbling blocks (scratch pads). At garden shops, those with green fingers (a green thumb) might pick up some courgette (zucchini), swede (rutabaga), or aubergine (eggplant) seeds. If you need a torch (flashlight), visit the ironmonger's (hardware store).

In Britain, fries are chips and potato chips are crisps. A beefburger, made with mince (hamburger meat), comes on a toasted bap (bun). For pudding (dessert), have some sponge (cake).

The British have a great way with names. You'll find towns with names like Upper and Lower Slaughter, Once Brewed, and Itching Field. This cute coziness comes through in their language as well. You'll visit "brilliant" (wonderful) sights that'll give you "goose pimples" (goose

Have a chin-wag (chat) with the English.

bumps). Your car will have a bonnet and a boot rather than a hood and trunk. You'll drive on motorways, and when the freeway divides, it becomes a dual carriageway. Never go anticlockwise (counterclockwise) in a roundabout. Gas is petrol, a truck is a lorry, and when you hit a tail-back (traffic jam), don't get your knickers in a twist (make a fuss)—just be patient and queue up (line up).

The British never say they have a two-week vacation, but many locals holiday for a fortnight, often in a homely (homey) rural cottage or possibly on the Continent (continental Europe). They might pack a face flannel (washcloth) and hair grips (bobby pins) in their bum bag (never a "fanny" pack—which refers to the most private part of a woman's anatomy). If it's rainy, they wear a mackintosh (raincoat) or an anorak (parka) with press studs (snaps).

If you get settled into a flat (apartment), you can post letters in the pillar box or give your mum a trunk (long-distance) call. If that's too dear (expensive), she'll say you're tight as a fish's bum. If she witters on (gabs and gabs), tell her you're knackered (exhausted) and it's been donkey's years (ages) since you've slept. After washing up (doing the dishes) and hoovering (vacuuming), you can have a plate of biscuits

Beware of severe dips!

(cookies) and, if you're so inclined, a neat (straight) whisky. Too much of that whisky will get you sloshed, paralytic, bevvied, wellied, ratted, popped up, or even pissed as a newt.

Then there is the question of accents. In the olden days, a British person's accent indicated his or her social standing. As Eliza Doolittle discovered in *My Fair Lady*, elocution could make or break you. Wealthier families would send their kids to fancy private schools to learn elocution. But these days, in a sort of reverse snobbery that has gripped the nation, accents are back. Politicians, newscasters, and movie stars have been favoring deep accents over the Queen's English. It's hard for American ears to pick out all of the variations and some accents are so thick they sound like a foreign language, but most Brits can determine what region a person is from based on his or her accent.

All across the British Isles, you'll encounter new words, crazy humor, and colorful accents. Pubs are colloquial treasure chests. Church services, sporting events, and local comedy shows are linguistic classrooms. The streets of Liverpool, the docks of London, and children's parks throughout the UK are playgrounds for the American ear. One of the beauties of touring Great Britain is the illusion of hearing a foreign language and actually understanding it . . . most of the time.

Bath: England's Cover Girl

PAUL RUNS the Star Inn, the most characteristic pub in the historic spa town of Bath. He keeps a tin of complimentary snuff tobacco on a ledge for customers. I try some, enjoying the sensation of a monkey dancing in my nose. Paul says English coal miners have long used snuff because cigarettes were too dangerous in the mines, and they needed their tobacco fix. He wants me to take the tin as a gift. On my way out, while keeping one eye on a drunk guy from Wales squeezing by me holding two big pints of the local brew over my head, I put the tin back on the ledge and assure Paul that I'll enjoy it the next time I stop by.

Walking home through the English mist, I think about how this very old town has become one of the most touristy places in Britain. Since ancient Roman times, when the town was called Aquae Sulis, its hot mineral water attracted society's elite. The town's importance spiked in 973, when the first king of England, Edgar, was crowned in Bath's Anglo-Saxon abbey, but reached a low ebb in the mid-1600s, when its

Bath's ancient Roman baths, now a museum

3,000 residents lived in a huddle of huts around the abbey, oblivious to the Roman ruins 18 feet below their dirt floors.

Then, in 1687, Queen Mary, fighting infertility, bathed here. Within 10 months she gave birth first to a son . . . and then to a new age of popularity for Bath. The revitalized town boomed as a spa resort. Local architect John Wood was inspired by the Italian architect Palladio to build a "new Rome." The town bloomed in the Neoclassical style, and streets were lined not with scrawny sidewalks but with wide "parades," where women in stylishly wide dresses could spread their fashionable tails. Bath became the Hollywood of Britain.

Today, the former trendsetter of Georgian England has more "government-listed" or protected buildings per capita than any town in England. It's a triumph of the Neoclassical style of the Georgian era, with buildings as elegant as the society they once housed.

In the morning, at my posh hotel, which fills one of a row of Georgian townhouses, I chat with the doorman, marveling at the uniform elegance of the buildings. He takes me aside and says, "The Georgians were all about facades. Both architecturally and as people . . . it was just

Bath's Royal Crescent—classic Georgian architecture

facades." He then walks me to the back garden, where the uniformity of the front gives way to a higgledy-piggledy mess. "The people back then were just the same," he says, "All fur, but no knickers."

The entire city, built of the creamy warm limestone called "Bath stone," beams in its cover-girl complexion. With the theme of facades in mind as I stroll through town, I see classical columns that supported only Georgian egos and false windows built in the name of balance. Two centuries ago, rich women wore feathered hats atop three-foot hairdos and the very rich stretched their doors and ground floors to accommodate this high fashion.

To get behind another of those classy facades, I drop by the Georgian house at No. 1 Royal Crescent. It's a museum that gives an intimate peek into the lavish lifestyles of the 18th century. I learn that high-class women shaved their eyebrows and carefully pasted on trimmed strips of furry mouse skin in their places. The kitchen, with all the latest Georgian gizmos, included a meat-spit that was powered—I kid you not—by a dog on a treadmill.

Another highlight is a stroll through four centuries of clothing trends in the Fashion Museum. Following the evolution of styles one decade at a time, from the first Elizabeth in the 16th century to the second Elizabeth today, comes with some fun trivia. I've always wondered what the line, "Stuck a feather in his cap and called it macaroni," from "Yankee Doodle" means. I learn the answer here.

For a taste of pompous aristocracy, I pop into the Pump Room for tea and scones with live classical music. I sip the curative Bath water from the elegant fountain. It tastes awful.

The highlight of my day is a worship service at Bath Abbey. The Anglican service is very "high Church," eloquent, and filled with song. I'm struck by the calls for sobriety, and the focus on repentance, with

Bath Abbey in action

repeated references to how we are such wretched sinners. But I also notice the strong affirmation of a rich heritage.

The Anglican worship ritual is carefully passed from one generation to the next. That continuity seems to be underlined by the countless tombs and memorials that line the walls and pave the floors. Many are worn smooth and shiny by the feet of centuries of worshippers. Both "the quick and the dead" in the congregation seem to raise their heads in praise as sunlight streams through windows. I understand why this church is nicknamed "the Lantern of the West."

Glowing Bath stone columns sprout honey-colored, fan-vaulting fingers, and cherubic boys in white robes and ruffs fill the nave with song, making it a ship of praise. The church is packed with townsfolk, proper and still. Sitting among them, I am no longer a tourist. The scene feels timeless. I gaze at the same windows, hoping for the inspiration that peasants sitting on these pews must have sought centuries ago.

The sermon is about Christian servanthood. The pastor's stern comment about the USA takes me by surprise: "If, after 9/11, that great Christian nation, the USA, took its responsibility to be a servant among nations seriously, how different our world would be today." When he's finished and the offering plate is passed, his gentility also catches me off guard: "If you're a visitor, please don't be embarrassed to let the plate pass. It's a way for our regular members to support our work here at Bath Abbey."

After the choir parades out, the huge central doors—doors I didn't even realize existed—are opened. Indoors and outdoors mingle, as the congregation spills out onto the main square and into their city.

If ever a city enjoyed looking in the mirror, Bath's the one. But I'm left thinking that it's not all narcissism. There's a beauty in this town that goes deeper than its facades. And if you manage to sniff out those offbeat experiences, you may even enjoy that sensation of monkeys dancing in your nose.

The Cotswolds:
Thatched Kingdom of Quaint

THE COTSWOLDS are crisscrossed with hedgerows, strewn with story-book villages, and sprinkled with sheep. Everything about them—the meadows, thatched roofs, churches, pubs, B&Bs, and even the tourist offices—is quaint. As a travel writer, I try not to use that word, "quaint." But this is England's quaintsville.

The Cotswolds are also walkers' country. The English love to walk the peaceful footpaths shepherds walked back when "polyester" only meant two girls. Hikers vigorously defend their age-old right to free passage. Once a year, the Ramblers, Britain's largest walking club, organizes a "Mass Trespass," when each of England's 50,000 miles of public footpaths is walked. By assuring each path is used at least once a year, they stop landlords from putting up fences. Most of the land is privately owned, but you're legally entitled to pass through, using the various sheep-stopping steps, gates, and turnstiles provided at each stone wall.

As with many fairy-tale regions of Europe, the present-day beauty of the Cotswolds was the result of an economic disaster. Wool was a huge industry in medieval England and the Cotswold sheep grew it best. Wool

A ramble through the Cotswolds offers timeless scenery.

money built lovely towns and palatial houses. Local "wool" churches are called "cathedrals" for their scale and wealth. Stained-glass slogans say things like "I thank my God and ever shall, it is the sheep hath paid for all."

Then came the rise of cotton and the Industrial Revolution. The wool industry collapsed, mothballing the Cotswold towns into a depressed time warp. Today, this most pristine English countryside is decorated with time-passed villages, gracefully dilapidated homes of an impoverished nobility, tell-me-a-story stone fences, and "kissing gates" no one should experience alone. Throngs of 21st-century romantics enjoy a harmonious blend of humanity and nature . . . and the Cotswolds are enjoying new prosperity.

In these small towns, everyone seems to know everyone. They're all ever so polite. Chatty residents commonly rescue themselves from a gossipy tangent by saying, "It's all very . . . ummm . . . yaaah."

Village pubs provide fuel (and memories) for hikers.

I use Chipping Campden as my home base. Just a few miles from the train station at Moreton-in-Marsh, it was once the home of the richest Cotswold wool merchants.

The great British historian G. M. Trevelyan calls Chipping Campden's High Street the finest in England. Walking its full length, I agree. As in most market towns, the street is wide enough to have hosted plenty of sheep business on market days. On one end are the top-end homes with, it seems, competing thatched roofs. I pass the 17th-century Market Hall, the wavy slate roofline of the first great wool mansion, a fine and free memorial garden, and, finally, the town's famous 15th-century Perpendicular Gothic "wool" church.

Nearby, Snowshill, Stanway, and Stanton are my nominations for the cutest Cotswold villages. Like marshmallows in hot chocolate, they nestle side by side.

Snowshill, a nearly edible little bundle of cuteness, has a photogenic triangular town center and a good pub. I enjoy observing the hikers, young and old, wandering through, much like the wayfarers from centuries past. And, as if standing by for the older hikers, the traditional red phone booth no longer offers a telephone . . . but a defibrillator.

Stanway is notable for its manor house. The Earl of Wemyss, whose family tree charts relatives back to 1202, opens his melancholy home—once so elegant and now wistful for times gone by—to visitors two days a week in the summer. His 14th-century Tithe Barn was where the peasants of the manor would give one-tenth of whatever they produced to their landlord. While motley peasants no longer gather here to pay their feudal "rents," the lord still gets rent from his vast landholdings and hosts community fêtes in his barn.

Stepping into the obviously very lived-in palace feels like stepping into a previous century. I see a demonstration of the spinning rent-collection table and marvel at the one-piece oak shuffleboard table in the great hall. I ask about the 1780 Chippendale exercise chair, and get an answer from the earl himself. He explains, "Half an hour of bouncing on this was considered good for the liver." He also shows me that the manor dogs have their own cutely painted "family tree," but then admits that his last dog, C. J., was "all character and no breeding."

The Earl of Wemyss welcomes travelers into his home . . . for a price.

This place has stories to tell. And so do the docents stationed in each room—who, even without fancy titles, can trace their histories back just as far as the lord of the manor. Talking to them, I'm reminded that seeking out one-on-one conversations like this is how I've really gotten to know and better understand England.

Stanway and neighboring Stanton are separated by a row of oak trees and grazing land, with parallel waves echoing the furrows plowed by generations of medieval farmers. Driving under a canopy of oaks and past stone walls and grazing sheep to get to Stanton is a joy.

In Stanton, flowers trumpet, door knockers shine, and slate shingles clap—cheering me up the town's main street. The church, which probably dates back to the ninth century, betrays a pagan past. Stanton is at the intersection of two ley lines (considered by many to come with mystical powers) connecting prehistoric sites. Churches such as

St. Michael

this one, built on pagan holy ground, are dedicated to St. Michael—the defender of the Church against pre-Christian spiritual threats. Michael's well-worn figure is above the door. Inside, I take a seat in the back pew and study the scene. Above the capitals decorating the columns leading to the altar, I see the pagan symbols for the moon and the sun. But it's Son worship that's long established here; the list of rectors behind me goes back to 1269. I finger the grooves cutting into the finely carved end piece of the pew, worn away by sheepdog leashes over the generations. Even today, a man's sheepdog accompanies him everywhere. Some things never change, especially in the Cotswolds.

Stanton's Church of St. Michael

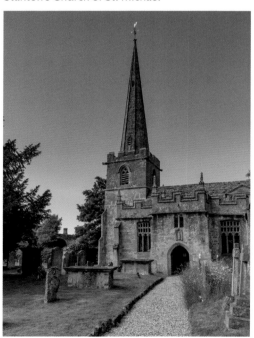

England's Lake District: Land of Great Hikes and Poets

I N ENGLAND'S Lake District, nature rules and humanity keeps a wide-eyed but low profile. At just about 30 miles long and 30 miles wide, it's a lush, green playground for hikers and poets alike. William Words-worth's poems still shiver in its trees and ripple on its ponds. There's a walking-stick charm about the way nature and culture mix here. Walk-ing along a windblown ridge or climbing over a rock fence to look into the eyes of a ragamuffin sheep, even tenderfeet get a chance to feel outdoorsy.

I've come here to enjoy some natural thrills and renew my poetic license. I focus on the northern lake of Derwentwater, with the nearby town of Keswick as my home base. It was an important mining cen-ter through the Middle Ages, but slate, copper, and lead gave way to Romantic poets and tree-hugging tourists in the 19th century. Keswick's fine Victorian buildings recall those Romantic days when city slickers first learned about "communing with nature."

Succumb to nature in England's Lake District.

A bald and bold hill called Catbells towers over Derwentwater. Often over the years, from a boat on the lake, I've looked enviously at hikers: tiny stick figures working their way up the ridge to that enticing 1,500-foot summit. Locals call these distant figures silhouetted against the sky at the summit "crag rats." With a free afternoon for a hike, I'm excited to finally become a crag rat myself. But the blustery weather conspires to keep me in. My B&B host loans me a better coat and eggs me on, saying, "The wind will blow the cobwebs out."

I venture up the ridge, leaning into the wind, passing the comedic baaing of sheep, and finally savoring that "king of the mountain" feeling—to stand all alone on the top of Catbells and to stoke someone else's crag-rat envy. The blustery weather reminds me of what I've learned about Britain: Don't wait for it to get better. Dress in layers and expect rain mixed with "bright spells." Drizzly days can be followed by long and delightful evenings. You can usually find convivial and atmospheric shelter at strategically placed pubs.

And, oh, the joy of a pub after a good hike. When my face is weatherstung and my legs ache happily with accomplishment, a pub's ambience sparkles even brighter and a good pint of beer is even more refreshing.

Friendly dogs are welcome at England's friendly pubs.

The ancient Castlerigg
Stone Circle near Keswick

Keswick's Dog and Gun pub, where "well-behaved dogs are welcome," is predictably full of hiking-partner pups. You can always pal up to an English pooch—I find they're happy to introduce you to their masters.

After a hearty pub dinner, I drive to the Castlerigg Stone Circle, three miles east of Keswick. Drenched in beauty, it stands like a mini Stonehenge. The majority of England's stone circles are here in the northern region of Cumbria. Castlerigg is one of the best and oldest in Britain. The circle, 90 feet across and 5,000 years old, has 38 stones mysteriously laid out on an axis between the two tallest peaks on the horizon. They most likely served as a celestial calendar for ritual celebrations.

I wander through this stone circle and imagine it in megalithic times—alive with people as ancient as King Tut, filling the clearing in spring to celebrate fertility, in late summer to commemorate the harvest, and in winter to mark the solstice and the coming renewal of light. A visit at dawn or sunset comes with solitude and leads to maximum "goose pimples."

Lingering in the Lake District, I can share my appreciation of nature with the crag rats, the poets, and the druids. While its charms are subtle, its rewards are great. Hiking along a ridge in the footsteps of Wordsworth, I feel recharged, inspired . . . and ready to write a poem.

York: Vikings, Bygone Days, and England's Top Church

I'M IN YORK, following Edwin, a wry and spry retired schoolteacher, into an overgrown turret in the city's ancient wall. Edwin stays active leading town walks and giving private tours. Today, he's taking me to his favorite places.

Fingering a red brick, Edwin explains that just as a scout counts the rings in a tree, we can count the ages of York by the layers of bricks in the city wall: Roman on the bottom, then Danish and Norman, and finally topped off with the "new" addition—from the 14th century.

Historians run around York like kids in a candy shop. And with a knowledgeable guide like Edwin bringing things to life, even non-historians find themselves exploring the past with a childlike wonder.

Strolling into the half-timbered town center, we stop at the medieval butchers' street called The Shambles. As if sharing a secret, Edwin nudges me under an eave and points out the rusty old hooks and says, "Six hundred years ago, bloody hunks of meat hung here, dripping and then draining into the gutter that still marks the middle of the lane. This

Street leading to York's Minster

slaughterhouse of commercial activity gave our language a new word. This was the original 'shambles.'"

I find English guides likeably chatty and opinionated. As Edwin and I explore York, I learn several ghost stories, what architectural "monstrosity" the "insensitive" city planners are about to inflict on the townsfolk, a bit of the local politics, and the latest gossip.

York is the most interesting town between London and Edinburgh. Edwin is ready with an explanation: In the Victorian Age, most big cities embraced the Industrial Revolution, tearing down their walls and inviting the train tracks to run right through their center. But the people of York kept their walls and required the train station to be built just outside the center. While less efficient at the time, this left the city a historic treasure cradled entirely within the surviving walls. Those York Victorians not only saved their wall, but they amped up its historic charm with a remodel, giving it fanciful crenellations and arrow slits.

Edwin and I head over to the York Castle Museum, where English memorabilia from the 18th, 19th, and early 20th centuries is cleverly displayed in a huge collection of craft shops, old stores, and bygone living rooms. Charles Dickens would feel right at home here. As towns were being modernized in the 1930s, the museum's founder, Dr. Kirk, recognized a threat to their heritage and collected entire shops and reassembled them here. In Kirkgate, the museum's most popular section, we wander down a century-old Lincolnshire street, popping in to see the butcher, baker, coppersmith, and barber.

Tempted at the old-time sweet shop in York's Castle Museum

The shops are actually stocked with the merchandise of the day. In the confectionery, we eavesdrop on English grannies giggling and reminiscing their way through the mouthwatering world of "spice pigs," "togo bullets," "hum bugs," and "conversation lozenges." The general store is loaded with groceries, the toy shop has old-time games, and the sports shop has everything you'd need for a game of 19th-century archery, cricket, or skittles. Anyone for ping-pong? Those Victorians loved their "whiff-whaff."

In the period rooms, three centuries of Yorkshire living rooms and clothing fashions paint a cozy picture of life centered around the hearth. A peat fire warms a huge brass kettle while the aroma of freshly baked bread fills a room under heavy, open-beamed ceilings. After walking through the evolution of romantic valentines and unromantic billy clubs, we trace the development of early home lighting from simple waxy sticks to the age of electricity. An early electric heater has a small plaque that explains, "How to light an electric fire: Switch it on!"

Dr. Kirk's "memorable collection of bygones" is the closest thing in Britain to a time-tunnel experience, except perhaps for our next destination, the Jorvik Viking Centre just down the street.

A thousand years ago, York was a thriving Viking settlement called Jorvik (YOR-vik). While only traces are left of most Viking settlements, Jorvik is an archaeologist's bonanza, the best-preserved Viking city ever excavated. Sail Disney's "Pirates of the Caribbean" north a thousand miles and back a thousand years, and you get Jorvik. More a ride than a

The National Railway Museum tracks the evolution of train travel.

museum, this exhibit drapes the abundant harvest of this dig in theme park cleverness. We ride a kid-pleasing people-mover for 12 minutes through the re-created Viking street of Coppergate. It's the year 975 and we're in the village of Jorvik. Everything—sights, sounds, even smells—has been carefully re-created. Next, our time-traveling train rolls through the actual excavation site, past the remains that inspired the reconstructed village. Stubs of buildings, piles of charred wood, and broken pottery are the time-crushed remains of a once-bustling town. Everything is true to the original dig. Even the face of one of the mannequins was computer-modeled from a skull dug up right here.

Our next stop is the thunderous National Railway Museum, which showcases 200 illustrious years of British railroad history. Fanning out from a grand roundhouse is an array of historic cars and engines, including Queen Victoria's lavish royal car and the very first "stagecoaches on rails." Exhibits on dining cars, post cars, Pullman cars, and vintage train posters creatively humanize the dawn of an exciting new age.

Edwin and I walk over the river toward the towering York Minster, stopping first at the romantic ruins of St. Mary's Abbey. A fragile arcade of pointed Gothic arches seems to hang from the branches of the trees that tower above. I remark to Edwin that it's striking how magnificently the Minster survives while only a single wall of this abbey church still stands. Edwin explains that Henry VIII, so threatened by the power of the pope, destroyed nearly everything that was Catholic—except the great York Minster. Thankfully, Henry needed a northern capital for his Anglican Church. Edwin then explains the Dissolution of the Monasteries. "Henry wanted more than a divorce. He wanted to be free from the power of the abbots and the monasteries and the pope in Rome. It was our first Brexit—and we got it in 1534." Then, playfully describing three bombastic leaders at the same time, he says, "It was spearheaded by a much-married, arrogant, overweight egomaniac." Edwin is playing with me, alluding to my president, but he is also describing the pompous, pro-Brexit British politician Boris Johnson along with Henry VIII. While 500 years apart, they both wanted to "be free" from Europe (from the pope and from the EU), which also meant sending no more money to Europe (in tithes to the Roman Catholic Church back then or taxes to

Brussels today). And they both wanted no more intrusions from Europe into their realm. In the 16th century under Henry and in the 21st century under Boris, for Britain, "leaving means leaving."

With that, we step into York's Minster, the pride of the city. It's one of the most magnificent churches in Britain and the largest Gothic church north of the Alps. Splashed with stained glass and graced with soaring ceilings, this dazzling church brilliantly shows that the High Middle Ages may have been dank, but they were far from dark.

The Minster is famous for its 15th-century stained glass, especially its Great East Window, which is the size of a tennis court. The window's fine details—far too tiny to see from the floor—were originally intended "for God's eyes only."

But Edwin has opera glasses. He pulls them from his satchel so I can study the window as he guides me: A sweeping story is told in more than 300 panels of painted and stained glass, climaxing with the Apocalypse. It's a medieval disaster movie—a blockbuster back in 1408—showing the end of world in fire and flood and pestilence . . . vivid scenes from the Book of Revelations. Angels trumpet disaster against blood-red skies. And there it is, the fifth panel up on the far left side . . . the devil giving power to the "Beast of the Apocalypse," a seven-headed, ten-crowned lion, just as it was written in the Bible. This must have terrified worship-

The Minster's Great East Window

pers. This British masterpiece was unprecedented in its epic scale, created a hundred years before Michelangelo frescoed the story of the beginning and end of time at the Sistine Chapel in Rome. One of the great art treasures of the Middle Ages, it's the work of one man: John Thornton of Coventry (who, I think, deserves a little of Michelangelo's fame).

In York, the church bell rings the ringer.

The church also holds a full carillon of 35 bells, so church-bell enthusiasts can enjoy a little ding-dong ecstasy during the weekly bell concerts. Edwin has another guiding appointment. But before leaving, he introduces me to a deacon, who delights in showing off this pride of the Minster. He leads me upstairs a few flights and into the bell tower to show off the biggest bell. We come to a stony room—vacant except for a fat, lifeless rope dangling from the ceiling. With childlike enthusiasm, the suddenly animated deacon begins pulling the rope. He reaches and reaches, pulling ever higher and ever lower, and I ready my ears for a thunderous sound. Suddenly the deacon clenches the rope and becomes airborne, soaring high above me as ear-shattering clanging rings throughout the town. Eventually landing back on the medieval wooden floor, he winks at me and says, "In York, our bell is so big it rings the ringer."

He invites me to attend the evensong service, reminding me that it's a good way to fully experience the York Minster. Later that evening I return, arriving early to get a prime seat. It's a spiritual Oz, with 40 boys singing psalms: a red-and-white-robed pillow of praise, raised up by the powerful pipe organ.

As the boys sing and the organ plays, I ponder the towering Gothic arches—stone stacked by locals 700 years ago, still soaring like hands folded in prayer. I whisper, "Thank God for York. Amen."

Blackpool: Britain's Coney Island

WHEN I TELL my British friends I'm going to Blackpool, their expressions sour and they ask, "Oh, God, why?" My response: Because it's a carnivalesque, tipsy-toupee, ears-pierced-while-you-wait place, where I can experience working-class England at play.

For over a century, until the last generation, Blackpool, located on the west coast north of Liverpool, was where the mill workers and miners of Yorkshire and Lancashire spent their holidays. Working blokes took their families to this queen of North England resorts hoping for good fun for the kids and a bit of razzle-dazzle entertainment for themselves.

Today, Blackpool's vast beaches are empty—too cold for comfort. But during the resort's heyday, life was cold: People expected to be cold at home, at work—and on their annual vacation. Even if the beach was cold, it was still the beach. People enjoyed sitting on the beach—just being there, breathing in what they thought was healthy air, looking out at the Irish Sea . . . in the cold. Today, with cheap airfare to Spain, even lowly workers know that warm beaches are an option . . . somewhere else.

While discount flights to the Costa del Sol have stolen most of its business, Blackpool parties on—tacky, tatty, and run-down, it struggles to remain England's glittering city of fun. It's ignored by American guidebooks—and many would say with good reason. But its "Seven Golden Miles" of beach promenade affords a fascinating glimpse of an England few travelers see.

An English family at the beach imagining sunshine

Blackpool is dominated by the Blackpool Tower. Shaped like a stubby Eiffel Tower, this giant amusement center seems to grunt, "Have fun." At the tip of this 518-foot-tall symbol of Blackpool is a grand view that's just smashing, especially at sunset.

The tower's gilded ballroom is festooned with old-time seaside elegance. A relay of organists keeps pensioners waltzing, fox-trotting, and doing the tango. Many of these dancers have been coming here regularly for 50 years. They're happy to share an impromptu two-step lesson with any curious visitor. Many more pay to sit with their fish-and-chips and mushy peas and watch.

Leaving the ballroom, I work my way through a string of noisy amusements on the waterfront promenade. Countless greedy doors open, trying every trick to get me inside. Huge arcade halls broadcast tape-recorded laughter and advertise free toilets. The randy wind machine under a wax Marilyn Monroe flutters her skirt with a steady breeze. The smell of fries, tobacco, and sugared popcorn wafts with an agenda around passersby. Aunt Sally boards give people with nothing interesting to report on Facebook silly holes to stick their heads through for an entertaining photo. Milk comes in raspberry or banana here and people under incredibly bad wigs look normal. I was told that I mustn't leave without having my fortune told by a Gypsy spiritualist, but learning she charges $10 per palm, I decide to read them myself.

Passing a bingo parlor, I hear the siren sounds of the caller—a woman's voice singing a mesmerizing melody: "Twenty-seven . . . two and seven . . . thirty-three . . . all the threes." As if hypnotized by the soothing tune, the roomful of zombies sip tea and hope for that big win. In the 1960s, gambling laws were loosened and suddenly bingo became a big hit in gambling-averse England.

Blackpool, its beach, and its tower

For a quick diversion, I hop a vintage trolley car to cruise the promenade. Riding the trolleys, which constantly rattle up and down the waterfront, is more fun than driving. While the old trolleys survive, the traditional horse carriages have been replaced with sugary pink Cinderella carriages. Little girls want to be princesses and demand drives change.

Each of the three amusement piers has its own personality. Are you feeling sedate? Head to the north pier. Young and frisky? Central pier. Dragging a wagon full of children? The south pier is for you. For a peaceful side of Blackpool, I hop out at the north pier, and stroll that venerable boardwalk out to sea where the only sounds are the gulls and the wind in my hair.

In 1879, back when the north pier was new, Blackpool became the first city in England to switch on electric streetlights. Now, it stretches its season into the autumn by illuminating its seven miles of waterfront with countless blinking and twinkling lights. The first time I saw the much-hyped "Illuminations" years ago, the American inside me kept saying, "I've seen bigger and I've seen better." But I filled his mouth with cotton candy and just had some simple fun like everyone else on my specially decorated trolley.

Blackpool claims to be England's second-best theater town (after London), so a fun part of my afternoon is deciding how I'll cap my day: with a play or an old-time variety show. When in the mood for variety, there are always a few dancing-girl, racy-humor, magic, and tumbling shows. I enjoy the "old-time music hall" shows: always corny, neither hip nor polished. It's fascinating to be surrounded by hundreds of partying

Backstage at a Blackpool drag show	A young-at-heart Blackpool blonde

British seniors, swooning again and waving their hankies to the predictable beat. Busloads of happy widows come from all corners of North England to giggle at the racy jokes. A perennial favorite is *Funny Girls*, a burlesque-in-drag show that delights footballers and grannies alike.

For me, Blackpool's top sight is its people. You experience England here like nowhere else. Grab someone's hand and a big stick of "rock" (rock candy), and stroll. Appreciate the noisy 20-somethings pulling down their pants to show off butt cheeks reddened by new tattoos. Ponder what might inspire someone to spend his golden years here, wearing plaid pants and a bad toupee.

A British friend once told me, "Blackpool is in the DNA of north England. It's a ritual where family memories are created and where those memories are passed through the generations. It's a place not to see but to do. You've got to eat the candy, ride the carousel, dance in the ballroom, walk the pier."

With that in mind, I hail my own private Cinderella carriage for a final ride down the promenade. Clip-clopping down the Golden Mile and feeling very pink, I think about how Blackpool is a scary thing to recommend. I probably overrate it. Many people, ignoring my "50 million flies can't be wrong" logic, think I do. If you're not into kitsch and greasy spoons, skip Blackpool. But if you're traveling with kids—or still are one yourself—splash in Britain's fun puddle. So many Brits do, even though few will admit it.

A Cinderella carriage . . . ready to make a commoner a princess

Mysterious Britain

O N MY FIRST trip to Dartmoor National Park, back when I was a student, word of the wonders lurking just a bit deeper into the moors tempted me away from my hostel in Gidleigh. I was told of an especially rewarding hike that would lead me to the mysterious Scorhill Stone Circle. Climbing over a hill, surrounded by ominous towers of craggy granite, I was swallowed up by powerful, mystical moorland. Hills followed hills followed hills . . . green growing gray in the murk.

Where was that 4,000-year-old circle of stone? I wandered in a scrub-brush world of greenery, white rocks, eerie winds, and birds singing unseen. Then the stones appeared. It seemed they had waited for centuries, still and silent, for me to visit.

I sat on a fallen stone and my imagination ran wild, pondering the people who roamed England so long before written history documented their stories. I took out my journal, wanting to capture the moment . . . the moor, the distant town, the chill, this circle of stones. I dipped my pen into the cry of the birds and wrote.

Avebury, one of Britain's many stone circles

That experience, 40 years ago, kicked off decades of my fascination with mysterious Britain. Dartmoor, Stonehenge, the Holy Grail, Avalon . . . there's an endlessly intriguing side of Britain steeped in lies, legends, and at least a little truth. Haunted ghost walks and Loch Ness Monster stories are profitable tourist gimmicks, but the cultural soil that gave us Beowulf, King Arthur, and Macbeth is fertilized with a murky story that goes back over 5,000 years—older, even, than Egypt's pyramids. With a little background, even skeptics can appreciate Britain's historic aura.

There are countless stone circles, forgotten tombs, man-made hills, and figures carved into hillsides whose stories will never be fully understood. Britain is crisscrossed by lines, called ley lines, connecting these ancient sites. Prehistoric tribes may have transported these stones along a network of ley lines, which some think may have functioned together as a cosmic relay or circuit.

Two hours west of London, Glastonbury is located on England's most powerful ley line. It gurgles with a thought-provoking mix of history and mystery. For the views, hike up the 500-foot-tall Glastonbury Tor (a grassy, conical clay hill capped with an old church tower), and you'll notice the

Glastonbury Tor attracts hikers and seekers.

remains of the labyrinth that made climbing the hill a challenge some 5,000 years ago.

In AD 37, Joseph of Arimathea, Jesus' wealthy tin-merchant uncle, supposedly brought a vessel containing the blood of Christ to Glastonbury, and with it, Christianity to England. (Joseph's visit is plausible because back then, merchants from the Levant came here to trade with the local miners.)

While that story is supported by fourth-century writings and accepted by the Church, the King Arthur and Holy Grail legends it inspired are not. Those medieval tales were cooked up when England needed a morale-boosting folk hero to inspire its people during a war with France. They pointed to the ancient Celtic sanctuary at Glastonbury as proof of the greatness of the fifth-century warlord, Arthur. In 1911, his supposed remains, along with those of Queen Guinevere, were dug up here, and Glastonbury was woven into the Arthurian legends. The Camelot couple was reburied in the abbey choir and their gravesite is a kind of shrine today. Many believe the Grail trail ends at the bottom of the Chalice Well, a natural spring at the base of the tor.

In the 16th century, Henry VIII, on a rampage against the power of the monasteries, destroyed Glastonbury Abbey. For emphasis, he hung and quartered the abbot, sending his body on four national tours . . . at the same time. Two centuries later Glastonbury rebounded. In an 18th-century tourism campaign, thousands signed affidavits stating that water from the Chalice Well healed them, putting Glastonbury on the tourist map.

Today, Glastonbury is a center for searchers. It's too out there for the mainstream church, but just right for those looking for a place to recharge their crystals. Since the society that built that labyrinth worshipped a mother goddess, the hill, or tor, is seen by many today as a symbol of the Sacred Feminine.

Along with its history, the geology contributes to the mystery of this land. Southern England's shoreline is lined by famed white chalk cliffs. And that same white chalk is just below a thin layer of topsoil all across the region. Eons ago, all it took was a shovel and a little hard work to peel away the soil and transform rolling hillsides into works of art—or messages.

Travelers to this day are entertained by giant white figures popping out of these grassy green slopes. Many are creations of 18th- and 19th-century Romantics acting out against the coldness of the Industrial Age, but a few of these figures have, as far as history is concerned, always been there. One figure is particularly eye-catching: The Cerne Abbas Giant, armed with a big club and an erection, is hard to ignore. For centuries, people fighting infertility would sleep on Cerne Abbas. As my English friend explained, "Maidens can still be seen leaping over his willy."

And fixed like posts into that same chalk subsoil are stone circles,

The eye-catching Cerne Abbas Giant

more souvenirs of England's misty, distant past. The most famous stone
circle, Stonehenge, is an hour's drive from Glastonbury. Built in phases
between 3000 and 1000 BC with huge stones brought all the way from
Wales, it still functions as a remarkably accurate celestial calendar.

A study of more than 300 similar circles in Britain found that each
was designed to calculate the movement of the sun, moon, and stars,
and even predict eclipses. These prehistoric timekeepers helped early
societies know when to plant, when to harvest, and when to party. Even
in modern times, when the summer solstice sun sets in just the right slot
at Stonehenge, pagans boogie.

Curiously, some of the particular "blue stones" used in Stonehenge
were found only in distant Wales. Why didn't the prehistoric builders
use what seem like perfectly adequate stones nearby? Consider those
ley lines. Perhaps a particular kind of stone was essential for maximum
energy transmission. How might these massive stones have been transported in a pre-industrial age? Various practical explanations have been
suggested, but there's no consensus among experts. Imagine instead
congregations gathering here 5,000 years ago, raising thought levels

and creating a powerful life force transmitted along the ley lines. Maybe the stones were levitated in Wales and rocketed a hundred miles to this spot. Maybe psychics really do create powerful vibes. Maybe not. It sounds unbelievable, but at one time, so did electricity.

Not far away, the stone circle at Avebury is 16 times the size of Stonehenge and about one-sixteenth as touristy (see photo on page 104). Visitors are free to wander among 100 stones, ditches, and mounds, and ponder these curious patterns from the past. Near Avebury is the 130-foot-high pyramid-shaped Silbury Hill. More than 4,000 years old, this man-made mound of chalk is a reminder that you've only scratched the surface of Britain's fascinating prehistoric and religious landscape.

Stonehenge, a celestial calendar marking the seasons for 4,000 years

More Neolithic wonders lurk in England's moors. While they inspire exploration, beware: you can get lost in these stark, time-passed commons. Directions are difficult to keep. It's cold and gloomy, as nature rises like a slow tide against anything human-built. A crumpled castle loses itself in lush overgrowth. A church grows shorter as tall weeds eat at the stone crosses and tilted tombstones. Over the centuries, the moors have changed as little as the longhaired sheep that still seem to gnaw on moss in their sleep.

One of England's wildest and most remote regions is in the southwest corner of the country. It's Dartmoor—that wonderland of powerfully quiet rolling hills that inspired me long ago. Near the Cornwall Peninsula in the county of Devon, it's crossed by only three main roads. Most of this area is either unused or shared by its 34,000 villagers as a common grazing land—a tradition that goes back to feudal days. Ordnance Survey maps show that Dartmoor is peppered with bits of England's mysterious past, including more Bronze Age stone circles and enigmatic megaliths than any other chunk of England. It's perfect for those who dream of enjoying their own private Stonehenge without barbed wire, police officers, parking lots, tourists, or port-a-loos.

Returning to Dartmoor on my last trip, I sat peaceful and alone on the same mossy stone I warmed the day I first experienced Scorhill Stone Circle in 1978. I recalled that day, at the age of 23, when I realized how many wonders in Europe were still undiscovered . . . hidden and unheralded. I remembered how, hiking home that evening, I decided that my calling was to find these places and to share them. That was the day I became a travel writer.

A prehistoric dolmen in Cornwall

Ireland's Dingle Peninsula:
The Next Parish Over is Boston

I ONCE MET an elfish, black-clad old man in the little town of Ventry, on Ireland's Dingle Peninsula. When I asked if he was born here, he paused, breathed deeply, and said, "No, 'twas about five miles down the road."

I asked him if he had lived here all his life.

He answered, "Not yet."

When I told him where I was from, a faraway smile filled his eyes as he looked out to sea and muttered, "Aye, the shores of Americay."

Dingle Peninsula gives the traveler Ireland in the extreme. It feels so traditionally Irish because it's part of a Gaeltacht, a region where the government subsidizes the survival of the Irish language and culture. While English is everywhere, the signs, songs, and chitchat are in Gaelic.

This sparse but lush peninsula marks the westernmost point in Ireland. Residents are fond of gazing out at the Atlantic and saying with a sigh, "Ahh, the next parish over is Boston."

Fishing once dominated Dingle, but tourists and moviemakers are well onto the region now. Several films feature the peninsula, including

Dingle's main drag—where nearly every other storefront is a pub

Ryan's Daughter and *Far and Away*. Its offshore islands were the hideout of an aging Luke Skywalker in the most recent *Star Wars* trilogy. What had been a trickle of visitors has surged into a flood as word of Dingle's musical, historical, gastronomical, and scenic charms spread.

About 30 miles around, the peninsula is just the right size for a day-long driving or cycling tour. Hopping on a bike, I assess the gathering storm clouds and zip up my parka. In Ireland, good and bad weather blow by in a steady meteorological parade. A little rain will just add to the experience. Circling these roads is like a trip through an open-air museum. The landscape is littered with a half-million sheep and dozens of monuments left behind by Bronze Age settlers, Dark Age monks, English landlords, and even Hollywood directors.

In the darkest depths of the Dark Ages, when literate life almost died in Europe, peace-loving, scholarly monks fled the chaos of the Continent and its barbarian raids. Sailing to this drizzly fringe of the known world, they lived out their monastic lives in lonely stone igloos or "beehive huts" that I pass on my ride.

Rounding Slea Head, the point in Europe closest to America, the rugged coastline offers smashing views of deadly black-rock cliffs. The crashing surf races in like white stallions.

I ponder the highest fields, untouched since the planting of 1845,

Gallarus Oratory, still watertight after 1,300 years

when the potatoes rotted in the ground. The vertical ridges of those bleak potato beds are still visible—a barren and godforsaken place. That year's Great Potato Famine eventually, through starvation or emigration, cut Ireland's population by a quarter.

I stop to explore the Gallarus Oratory, a stone chapel dating from AD 700 that's one of Ireland's best-preserved early Christian monuments. Its shape is reminiscent of an upturned boat. Finding shelter inside as a furious wind hurls rain against its walls, I imagine 13 centuries of travelers and pilgrims standing where I am, also thankful for these watertight dry-stone walls.

When the squall blows over, I continue up the rugged one-lane road from the oratory to the crest of the hill, then coast back into Dingle town—hungry, thirsty, and ready for a pub crawl.

Of the peninsula's 10,000 residents, 1,500 live in Dingle town. Its few streets, lined with ramshackle but gaily painted shops and pubs, run up from a rain-stung harbor. During the day, teenagers—already working on ruddy beer-glow cheeks—roll kegs up the streets and into the pubs in preparation for another tin-whistle music night. "Pub" is short for "public house." A convivial mix of good *craic* (that's the art of conversation, pronounced "crack") and local beer on tap complements the music. People are there to have a good time and visitors from far away are considered a plus.

A ruined church on Dingle Peninsula

In Dingle town, when the sun goes down, traditional music fills the pubs.

In Dingle, there's live music most nights in half a dozen pubs. There's never a cover charge. Just buy a beer and make yourself at home. The Small Bridge Bar and O'Flaherty's are the most famous for their atmosphere and devotion to traditional Irish music. But tonight—and most nights—I make a point to wander the town and follow my ears. Traditional music is alive and popular in Ireland. A "session" is when musical friends (and strangers who become friends) gather and jam. There's generally a fiddle, flute or tin whistle, guitar, *bodhrán* (goat-skin drum), and maybe an accordion.

I follow the music into a pub and order a pint. The music churns intensely, the group joyfully raising each other up one at a time with solos. Sipping from their mugs, they skillfully maintain a faint but steady buzz. The drummer dodges the fiddler's playful bow. The floor on the musicians' platform is stomped paint-free and barmaids scurry through the commotion, gathering towers of empty, cream-crusted glasses. With knees up and heads down, the music goes round and round. Making myself right at home, I "play the boot" (tap my foot) under the table in time with the music. When the chemistry is right, live music in a pub is one of the great Irish experiences.

The Irish like to say that in a pub, you're a guest on your first night; after that, you're a regular. That's certainly true in Dingle . . . the next parish over from Boston.

Belgium and the Netherlands

THE LOW COUNTRIES have always expected the most out of life. Pioneers in freedom, the Dutch rid their land of popes and foreign kings. Hardworking and innovative, they built their nation by taking land from the sea. And from that below-sea-level homeland, they sailed—reaching out across the world—to build an empire and earn a Golden Age.

Perhaps because of their high expectations, the people of the Low Countries have also developed a knack for wringing as much joy as possible out of life while playing the cards they were dealt. Belgium has mastered the fine art of beer, chocolate, and church-bell chimes. And the Netherlands, with some of Europe's finest cityscapes, takes a practical approach to the challenges of prostitution and drugs—in a way that both fascinates and challenges visitors.

Careening from windmills to coffeeshops, and from austere to hedonistic, these stories capture Dutch life below sea level, from the seat of a bike, and on strolls along windy dikes. Traveling in the Low Countries always makes me reconsider things I've never before questioned.

Windmill at Netherlands Open-Air Museum, in Arnhem

Bruges: Pickled in Gothic

WITH A SMILE, the friendly shopkeeper hands me a pharaoh's head and two hedgehogs. Happily sucking the liquor out of a hedgehog, I walk out of the small chocolate shop with a €3 assortment of Bruges' best pralines—chocolate treats with sweet fillings.

Belgian chocolate is considered Europe's finest. And in Bruges, locals boast that their chocolate is the best in Belgium. I'm always tempted by the treats in display windows throughout town. Godiva's chocolate is thought to be the best big-factory brand, but for quality and service, I drop by one of the many family-run shops. (I pray for cool weather in Belgium because quality chocolate shops close down when it's hot.)

Gourmet chocolate and a Bruges temptress

Free time to explore Bruges always puts me in a fun-loving mood. With Renoir canals, pointy gilded architecture, and stay-awhile cafés, the marvelously preserved medieval town is a delight. Where else can you bike along a canal, munch mussels, drink fine monk-made beer, see a Michelangelo statue, and savor heavenly chocolate, all within 300 yards of a bell tower that rings out "Don't worry, be happy" jingles?

The town is Bruges (broozh) in French and English, and Brugge (BROO-gah) in Flemish. Before it was French or Flemish, the name was a Viking word for "wharf" or "embankment." Right from the start, Bruges was a trading center. By the 14th century, it had a population of 35,000 (comparable to London's) and the most important cloth market in northern Europe. By the 16th century, silt had clogged the harbor and killed the economy. Like so many of Europe's small-town wonders, Bruges is well-pickled because its economy went sour. But rediscovered by modern-day tourists, Bruges thrives.

The serene side of Bruges from a canal-boat tour

The colorful heart of the city, Market Square, is ringed by great old gabled buildings. Since 1300, it has been crowned by a leaning bell tower with a famous set of musical bells. Climbing its 366 steps rewards me with a commanding view and a chance to peek into the carillon room. I time my climb to be there on the quarter hour. That's when the giant revolving barrel with movable tabs jerks into motion and mechanically rings the 47 bells to play the tune *du jour*.

Marveling at the medieval contraption doing its musical thing, I meet the carillonist who explains how the adjustable tabs are moved one way to ring different bells and the other way to make different rhythms. For concerts, the barrel is disengaged, which then engages the manual keyboard. About to leave, I shake his hand . . . and realize it's deformed by a

Gabled buildings line Market Square in Bruges.

massive callous making his little finger twice the normal width. Noticing my reaction, he says, "That's from lots of practice . . . a carillonist plays the keyboard with fists and feet rather than fingers." Then he reminds me there's a free concert tonight at eight.

Scampering down the spiral steps, I realize I need to be quick to see the remaining sights and still have time for the brewery tour. Thankfully, everything's very close.

The Basilica of the Holy Blood is named for its relic of the blood of Christ, which, according to tradition, was brought to Bruges in 1150 after the Second Crusade. The City Hall has the oldest and most sumptuous Gothic hall in the Low Countries. The Gruuthuse Museum is a wealthy brewer's home, filled with everything from medieval bedpans to a guillotine. The Church of Our Lady has a brick tower that rockets high above anything else in town—standing as a memorial to the power and wealth of Bruges in its heyday. The church holds a delicate *Madonna and Child* by Michelangelo. Bought with money made from Bruges' lucrative cloth trade, it's said to be the only statue by the artist to leave his native Italy during his lifetime.

I step into the De Halve Maan brewery just in time for the last English-language tour of the day. This is a handy way to pay my respects to the favorite local beer: Brugse Zot. The happy gang at this working family brewery posts a sign reminding their drinkers: "The components of our beer are vitally necessary and contribute to a well-balanced life pattern. Nerves, muscles, visual sentience, and a healthy skin are stimulated by these in a positive manner. For longevity and life-long equilibrium, drink Brugse Zot in moderation!" Like any good beer tour, it finishes with a proud tasting.

Belgians, who seem to speak better English after a beer, love to show off their beer expertise. The man at the bar gives me an earful. "Our country has more than 350 types of beer. That's the most. And each beer must be served in the right glass. If they don't have the correct glass, I will order a different beer. Look at our variety," he says, handing me a menu of what's available. "Dentergems is made with coriander and orange peel. Those who don't usually like beer might enjoy our fruity brews: cherry-flavored *kriek* and raspberry-flavored *frambozen*."

I tell him I like the complex and creamy, monk-made Chimay.

He says, "Me as well. Brewed by Trappist monks, the Chimay could almost make celibacy livable . . . almost."

I walk off my beer buzz with a stroll through the *begijnhof*—a tranquil courtyard of frugal little homes. For reasons of war and testosterone, there were more women than men in the medieval Low Countries. The religious order of Beguines gave women (often single or widowed) a dignified place to live and work. While there are no longer Beguines, many *begijnhofs* survive—taken over by town councils for subsidized housing, or—like this one—still church-owned and housing nuns. Walking beneath the wispy trees of the charming *begijnhof* almost makes me want to don a habit and fold my hands.

It's been a full day, but I'm not quite ready for my hotel room. Stopping by a waffle stand, I get a Belgian waffle to go. Grabbing a wooden bench in the little courtyard under the bell tower, I'm just in time for the evening carillon concert. As the bells ring, I imagine the musician's massive calloused hands hard at work. Eating the last sweet strawberry on my waffle, I ponder how, even though this Gothic town is a thousand years old, it makes me feel like a kid.

Night falls in Bruges as the carillon plays.

Flabbergasted in a Haarlem B&B

I'M HANGING OUT in the living room of my B&B in the Amsterdam suburb of Haarlem with my hosts Hans and Marjet. Reaching for my Heineken, I notice it sits on a handbook the Dutch government produces to teach prostitutes about safe sex. Thumbing through it, I say to Hans, "It's both artistic and explicit."

"It's Victoria without the secret," he whispers playfully.

"Isn't this shocking to a lot of people?" I ask.

Marjet and Hans

"Only to the English and the Americans," he replies. "Remember, this is Holland. Last night we saw a local TV documentary. It was about body piercing, in full graphic detail—tits, penises, everything. Last week there was a special on the Kama Sutra. Sexual gymnastics like I had never seen. To us Dutch, these were only two more documentaries . . . no big deal. Perhaps these would have been big hits on American TV."

"I don't know," I say, realizing that I was finding the handbook more interesting than Hans. "But you know what the most-visited page on my website is? A goofy little article comparing Amsterdam's two sex museums."

"Sex is not clickbait here. It's not a taboo in Holland," says Marjet. "But we are not reckless with sex, either. The Dutch teen pregnancy rate is one-half the American rate."

Staying in a B&B saves money. As a bonus, I find that B&B hosts are often great students of intercultural human nature and love to share their findings. They give me an intimate glimpse of a culture I couldn't get from the front desk of a hotel.

This is certainly true of Hans and Marjet, who encourage guests to make themselves thoroughly at home. And in their living room, with its well-worn chairs, crowded books, funky near-antiques, and an upright piano littered with tattered music, it's easy to feel at home.

Hans and Marjet live in three rooms and rent out five. Hans would like a little more living space. Like his neighbors, he could glass-in his tiny backyard, but he couldn't bear trading away his lush but pint-sized garden. Bringing me another beer, he asks, "How long do you stay here this time?"

Hans discusses cultural quirks.

"Not long enough" is my regular response. I'm Hans' pet Yankee. He's on a personal crusade to get me to relax, to slow down. To Hans, I am the quintessential schedule-driven, goal-oriented American.

Hans provides more insight into the cultural differences of their guests. "We Dutch are in the middle," he says. "We are efficient like the Germans—that's why there are many American companies here in Holland. But we want to live like the French."

"And crack jokes like the English," adds Marjet. "Everybody here admires the British sense of humor. We watch BBC for the comedies."

Hans sees cultural differences in their guests' breakfast manners, too. "Americans like hard advice and to be directed. Europeans—especially the Germans—they know what they want. The French take three days to defrost. But Americans talk and make friends quickly. Europeans, even with no language differences, keep their private formal island at the breakfast table."

Pointing to their two kitchen tables, he continues. "If there are Germans sitting here and Americans there, I break the ice. Introducing the Americans to the Germans, I say, 'It's okay, they left their guns in the States.' We Dutch are like the Germans—but with a sense of humor."

Getting back to our talk about how different cultures approach sex,

Marjet says to Hans, "Tell Rick the 'Dutch boys on the English beach' story. This body stuff may be stressful to Americans, but it sends the English under their pillows."

"As a schoolboy I traveled with a buddy to England," Hans begins. "We changed our pants on the beach without the towel hassle—no problem. We're good Dutch boys. As usual, the beach had an audience: bench-loads of retired Brits enjoying the fresh air, suffering through their soggy sandwiches. When my friend began changing into his swimsuit, all the people turned their heads away. Amused by our power to move the English masses, we repeated the move. I pulled my trousers down and all the heads turned away again."

Marjet, laughing like she's hearing the story for the first time, says, "We don't see many English on our beaches."

"We get mostly Americans," says Hans.

"We'd be happy to fill our house with only Americans," says Marjet. "Americans are easy to communicate with. They're open. They taught me to express myself, to say what I really think."

Hans breaks in with a Tony the Tiger tourist imitation, "Oh wow, this is grrreat! What a grrreat house you have here!"

"Americans get flabbergasted," Marjet adds.

"The English don't know how to be flabbergasted," says Hans.

"I think you nearly flabbergasted them on that beach," Marjet says. "When we visited Colorado, my trip went better when I learned to say 'wow' a couple of times a day."

Curling comfortably in the corner of the sofa, tucking her legs under her small body, Marjet explains, "When an American asks, 'How are you?' we say, 'Okay,' to mean 'good.' The American says, 'That doesn't sound very good.' We explain, 'We're European.'"

Hans says, "Then the American replies, 'Oh, yes—you're honest.'"

Fascinated by the smiley-face insincerity of America, Marjet says, "In the US, even supermarket shopping bags have big 'smile and be a winner' signs."

"It's true," I agree. "Only in America could you find a bank that fines tellers if they don't tell every client to 'Have a nice day.'"

Hans says, "Did you know that the Dutch are the most wanted workers at Disneyland Paris? This is because most Dutch are open-minded. We can smile all day. And we speak our languages."

Marjet explains, "In Holland when someone asks, 'Do you speak your languages?' they mean: Do you speak French, German, and English, along with Dutch?"

Hans continues. "And for us, acting friendly is maybe less exhausting than for the French. Can you imagine a French person having to smile all day long?"

Hans tops off my glass of Heineken. "God created all the world. It was marvelous. But France . . . it was just too perfect. So he put in the French to balance things out."

"And Canada could have had it all: British culture, French cuisine, American know-how," says Marjet. "But they messed up and got British food, French know-how, and American culture."

As I climb the steep Dutch stairs to my bedroom in the loft, I ponder the value of friends on the road. The most memorable moments of this day came after I was done sightseeing.

Market Square in Haarlem

Going Dutch . . . in Holland's Polder Country

Today my longtime Dutch friends Hans and Marjet are driving me through polder country. In these vast fields reclaimed from the sea, cows graze, narrow canals function as fences, and only church spires and windmills interrupt the horizon.

Hans is behind the wheel. He injects personality-plus into all he does, whether running a B&B or guiding Americans around Holland. Bouncy Marjet has a head of wispy strawberry-blonde hair, red tennis shoes, and a talent for assembling a Salvation Army-chic outfit for under $20.

As he drives, Hans talks about how people, including himself, call the entire country "Holland" when Holland actually comprises just two of the 12 provinces that make up the Netherlands. He says, "That'd be like me calling America 'Texas.'" I bring up that most of America's cliché images of the Netherlands come from the region properly referred to as Holland.

Looking out at the polder country, I remember that the word "Netherlands" means "lowlands." This country occupies the low-lying delta near the mouth of three of Europe's large rivers, including the Rhine. In medieval times, inhabitants built a system of earthen dikes to protect their land from flooding caused by tides and storm surges. The fictional story of the little Dutch boy who saves the country by sticking his finger in a leaking dike summed up the country's precarious situation. Many Americans know this story from a popular 19th-century novel, but Hans says few Dutch people have ever heard of it. In 1953, severe floods breached the old dikes, killing 1,800 and requiring a major overhaul of the system.

Chatting as we drive, I'm struck by how 10 minutes from Amsterdam, you can be in this wide-open polder land. It's early summer, and the landscape is streaked with yellow and orange tulip fields.

Hans points out a quaint windmill along a sleepy canal. An old mill like this was used to turn an Archimedes screw in order to pump the polders dry. After diking off large tracts of land below sea level, the Dutch harnessed wind energy to lift the water up and out of the enclosed area,

Filming my show: "The Dutch claim if you stand on a chair you can see all across the Netherlands."

divert it into canals, and drain the land. They cultivated hardy plants that removed salt from the soil, slowly turning marshy estuaries into fertile farmland. The windmills later served a second purpose for farmers by turning stone wheels to grind their grain.

This area, once a merciless sea, is now dotted with tranquil towns. Many of the residents here are actually older than the land they live on, which was reclaimed in the 1960s. The old-time windmills, once the conquerors of the sea, are now relics, decorating the land like medallions on a war vet's chest. Today, they've been replaced with battalions of sleek, modern wind turbines.

Several other Dutch icons came directly from the country's flat, reclaimed landscape. Wooden shoes *(klompen)* allowed farmers to walk across soggy fields. They're also easy to find should they come off in high water because they float. Tulips and other flowers grew well in the sandy soil near dunes.

We head seaward, driving past sprawling flower-mogul mansions, then through desolate dunes. The little road dwindles to a sandy trailhead. Hans parks the car and we hike to a peaceful stretch of North Sea beach. Pointing a stick of driftwood at a huge seagoing tanker, Hans says, "That ship's going to the big port at Rotterdam. We're clever at trade. We have to be—we're a small country."

Ships dredge sand to strengthen dikes.

The Netherlands welcomes the world's business, but the country is not designed for big shots. Hans explains, "Being ordinary is being prudent. We Dutch say a plant that grows above the grains gets its head cut off. Even our former queen prefers to do her own shopping."

While Hans and I talk, Marjet skips ahead of us on the beach, collecting shells with the wide-eyed wonder of a 10-year-old. "Cheap souvenirs," Hans teases. One cliché the Dutch don't dispute is their frugality. Hans quizzes me: "Who invented copper wire?"

I know that one. "Two Dutch boys fighting over a penny."

Hans points up the coast at a huge arc of mud shooting up from a ship. "We're moving mountains of sand and mud to make our dikes stronger against the sea." The frugal Dutch are, at heart, pragmatic. They spend their money smartly. In this era of global warming and rising sea levels, the Dutch are spending billions to upgrade their dikes and bulk up their beaches to hold back the sea. All this technological tinkering with nature reminds me of a popular local saying: "God made the Earth, but the Dutch made Holland." They made it and they're determined to keep it.

Marjet scuffs through the sand, her pockets full of seashells, her scarf flapping in the wind like a jump rope. Under big, romping white clouds, I think, "Everything's so . . . Dutch."

Windmills helped reclaim land from the sea.

Pedaling Through Amsterdam

SIGHTSEEING ISN'T just seeing. To get the full experience of a place, you need to feel, hear, taste, and smell it. On this visit to Amsterdam, I'm making a point to focus on sensual travel. It's a city made to engage all of the senses.

I always rent a bike here. I want to feel the bricks and pavement beneath two wheels. The lack of hills and the first-class bike-lane infrastructure makes biking here a breeze. The clerk at the rental shop must be tired of explaining why they don't carry mountain bikes in this flat land. When I ask, he responds—in classic Dutch directness—"Mountain bikes in the Netherlands make no sense at all. When a dog takes a dump, we have a new mountain. You pedal around it . . . not over. It's no problem."

I ride off along the shiny wet cobbles, my Amsterdam experience framed by my black bike's handlebars. I get pinged by passing bikes and ping my bell to pass others. When it comes to bike bells, there's no language barrier. For my own safety, I wish I had a bigger periphery, as cars, trams, bikers, and pedestrians seem to float by from all directions

A boat glides through a canal lined by bikes.

Bikes: the preferred transport

in silence—their noise lost in the white noise of breezing through this dreamy city on two wheels.

Reaching the Red Light District, I stop to use a classic old street-corner urinal. It's painted a deep green and designed to give the user plenty of privacy from the neck down and a slice-of-Amsterdam view at the same time. The pungent smells of pot smoke and someone else's urine compete with the dank smell of the canal. I remember one of the new Amsterdam facts I've learned: A handful of people drown in the canals each year. When their bodies are finally dredged up, very often, their zippers are down. They were very drunk and, rather than using the civilized urinal as I did, they used the canal . . . their final mistake. Across the lane, an abundant woman in a cliché of lingerie eyes me seductively from a window, framed in red. I think to myself, "This is probably the most unforgettable trip to a urinal I'll ever have in my life."

Pedaling on, I notice that the Red Light District is now a little more compact than I remember. Spliced in among the windows displaying enticing women are other windows promoting fashion and contemporary art. Amsterdam's leaders recognize that legalized marijuana and prostitution are part of the city's edgy

The top floor of a garage for bikes in downtown Amsterdam

charm, but are also working to rein in the sleaze. They're not renewing some Red Light District leases, instead giving them to more preferable businesses.

Continuing on my ride, it strikes me that much of Amsterdam still looks like it did three or four centuries ago, during the Dutch Golden Age, when this was the world's richest city.

I continue on to a square called Museumplein where Amsterdam's three big art museums are gathered—and selfie-crazed millennial tourists gather around the red-and-white "I AMsterdam" letters, which are as tall as people.

I stop a moment to take in the square. Long lines plague the Dutch Master-filled Rijksmuseum and Van Gogh Museum—both understandably popular. There's rarely a wait at the Stedelijk Museum, nicknamed "the bathtub" because of the striking shape of its modern architecture. Inside are 20th-century favorites (Dalí, Picasso, Kandinsky) and crazy contemporary art. I'm not a big fan of the abstract style, but the artwork at the Stedelijk is really fun (perhaps really, *really* fun if you're into marijuana—sold with a smile in the city's many "coffeeshops").

The sounds of Amsterdam's knack for good living seem to surround

Vondelpark, Amsterdam's playground

the museum district. Underneath the Rijksmuseum, in a public passage-way, street musicians seem to be performing everything from chamber music to Mongolian throat singing. Around the corner, a man in a top hat cranks away on his candy-colored street organ. Mesmerized children watch its figurines jingle and jangle to the jaunty music as it slowly grinds through its perforated song boards.

The city's biggest green space, Vondelpark, is just a short pedal away. I roll by snippets of Dutch conversation—families with kids, romantic couples, strolling seniors, and hippies sharing blankets and beers.

By now my sense of taste is ready for a little attention. Thinking about the options, I consider *rijsttafel* (literally "rice table"), a ritual dish for tourists in Holland. Not a true Indonesian meal, it's a Dutch innovation designed to highlight the best food of its former colony—specifically to show off all the spices that in some ways originally motivated the colonial age. The dinner includes 20 dishes and a rainbow of spices with white rice to mix and mingle on your plate and palate. Working your way through this tasty experience, it's clear why the Dutch called Indonesia "The Spice Islands."

In the mood for something more historically Dutch, I opt instead for a snack of herring with pickles and onions. Later, I indulge my taste buds at a cheese-tasting class. After a short video that's somewhere between a cheese commercial and dairy soft porn, I guillotine six different local cheeses studying, smelling, and tasting them with a wine accompaniment.

My final experience: some Dutch booze. While the 20-somethings line up for the Heineken Experience—a malty, yeasty amusement ride of a brewery tour—I join an older crowd at the slick House of Bols: Cocktail & Genever Experience. Here, I learn about the heritage of Dutch gin *(genever)*, and test my olfactory skills at a line of 36 scents. I fail miserably, my nose identifying only one scent: butterscotch. I console myself by designing the cocktail of my dreams at a computer kiosk and taking the recipe printout to the nearby barista, who mixes a Dutch gin drink that's uniquely mine.

Pedaling back to my hotel, rattling over those shiny cobbles just inches from the murky canals, I'm thankful I turned down that one last gin.

Dutch Tolerance: Red Lights and Pot Shops

AMSTERDAM is a laboratory of progressive living, bottled inside Europe's finest 17th-century city. Like Venice, this city is a patchwork quilt of elegant architecture and canal-bordered islands anchored upon millions of wooden pilings. But unlike its dwelling-in-the-past, canal-filled cousin, Amsterdam sees itself as a city of the future, built on good living, cozy cafés, great art, street-corner jazz . . . and a persistent spirit of live-and-let-live.

During its Golden Age in the 1600s, Amsterdam was the world's richest city, an international sea-trading port, and a cradle of capitalism. Wealthy burghers built a planned city of tree-shaded canals lined with townhouses topped with fancy gables. The atmosphere they created attracted a high-energy mix of humanity: Immigrants, Jews, outcasts, and political rebels were drawn here by its tolerant atmosphere. Sailors—so famously hard-living and rowdy—were needed to man the vast fleet of merchant ships. And painters like young Rembrandt found work capturing that atmosphere on canvas.

I approach Amsterdam as an ethnologist observing a unique culture. A stroll through any neighborhood is rewarded with slice-of-life scenes that could rarely be found elsewhere. Carillons chime from church

Sailors and strip joints in the Red Light District

towers in neighborhoods where sex is sold in red-lit windows. Young professionals smoke pot with impunity next to old ladies in bonnets selling flowers. Each block has a quirky and informal custom of neighbors looking out for neighbors, where an elderly man feels safe in his home knowing he's being watched over by the sex workers next door.

Prostitution has been legal since the 1980s (although streetwalking is still forbidden). The women are often entrepreneurs, running their own businesses and paying taxes. Women usually rent their space for eight-hour shifts. A good spot costs $150 for a day shift and $250 for an evening. Popular prostitutes charge $50-70 for a 20-minute visit. Many belong to a union called the Red Thread.

The rooms look tiny from the street, but most are just display windows, opening onto a room behind or upstairs with a bed, a sink, and little else. Prostitutes are required to keep their premises hygienic, avoid minors, and make sure their clients use condoms. If a prostitute has a dangerous client, she pushes her emergency button and is rescued not by a pimp, but by the police.

The Dutch are a handsome people—tall, healthy, and with good posture. They're open, honest, refreshingly blunt, and ready to laugh. As connoisseurs of world culture, they appreciate Rembrandt paintings, Indonesian food, and the latest French films, but with a down-to-earth, blue-jeans attitude.

While smoking tobacco is not allowed indoors, the Dutch seem to smoke more cigarettes than anyone in Europe. Yet somehow, they are among the healthiest people in the world. Trim and wiry Dutch seniors sip beers, have fun blowing smoke rings, and ask me why Americans have a love affair with guns and kill themselves with Big Macs.

While the Dutch smoke a lot of tobacco, they smoke less marijuana than the European average. Although hard drugs are illegal, a joint causes about as much excitement here as a bottle of beer. Still, following an ethic of pragmatic harm reduction rather than legislating morality and pushing incarceration, the government allows the retail sale of pot. The Dutch think the concept of a "victimless crime" is a contradiction in terms. If a tipsy tourist calls an ambulance after smoking too much pot, medics just say, "Drink something sweet and walk it off."

Throughout Amsterdam, you'll see "coffeeshops"—pubs selling marijuana—with menus that look like the inventory of a drug bust.

Most of downtown Amsterdam's coffeeshops feel grungy and foreboding to American travelers who aren't part of the youth-hostel crowd. But the places in local neighborhoods and small towns around the countryside feel much more inviting to people without piercings and tattoos.

Coffeeshops sell marijuana.

Paradox is the most *gezellig* (cozy) coffeeshop I've found in Amsterdam—a mellow, graceful place. The managers, Ludo and Wiljan, and their staff are patient with descriptions. With each visit, they happily walk me through their menu. The juice is fresh, the music is easy, and the neighborhood is charming.

It's become a ritual for me now to drop by Paradox and check in with Ludo and Wiljan with each visit to Amsterdam. I grab a wicker chair just outside their door. Framed in the jungle of lush vines that decorates the storefront, I sit and observe the metabolism of the neighborhood. I think about how challenging societal norms—with a pinch of shock here and a dash of tolerance there—leads to progress. I'm grateful that this city's bold experiment in freedom continues.

For the gardener on your gift list?

A Coffeeshop Conversation in Amsterdam

WANDERING AROUND Amsterdam, every few blocks you pass a window full of plants displaying a red, yellow, and green Rastafarian flag—both indications that the coffeeshop doesn't sell much coffee. These days, "coffeeshop" refers to a place where the Dutch gather to buy and smoke marijuana. I duck into one of these coffeeshops to get the latest.

A round table at the front window is filled with a United Nations of tourists sharing travelers' tales stirred by swizzle sticks of smoke. From the looks of the ashtray, they've been here a while. The table is a clutter of tea cups, maps, and guidebooks.

Taking a seat at the bar next to a leathery 40-something biker and a college-age kid with two holes in his body for each one in mine, I feel more like a tourist than I have all day. The bartender, Pieter—sporting a shaved head and a one-inch goatee—greets me in English and passes me the menu.

Swarte Marok, Blond Marok, White Widow, Northern Light, Stonehedge, Grasstasy . . . so many choices on the menu, and that's just the *wiet* (marijuana). Hashish selections fill the bottom half of the menu. I point to a clipped-on scrap of paper. "What's *Aanbieding: Swarte Marok?*"

"Today's special is Black Moroccan," Pieter says.

Above me dangles a tiny Starship Enterprise from a garland of spiky leaves. And behind Pieter stands a row of much-used and apparently never-cleaned bongs, reminding me of the hubbly-bubblies that litter Egyptian teahouses. With a flick of my finger, I set the Enterprise rocking.

Pieter says, "Access to the stars. That's us."

When I marvel at how open-minded the Dutch are, Pieter explains, "We're not open-minded, just tolerant. There's a difference. *Wiet* is not legal . . . only tolerated."

I ask, "Does this tolerance cause a problem?"

Handing a two-foot-tall bong and a baggie of leaves to a woman whose huge dog is tied to the bike rack outside, Pieter says, "My grandmother has an old pipe rack. It has a sign: 'A satisfied smoker creates no problems.'"

"That was tobacco, wasn't it?"

"Yes, it's from the 1860s. But this still applies today."

I ask the guy with all the holes why he smokes here.

Speaking through the silver stud in his tongue, he says, "Some young people hang out at coffeeshops because their parents don't want them smoking at home, others come here to smoke pot with their parents. I come here for the coffeeshop ambience."

The older guy in leather laughs. "Yeah, ambience with a shaved head," he says, as Pieter hands him his baggie to go.

I ask about the sign with a delivery boy on it.

"In Holland, we have pot delivery services," Pieter explains, "like you have pizza delivery in America. Older people take out or have it delivered."

A middle-aged woman hurries in and says, "Yellow Cab, please."

Pieter hands her a baggie saying, "I cut you a fat bag."

With a *"Dank u wel*, Pieter," she tosses it into her shopping tote and hurries out.

In the Netherlands, pot users go to coffeeshops—not jail.

"We have lots of states where recreational pot is legal but a coffeeshop like this is not possible yet in the United States," I say.

"I know," Pieter agrees. He shows me snapshots of Woody Harrelson and Willie Nelson, each hanging out in this obscure little coffeeshop, and continues. "America's two most famous pot smokers told me all about America."

The kid chimes in. "Hollanders—even those who don't smoke—they believe soft drugs . . . you know, pot, hash . . . it shouldn't be a crime."

"What do your parents think?" I ask.

"They think the youth have a problem. My dad says, 'Holland will get the bill later on.'"

"And other countries . . . doesn't legal pot in Holland cause them a problem?" I ask.

"Actually, it's not legal here," he reminds me, "just tolerated. Officially, we can't legalize anything because your country made these world treaties."

"The French complain about Holland's popularity with drug users, but they have a worse problem with illegal drugs," Pieter adds. "Here,

An array of joints for sale

the police know exactly what's going on and where."

"But what about hard drugs?"

"These are the problem. Europe comes to Holland for more than the pot. Most Dutch agree that these hard drugs should be illegal. We Dutch—I think because pot is tolerated—handle our drugs better than the kids who travel here to get high. But, like everywhere, we have a hard drug problem."

At this coffeeshop, you order at the bar.

Pieter points to a chart on the wall that shows how to avoid bad XTC pills. "The police give us this chart. My English friends cannot believe they help in this way. They call our *Politie* the 'polite-ies.' We work with the police and they are thankful. It is helpful for our community."

"You don't see the Dutch dying from heroin overdoses," Pieter continues. "But every time I read the newspaper it seems another German is found dead on the floor of a cheap Amsterdam hotel room.

"But pot," he says, fingering a perfectly rolled joint, "this is not a problem."

"In many states, American prisons are filled with pot offenders," I tell him.

"Take your choice," he says. "Allow for alternative ways of living or build more prisons. Here in Holland, pot is like cigarettes. We smoke it. We pay taxes. We don't go to jail."

Switzerland and Austria

THE HIGH-ALTITUDE thrills of the Alps are matched by the high cultural thrills of Vienna. And, whether I'm standing all alone atop an alpine bluff or enjoying standing room only at the opera, both make me want to raise my arms high and sing for joy.

In Austria, culture, history, and nature mix it up as if they shared the same crib. The capital, Vienna, comes with a fine symphony, exquisite chocolate cakes, and an enduring Habsburg heritage. And just up the Danube, in the alpine foothills, sword-fern fantasies in ruined castles make boyhood dreams come true.

In neighboring Switzerland, life is viewed differently from the scalps of the Alps. Respecting the power of nature while conquering it with cables and cogwheels, the Swiss have taken Europe's most rugged land and made it theirs. Exploring a humble village where nearly everyone has the same last name, where life is accompanied by an orchestra of cowbells, and where farmers ride down the mountain on tarp-loads of freshly cut hay, you find traditional culture survives most vividly in the high country. In the Alps, you can taste the mountain flowers in the cheese.

Hiking in Switzerland's Berner Oberland

Gimmelwald: The Swiss Alps in Your Lap

O N THE TRAIN heading south from Interlaken into the high country, the Swiss woman sitting across from me asks where I'm going. When I say "Gimmelwald," she assumes I mean the famous resort in the next valley, and says, "Grindelwald, that's very nice." When assured that Gimmelwald is my target, she leans forward, widens her eyes, and—with her sing-song Swiss German accent—asks, "*Und* how do you know Gimmelvald?"

The traffic-free village of Gimmelwald hangs nonchalantly on the edge of a cliff high above Lauterbrunnen Valley. This sleepy village has more cow troughs than mailboxes.

Gimmelwald is an ignored station on the cable-car route up to the spectacular mountain peak, the Schilthorn. The village should be built to the hilt. But, led by a visionary schoolmaster, the farming community managed to reclassify its land as an "avalanche zone"—too dangerous for serious building projects. So, while developers gnash their teeth, sturdy peasants continue to milk cows and make hay—enjoying a lifestyle that survives in a modern world only by the grace of a government that subsidizes such poor traditional industries.

Gimmelwald is a community in the rough. When I arrive, I take a quick "welcome back" walk—a tour of the whole town takes about 15 minutes. Its two streets, a 700-year-old zig and zag, are decorated by drying laundry, hand-me-down tricycles, and hollowed stumps bursting proudly with geraniums. Grandpas, like white-bearded elves, set aside hand-carved pipes to chop firewood. Children play "barn" instead of "house." And a little boy parks his toy car next to his dad's tank-tread mini tractor—necessary for taming this alpine environment. Stones sit like heavy checkers on old rooftops, awaiting nature's next move. While these stones protect the slate from the violent winter winds, in summer it's often so quiet that you can hear the cows ripping tufts of grass.

Traditional log-cabin homes line the lanes. Their numbers are not addresses, but fire insurance numbers. The troll-like hut aging near the cable-car station is filled with rounds of Alp cheese, also aging. Small as

A farmer loads up his tarp for a hayride directly to the barn.

Gimmelwald is, it still has daily mail service. The postman drops down from neighboring Mürren each day (by golf cart in summer, sled in winter) to deliver mail and pick up letters at the communal mailbox. Most Gimmelwalders have one of two last names: von Allmen or Feuz. I'm told that to keep prescriptions and medical records straight, the doctor in nearby Lauterbrunnen goes by birthdate first, then the patient's name.

Watching two schoolboys kick a soccer ball just a few steps from the cliff's edge, I enjoy the thought that there's nothing but air between Gimmelwald and the rock face of the Jungfrau directly across the valley. Over there, small avalanches look and sound like distant waterfalls. Village kids have likely learned the hard way: Kick that ball wrong and it ends up a mile below on the Lauterbrunnen Valley floor.

My Gimmelwald walk comes with the sweet smell of freshly cut hay. The townspeople systematically harvest the steep hillside, with entire families cutting and gathering every inch of hay. After harvesting what the scythe can reach, they pull hay from nooks and crannies by hand. Half a day is spent on steep rocks harvesting what a machine could cut in two minutes on a flat field. It's tradition. For locals, cutting the hay is like breathing . . . and there's one right way to do it.

Climbing from zig to zag, I witness a first for me: A farmer at the top of town has filled his big blue tarp with a mountain of hay the size of a small car. Directly below him is his barn with a bridge leading to its loft—the door open like the mouth of a hungry child. Nonchalantly, as if he does this every day, the farmer climbs onto the hay and rides it like a sled steeply down the field to the little bridge where his son awaits. Together, they drag the load into the loft and close the door.

To inhale the Alps and really hold it in, I sleep high in Gimmelwald. Poor but pleasantly stuck in the past, the village has a creaky hotel, happy hostel, decent pension, and a couple of B&Bs. Walter Mittler's Hotel Mittaghorn, sitting at the top end of Gimmelwald, has long been my favorite. The weather-stained chalet has eight pint-sized balconies and a few tables shaded by umbrellas on its small terrace. Everything comes with huge views. Sitting as if anchored by pitons in the steep, grassy hillside, the hotel is disturbed only by the cheery chatter of hikers and the two-stroke clatter of passing mini tractors. On Walter's terrace, I grab a table next to a group of Alp-aholics from the village's youth hostel. While they compare notes on nearby hikes and team up for tomorrow's adventures, I sip a coffee schnapps and watch rays from the setting sun warm the mountaintops as the moon rises over the Jungfrau.

Suddenly, the bright modern cable car swooshes by with 30 tourists gawking out the windows. Walter joins me with a drink and tells me a local tale illustrating how the Schilthornbahn is good for more than tourism. In Gimmelwald, the modern world began in 1965 with

the arrival of the cable car. Before that, mothers ready to give birth had to hike an hour downhill to the valley floor for a ride into Interlaken. Many mothers didn't make it all the way to the hospital. Just outside of Interlaken, a curve in the road is named for Zita, a Gimmelwald baby . . . born right there.

Today, the Schilthornbahn remains the

all-powerful lift that connects Stechelberg on the valley floor with the mountain communities of Gimmelwald and Mürren on its way to the 10,000-foot Schilthorn summit. This lift shuttles life's essentials—mail, bread, and coffins—plus skiers, hikers, schoolkids, and hang gliders, along with all those tourists—to and from each community.

Sleek lifts transport locals and visitors alike.

The next morning, I decide to start my day by riding the cable car up to the summit of the Schilthorn, which is capped by a restaurant called Piz Gloria. Lifts go twice hourly, involve two transfers, and take 30 minutes. Inside the gondola, watching the altitude meter go up, up, up comes with a soundtrack: my ears popping.

Reaching the top, I head to an unforgettable breakfast. Every table in the revolving restaurant comes with a thrilling and eventually 360-degree view. The experience never gets old. I sip my coffee slowly to enjoy one complete circle. Then, I drop into the theater to see clips from the James Bond movie *On Her Majesty's Secret Service*, in which it seems that this same restaurant is blown up. Finally, I go outside for the real thrills . . . to frolic on the ridge. A combination of the thin air and watching hang gliders jump into airborne ecstasy always stokes my pumping heart.

Now it's time to head back down the mountain. While it's possible to hike down from the top, I've found that the first gondola station below the summit, Birg, is the best jumping-off point for a high-country hike. Leaving Birg, I hike down toward Gimmelwald. Within a couple minutes, I'm surrounded by a harsh alpine world. After skidding through a patch of loose shale, I stop for a moment—just to hear the sound of the tumbling pebbles eventually grow silent and be replaced by the distant tinkling of cowbells and a cascading stream. As I hike gingerly along the edge of a ridge, dramatic valleys stretch to my left and right while, high above, icy Alps pop against a brilliant blue.

A revolving restaurant caps the Schilthorn.

If the quality of a church is a matter of how close you feel to God, being high in the Alps just might be Europe's ultimate cathedral. A day like today, with a perch like this, has holy rollers doing cartwheels and even Lutherans raising their hands.

After a steep descent, I step out of the forest and reach the village I call home. The finish line is a bench that sits where the trail hits the tiny paved lane that marks the high end of Gimmelwald. This bench is one of my favorite "savor Europe" spots: the right place to just sit still and take it all in. Cows munch, ignoring the view. The little resort of Mürren crowns a bluff above me on the left, keeping all the fancy tourists where they belong. Directly across the valley, a river bursts out of a glacier. Below that, in a lonely meadow, an alpine farm that has intrigued me for years still sits high above the tree line, forever alone amid distant flecks that must be cows and goats. Below me, the village schoolyard comes with the happy noise of children at play. Suddenly, Christian, a farmer (and the town's go-to accordion player), rumbles by. He's coming back from the fields in his mini truck towing a wobbly wagonload of hay. His kids bounce on top like happy cartoons.

Ideal for sweet dreams high in the Alps

Enjoying this alone is a delight. But sharing this bench with the right travel partner, the sun of a daylong hike ruddy on your smiling faces, is even better. There are many peaks and ridges in Switzerland offering high-elevation thrills . . . but at the end of the day, I love kicking off my boots in storybook-perfect Gimmelwald.

In Search of Edelweiss

I**T'S A GLORIOUS** Swiss Alps morning. I'm spending my day walking with my schoolteacher friend, Olle, exploring the alpine landscape surrounding his home in Gimmelwald. Before we're too far along, I realize I'm getting a blister.

Opening his rucksack on a rock, Olle asks me to take off my shoe and sock. Muttering that he can't believe how tourists tackle these mountains without good hiking boots, he fits some moleskin around my tender toe. As Olle works, I lie back on the rugged tufts of grass growing through the pebbly shale.

We continue on, following a faint path along the ridge. I stop every few steps to enjoy vast views of the Schilthorn on our left and the Jungfrau on our right. Olle takes on his teacher's voice: "We respect nature more than the tourists do. When there's an avalanche warning, we take the gondola down. Tourists continue sledding. There are many accidents. In Lauterbrunnen, maps show red flags for places of mountain injuries and black ones for deaths." Pointing to the towering rock cliff of the mountain over the valley directly ahead of us, he says, "The Eiger is solid black."

As I squint up at a wasp-like helicopter, Olle answers my question before I ask it. "Those are mostly sightseeing trips. But even sightseeing trips are related to mountain rescue. As they show a tourist around, they are practicing for emergency rescues."

"Are there really dead climbers hanging from ropes on the Eiger?" I ask.

"Yes," says Olle. "It's sad when bodies are finally recovered. They look like they did when we saw them last, except with a very light beard. You can tell from the beard how long they lived. The family has to identify them."

The weather can turn at any time. Just last month, a storm hit fast. Within a few minutes, five people died: three mountaineers on the Eiger, one on the Mönch, and one in the air—a paraglider.

I tell Olle of a harrowing experience I had back in my youth-hostel days. We'd hike up the Schilthorn from the hostel with a plastic bag, sit on the bag, and slide down the glacier—breathtaking fun. As a reckless young tour guide, I'd lead my groups down the mountain in the same way.

One day, late in the season, sliding on an icy but smaller-than-usual sliding field, I started going out of control. Hurtling directly toward the rocky edge, I didn't know what to do, but I did know I had to do something. After almost too much time to consider my options, I dug my hands like brakes into the rocky ice. Going through several degrees of burn in a matter of seconds, I ground to a halt with blackened, blistered, and bleeding hands—and a bloody butt.

My group heralded me as a hero. But in the doctor's office in Mürren, I was scolded as a fool, the whipping boy for all the stupid tourists who disrespect the power of the mountain. The doctor didn't even bother to clean my hands. He lectured me, sprayed something on my wounds, and bandaged me. I left knowing that the little bits of Schilthorn embedded in my palms would come out only in the pus of a later infection.

Olle nods, as if in support of the doctor, and says, "This happens many times."

He tells me that even cows become victims of the mountains, occasionally wandering off cliffs. Alpine farmers expect to lose some of their

Gimmelwald, built in an avalanche zone yet specializing in alpine tranquility

cows in "hiking accidents." These days, cows are double the weight of cows a hundred years ago and no less stupid. If one wanders off a cliff in search of greener grass, the others follow. Farmers tell their sons about the time at the high Alp above Gimmelwald when a dozen cows performed this stunt . . . and died like lemmings. Helicopters recover the dead cows, flying them out, but because the meat must be drained of blood immediately for human consumption, it's wasted. It's meat fit only for dogs.

As we continue our walk, a pastel carpet of flowers trims the scene: golden clover, milk kraut, bellflowers, daisies. "For me, it's like meeting old friends when the flowers come out again in the spring," Olle says. All but abandoning me for the flowers, he rummages through his rucksack and pulls out a weathered handbook describing the local flora. "My bible," he says. "When the cows eat this grass with all these flowers . . . it is a good mix for the milk."

"Okay, Rick, you will now risk your life for a flower." He leaves the trail and creeps over an edge and out of sight to find an edelweiss. Loose rocks, huge drop, no helicopter in sight . . . I don't really care about finding edelweiss.

For Olle, the flowers coloring the meadow are his friends.

Then I hear Olle holler, "Yes, I found some! Come around."

Feeling fat and clumsy, I leave the trail. Pulling gingerly at weed handholds, I work my way around a huge rock and across a field of loose shale. Olle comes into view, looking younger than he did a moment ago.

"There are three edelweiss here. But this is a secret for only you and me. This spot must not go in your guidebook." At this point I am not concerned about my guidebook, only my survival. Olle grabs my hand with hands that have grown strong and tough after 14 years of high-altitude village life.

As if to pump up the drama, he whispers, "For me, it would not be a hike without a little danger."

"That's why your school is so small," I whisper under my breath.

"*Edelweiss.* It means 'noble white.' In the valley, it's noble gray. Only at high elevations do they get this white. UV rays give all flowers brighter colors at this altitude." Creeping with me to the ledge, Olle gently bends three precious edelweiss toward the sun. Pinching off a petal, he assures me, "This will not affect reproduction."

Petting a petal gently, I note that it feels like felt.

"Yes, like felt," Olle agrees. "This protects the plants from dehydration. I collect and press flowers but have never pressed an edelweiss. Edelweiss has been picked nearly to extinction."

As we struggle back to the trail, Olle talks on. "Here in Switzerland we are getting serious about our environment. Twenty years ago, our rivers and lakes were very polluted. Today you can nearly drink out of Lake Thun. Now we understand. You don't pee in your living room, do you?"

I assure him that I do not.

Finally reaching the safety of the trail, we walk more quickly, with ease. "Do farmers mind if we walk through their property?" I ask.

"This is a human right—to walk through the land," Olle says. His environmental passion crescendos with his voice. "When I was in Boston, I asked, 'How can I get to the lake?' They told me, 'You can't, it is private.' That is for me perverse. This is unthinkable here in Switzerland. We are guests of this Earth." Like welcome guests, we make ourselves at home, stopping at a peak that stands dramatically high above Gimmelwald. Olle shares a snack as we sit quietly to savor our perch.

Switchbacking steeply back down, we pass through a thick forest and step out at the top end of Gimmelwald. We're cheered on by a fragrant finale . . . a field vibrant with flowers, grasshoppers, bees, crickets, moths, and butterflies.

Olle says, "This year farmers obeyed tradition and not their eyes. They waited too long and had to take cows directly to the high Alps. They skipped this lower field. For these flowers, it is a fine year—no hungry cows."

Switzerland embraces its traditions with such gusto that locals like Olle fear visitors think it's an underdeveloped nation. It's certainly not. And the good news: The traditional alpine culture survives most heartily—like edelweiss—in its most remote corners.

Goats like the flowers, too.

Dangling from a Swiss Cliff

DANGLING FROM a sheer cliff a thousand feet above the valley floor, I pause and look down at my boots, each numbly clinging to a rebar step—which, like giant staples, are tacked across the rock face. Between my legs, like little specks on the valley floor, I see tiny cows doing their part for the Swiss cheese industry. To my left, my mountain guide patiently waits, keeping a wary eye on me. To my right, my Swiss friend Simon laughs, saying, "Hand me your camera."

I know I need a photo to capture this amazing scene. But I don't want to have anything to do with grabbing my camera or posing. I am terrified.

I'm back in my favorite corner of Switzerland: the Berner Oberland. When I arrived, it occurred to me that I'd already ridden the lifts and hiked all the trails in the area. But there was one experience that I had yet to do: traverse the cliffside cableway called the *via ferrata*. This morning, Simon and I pulled on mountaineering harnesses and clipped our carabiners onto the first stretch of a nearly two-mile-long cable, setting off with a local guide on the "iron way" from Mürren to Gimmelwald.

The route does not follow the top of the cliff that separates the high country from Lauterbrunnen Valley. It takes us along the very side of the cliff, like a tiny window-washer on a geological skyscraper. The "trail" ahead of us is a series of steel rebar spikes jutting out from the side of the cliff. As I make my way, I alternate my two carabiners from segment to segment along the sturdy steel cable. For me, physically, this is the max. I am almost numb with fear. After one particularly harrowing crossing—gingerly taking one rebar step after another—I say to the guide, "Okay, now it gets easier?"

Buckled up as we embark on the *via ferrata*

Trying not to look down

"No," he says. "Now comes *Die Hammer Ecke!*" Translated into English, this means "The Hammer Corner." This name does not calm my fears.

For a couple hundred yards, we creep across a perfectly vertical cliff face—feet gingerly gripping rebar steps, hands tight on the cable. Miniature cows and a rushing river are far below me, the cliff face rockets directly above me, and a follow-the-cable horizontal path bends out of sight in either direction.

As I inch along the cliff, my mind flashes back to my many adventures with Simon over the years. Living high on the peaks of Europe, the Swiss are experts at living with nature—and Simon is always eager to share with me the Alps in all their moods. On recent visits, a new theme has emerged: the clear impact of climate change on their world. To people like Simon, who live so close to nature, the physical changes resulting from strange and changing weather is an increasingly troubling reality.

On one of my visits, we rode the early-morning lift to Männlichen, high on the ridge above Grindelwald and Lauterbrunnen, and stepped off and into a visual symphony: Before us towered the mighty Eiger, Mönch, and Jungfrau. Simon, who'd worked at Männlichen's mountaintop restaurant as a kid and still bikes here a couple of nights a week, spoke of the subtle changes he'd noticed here. Walking by a glacial pond, he recalled how, during his childhood, there would be hundreds of frogs singing. Now there are none.

At one time, a ski lift required just a few towers. Now, a swath is cut right up the mountain as each lift is plumbed with snowmaking gear. Big water pipes stick out of the concrete foundations, seeming to trumpet a new age. You won't have ski resorts in the future without artificial snow. Today, the Swiss ski industry is in crisis: A third of the lifts are losing money, a third are in trouble, and only a third are good business. Simon

Thrilling . . . a real cliff-hanger of a hike

gave me a trick postcard. Wiggling it made the glacier come and go. The valley in 1900 . . . filled with ice. The same valley today . . . dry, with a shrunken glacier hanging like a thirsty dog's tongue over the top of the valley high in the distance.

On another hike, as we gazed up at the North Face of the Eiger, Simon told me of speed climbers leaving Interlaken on the early train to the base, scaling this Everest of rock faces, and getting back to Interlaken in time for a late-afternoon business meeting. But as the permafrost thaws, there are more falling rocks, and mountain guides are abandoning once-standard ascents that are no longer safe.

With Simon, I've experienced calm, cool mornings giving way to freak afternoon hailstorms. One time, nervous locals scrambled like squirrels as the sky got dark and then . . . *bam!* Typhoon in the Alps. Flower gardens were hammered into pulp. The road became a river of flowing hail balls, leaves, and petals. Fifteen minutes later, the storm was over, leaving behind casualties: Fabric on chairs was ripped, an entire wall of old windows was left jagged, birds were stripped of their feathers and knocked silly. Car rooftops were blanketed in dents, and windshields were alligatored. With a black humor many Europeans have about climate change, Simon joked, "It's no problem—we Swiss are the most insured people in the world."

Back up on the *via ferrata,* I reach the end of my terrifying journey. Taking that last step, I triumphantly unclip my carabiner for the last time and hug our guide like a full-body high-five. Vivid experiences like this one are a hallmark of travel in the Swiss Alps. I only hope that future generations can enjoy this glorious landscape, too.

Café Chitchat, Chocolate Cake, and the Vienna Opera

MUNCHING Europe's most famous chocolate cake—the *Sacher torte*—in Café Sacher, across from Europe's finest opera house, I feel underdressed in my travel wear. Thankfully, a coffee party of older ladies, who fit right in with the smoked mirrors and chandeliers, make me feel welcome at their table. They're buzzing with excitement about the opera they are about to see—even bursting into occasional bits of arias.

Loni, the elegant white-haired ringleader, answers my questions about Austria. "A true Viennese is not Austrian, but a cocktail," she says, wiping the brown icing from her smile. "We are a mix of the old Habsburg Empire. My grandparents are Hungarian." Gesturing to each of her friends, she adds, "And Gosha's are Polish, Gabi's are Romanian, and I don't even know what hers are."

Vienna's beloved *Sacher torte*

"It's a melting pot," I say.

They respond, "Yes, like America."

For 600 years, Vienna was the head of the once-grand Habsburg Empire. In 1900, Vienna's nearly two million inhabitants made it the world's sixth-largest city (after London, New York, Paris, Berlin, and Chicago). Then Austria started and lost World War I—and its far-flung holdings. Today's Vienna is a "head without a body," an elegant capital ruling tiny Austria. The average Viennese mother has one child and the population has dropped to 1.8 million.

I ask Loni about Austria's low birthrate.

"Dogs are the preferred child," she says, inspiring pearl-rattling peals of laughter from her friends.

Sharing coffee and cake with Viennese aristocracy who live as if

Showing live opera on an outdoor screen brings high culture to more people.

Vienna were an eastern Paris, and as if calories didn't count, I'm seeing the soul of Vienna. Vienna may have lost its political clout, but culturally and historically, this city of Freud, Brahms, a gaggle of Strausses, Empress Maria Theresa's many children, and a dynasty of Holy Roman Emperors remains right up there with Paris, London, and Rome.

As far back as the 12th century, Vienna was a mecca for musicians, both secular and sacred. The Habsburg emperors of the 17th and 18th centuries were not only generous supporters of music but also fine musicians themselves (Maria Theresa played a mean double bass). Composers such as Haydn, Mozart, Beethoven, Schubert, Brahms, and Mahler gravitated to this music-friendly environment. They taught each other, jammed together, and spent a lot of time in Habsburg palaces. Beethoven was a famous figure, walking—lost in musical thought—through Vienna's wooded parks.

After the defeat of Napoleon, the Congress of Vienna in 1815 shaped 19th-century Europe. Vienna enjoyed its violin-filled belle époque, which shaped our romantic image of the city: fine wine, cafés, waltzes, and these great chocolate cakes. The waltz was the rage and "Waltz King"

Johann Strauss and his brothers kept Vienna's 300 ballrooms spinning. This musical tradition created the prestigious Viennese institutions that tourists enjoy today: the opera, Boys' Choir, and great Baroque halls and churches, all busy with classical concerts.

As we split up the bill and drain the last of our coffee, the women take opera tickets out of their purses in anticipation. "Where will you be sitting?" Loni asks.

"Actually I'll be standing," I say. "I've got a *Stehplatz*, a standing-room-only ticket."

The women look at me kindly, perhaps wondering if they should have paid for my cake and coffee.

"A *Stehplatz* is just €4. So I have money left over for more *Sacher torte*," I tell them with a smile. What I don't say is that, for me, three hours is a lot of opera. A *Stehplatz* allows me the cheap and easy option of leaving early.

Leaving the café, we talk opera as we cross the street. The prestigious Vienna Opera isn't backed in the pit by the famous Vienna Philharmonic Orchestra, but by its farm team: second-string strings. Still, Loni reminds me, "It's one of the world's top opera houses." Even with 300 performances a year, expensive seats are normally sold out—mostly to well-dressed *Sacher torte*-eating locals.

Saying goodbye to my new friends, I head for the standing-room ticket window. Cackling as old friends do, they waltz through the grand floor entrance and into another evening of high Viennese culture.

Vienna's elegant Opera House

The Castles of Boyhood Dreams

SOUTH OF MUNICH in the foothills of the Alps is Hohenschwangau Castle. It was "Mad" King Ludwig's father's castle—and Ludwig's boyhood summer home. When his father died, Ludwig became king. He was just a boy, 19 years old. And rather than live with the frustrations of a modern constitution and a feisty parliament in Munich reining him in, King Ludwig II spent his next years lost in Romantic literature and operas . . . hanging out here with composer Richard Wagner as only a gay young king could.

The king's bedroom was decked out like a fairy tale. The walls were painted in 1835 by a single artist, who gave the place a romantic, Tolkien fantasy feel. Lounging nymphs still flank the window and stars twinkle from the ceiling. A telescope stands as it did for the king, trained on a pinnacle on a distant ridge where Ludwig dreamed of building his ultimate castle fantasy: Neuschwanstein. On my first visit here, squinting through that telescope at Neuschwanstein (which had also inspired a boy named Walt Disney), I could relate to the busy young king. Bound by schoolwork and house rules rather than a constitution and parliament, with a stretched-out turtleneck and zits rather than crowns and composer friends, I too built a castle.

My piano-crate castle (circa 1967)

What I had that Ludwig lacked was a father who imported pianos. Shipped from Germany, they came encased in tongue-in-groove pine, sealed in a thick envelope of zinc sheeting. My wooden tree house was my castle: walls decorated with romantic 1968 magazines, the nails shining through the ceiling just long enough to bloody intruding bullies taller than me. Taking full advantage of those sliding pine boards, I could see who was coming. With a shiny zinc roof, my palace was the envy of other little kings. There was no tree house like it. Then, someone purchased the vacant lot next to our house, and I had to tear my tree castle down. At the time, I considered it the worst day of my life. Not long after, I embarked on my first no-parents trip to Europe. Touring Neuschwanstein, I relived my loss.

On that same trip, just over the border in Austria near the town of Reutte, I found another castle: the brooding ruins of the largest fort in Tirol—Ehrenberg. This impressive complex was built to defend against the Bavarians and to bottle up the strategic "Via Claudia" trade route that cut through the Alps here, connecting Italy and Germany since ancient times. One castle crowned its bluff while another was high above on the next peak. Exploring the ruins, I climbed deep into a misty forest littered with meaningless chunks of castle wall—each pinned down by pixy-stix trees and mossy with sword ferns. This once strategic and powerful fortress had somehow fallen apart and was slowly being eaten by the forest.

With Armin and hill-topping Ehrenberg Castle

My friend Armin Walch, an archaeologist who lives in Reutte, had a vision to bring these ruins to life. He was born the same year as me and pursued his project like the Indiana Jones of castle scholars. Today, with

Knighted Sir Rick of Ehrenberg

European Union funding, he's cut away the hungry forest to reveal and renovate what he calls the castle ensemble. And it's open for business, enabling countless children to live out their medieval fantasies, leaping from rampart to rampart with sword ferns swinging.

On my last visit, I was honored for bringing so many visitors to this remote corner of Austria over the years. With Armin as the jovial master of ceremonies, the town's hoteliers and tourism folks gathered in the castle like a council of medieval lords. Together we ate smoked game and rustic cheese with coarse bread. We swilled wine and clinked pewter mugs. I gave an impromptu speech about the wonders of Americans climbing through history far from home. Then I knelt before a man in armor who drew a shiny sword with my name etched upon it, and was knighted—Sir Rick, first knight of Ehrenberg.

The sword was my gift. It was solid and sparkled with sentiment. I loved how it felt in my hand as I swung it back and forth, cutting through the air—and how it symbolically wove together my tree-house childhood, my love of history, my longtime connection with Reutte, and Armin's vision. But the last thing I needed was to be packing a big sword through the rest of my trip. So I requested that my sword stay in the museum as a special exhibit on the castle-loving boy from Seattle who fell in love with the Ehrenberg ruins and then grew up to bring decades of American travelers to Reutte with his guidebooks.

On the way back to my hotel, Armin took me to his house for a drink. As a talented architect, he had cleverly hidden his sleek, futuristic, and creative pad behind a humble old-town facade. It was a royal domain for his family—two kids cozy on the carpet and a beautiful wife. Armin had bedazzled her at the university in Vienna and brought her here to remote Reutte with promises of a queenly life and a bitchin' castle.

Armin and I climbed boyishly to his rooftop—a perch he designed to view Ehrenberg. Together we shared a glass of schnapps flavored with local herbs and peered through his telescope at our favorite castle complex—now illuminated by powerful floodlighting. In his youth—before he excavated it—almost no one knew about the fortress that hid beneath the trees on the mountain. Nudging me aside, Armin took his turn squinting through his telescope. Happy as two boys in a tree house, like two Romantic-age princes, we marveled at this castle of his dreams.

A perch for daydreams amid castle ruins

Germany

GERMANY is a place that romantics, beer lovers, and historians alike adore. Traveling here is a lesson in contrasts. We celebrate the freedom after the fall of the Berlin Wall, make pilgrimages to death camps, and ponder how a great power remembers its dead when they were the bad guys. Beer maids with massive pretzels sell slinky radishes while nostalgic drunks in beer halls strike up easy conversation. We get naked with strangers lit by sunbeams under dreamy domes of 19th-century spas. A Night Watchman leads us back into the Middle Ages with an enchanting lantern. And speed demons rocket past us on the autobahn as they race to the wine garden to suddenly become experts in lethargy . . . standard-setters of conviviality under chestnut trees.

Burg Eltz, on Germany's Mosel River

Munich: Where Thirst is Worse than Homesickness

Heading for the Hofbräuhaus in Munich, I mention to my Bavarian friend, Friedrich, that I'd love to give this venerable beer hall some significance in my guidebook description. Unconvinced that "significance" is worth seeking at a beer hall, he quotes Freud: "Sometimes a cigar is just a cigar." Stepping through its stubby stone arcade, we wade through the commotion of a thousand people—eating, drinking, yelling, and laughing—to the center of the cavernous hall.

The smoke-stained ceiling painting, repaired after WWII bomb damage, is an evocative mesh of 1950s German mod: Bavarian colors, cheery chestnuts, and old-time food, drink, and music. A slogan arcing across the ceiling above the oompah band reads, *Durst ist schlimmer als Heimweh* ("Thirst is worse than homesickness"). Friedrich explains: "Drink a beer, and you worry no more."

Many of my most vivid, if still a bit fuzzy, Munich memories are set in beer halls. Locals always seem up for a visit. And for traditional Bavarian fun, nothing beats this scene, complete with rivers of beer, cheap food, noisy fun, and oompah music.

The music is loud. The musicians' shiny lederhosen accentuate huge bellies, which in turn accentuate bird-like legs. With knowing smirks, they conduct a musical liturgy from the stage. The boisterous crowd rises to its feet in well-practiced unison for the beer hall anthem, *"Eins, zwei, zuffa."* ("One, two, drink.") This is followed by a ritual of

In a Bavarian beer hall, you'll find men in lederhosen and beer in one-liter mugs.

Beer maids stay busy.

clinking and drinking. The hefty glass mugs clink solidly, encouraging that very Teutonic sport of toasting.

Friedrich and I settle in at a long table and survey the chaos. Apart from the "under 35" party tour groups, it's a three-generations-together scene. Kids build houses out of beer coasters while moms sip *Radler*s, a nearly dainty mix of beer and lemonade, and old-timers sport felt hats festooned with pins and feathers.

Beer halls give you what you need. If you don't have a partner, you can talk to yourself. One guy tries doggedly to hold his head up. His neighbor peers down at his spiral-carved radish as if he dropped a thought into it. Another man, with a mouthful of pretzel, really believes the band is following his dramatic conducting.

I ask Friedrich if they sell half-liters. He says, "This is a *Biergarten,* not a kindergarten." Soon a busy beer maid brings us each the standard full *Mass,* or liter glass (about a quart, nearly what we'd call *ein pitcher*). She

One of 14 massive beer-hall tents at Munich's Oktoberfest

scurries between tables, plopping down dinners and garnishing them with mustard packets pulled from her cleavage. I look over at Friedrich. Finishing a giant swig from his giant beer and licking the foam from his upper lip, he says, "Only in Bavaria."

Women laugh at men using urinals.

Beer halls are craziest during Oktoberfest, but you can dance to raucous bands, munch massive pretzels, and hone your stein-hoisting skills any time of year.

Beer halls always impress me with their long ranks of urinals. Often, life-size posters of dirndl-clad maidens are hung from high on the walls, pointing down and laughing at the men with their zippers down.

Watching the legions of happy beer-drinkers, it occurs to me that, unlike with wine, more money doesn't get you a better beer. Beer is truly a people's drink—and you'll get the very best here in Munich. Each connoisseur has a favorite brew and doesn't have to pay more to get it . . . they simply go to the beer hall that serves it.

Many beer halls have a big wooden keg out on display, but these days most draw beer from huge stainless-steel dispensers. If you're at a beer hall that uses classic old wooden kegs, your evening comes with a happy soundtrack: Every few minutes you'll hear a loud *whop!* as they tap a new keg. Hearing this, every German there knows they're in for a good, fresh mug.

Gemütlich is the perfect word for Bavaria's special coziness. It's a knack for savoring the moment. A beer hall is a classic *gemütlich* scene. Spend an evening clinking mugs with new friends, immersed in this boisterous and belching Bavarian atmosphere. The warm and frothy memories are yours for the taking.

Battleground Bacharach

CRUISING DOWN the romantic Rhine River, we dodge the treacherous reefs that spelled disaster for ancient sailors distracted by the fabled Lorelei siren. We dock at the half-timbered town of Bacharach, where I jump out. Bacharach, wearing a castle helmet and a vineyard cape, is a typical Rhine village. It lines the river and fills its tiny tributary valley with a history you can hook arms with in a noisy *Weinstube*.

"Bacharach" means "altar to Bacchus." The town and its wine date from Celtic and Roman times. Local vintners brag that the medieval Pope Pius II preferred Bacharach's wine and had it shipped to Rome by the cartload. Today, tourists drink it on the spot.

For each wine festival, Bacharach installs an honorary party mayor. He's given the title of Bacchus. The last Bacchus, one of the best wine gods in memory, died a year ago. Posters left up as a memorial, it seems, show his pudgy highness riding a keg of Riesling, wearing a tunic, and crowned with grapes as adoring villagers carry him on happy shoulders.

Bacharach on the Rhine and its 600-year-old Altes Haus

Bacharach's annual wine fest is the first weekend of October, just before the harvest. Its purpose is to empty the barrels and make room for the new wine, a chore locals take seriously.

The festival is months away, but the dank back alleys of Bacharach smell like the morning after. I drop my bag at Hotel Kranenturm, then head back to the boat dock. I've arranged a private walk through town with Herr Jung, Bacharach's retired schoolmaster.

The riverfront scene is laid-back. Retired German couples, thick after a lifetime of beer and potatoes, set the tempo at an easy stroll. I gaze across the Rhine. Lost in thoughts of Bacchus and Roman Bacharach, I'm in another age . . . until two castle-clipping fighter jets from a nearby American military base drill through the silence.

The Rhine Valley is stained by war. While church bells in Holland play cheery ditties, here on the Rhine they sound more like hammers on anvils. At bridges, road signs still indicate which lanes are reinforced and able to support tanks. As the last of the World War II survivors pass on, memories fade. The war that ripped our grandparents' Europe in two will become like a black-and-white photo of a long-gone and never-known relative on the mantle.

I pause at Bacharach's old riverside war memorial. A big stone urn with a Maltese cross framed by two helmets, it seems pointedly ignored by both the town and its visitors. Even when it was erected to honor the dead of Bismarck's first war in 1864, its designer sadly knew it would need to accommodate the wars that followed: Blank slabs became rolls of honor for the dead of 1866, 1870, and 1914–18.

Herr Jung arrives and I ask him to translate the words carved on the stone.

"To remember the hard but great time . . . " he starts, then mutters, "Ahh, but this is not important now."

Herr Jung explains, "We Germans turn our backs on the monuments of old wars. We have one day in the year when we remember those who have died in the wars. Because of our complicated history, we call these lost souls not war heroes but 'victims of war and tyranny.' Those who lost sons, fathers, and husbands have a monument in their heart. They don't need this old stone."

Rolf Jung is an energetic gentleman whose glasses seem to dance on his nose as he weaves a story. When meeting my tour groups for guided walks, he greets them as he did his class of fifth-graders decades ago, singing like a German Mr. Rogers: "Good morning, good morning, to you and you and you . . . " Like so many Europeans, he has a knack for finding dignity and pride in his work, no matter how grand or small the job. A walk with Herr Jung always makes me feel good about Europe.

As I ponder the memorial, he quotes Bismarck: "Nobody wants war, but everyone wants things they can't have without war."

Herr Jung looks past the town's castle, where the ridge of the gorge meets

Herr Jung leads a group through Bacharach.

the sky and says, "I remember the sky. It was a moving carpet of American bombers coming over that ridge. Mothers would run with their children. There were no men left. In my class, 49 of the 55 boys lost their fathers. My generation grew up with only mothers.

"I remember the bombings," he continues. "Lying in our cellar, praying with my mother. I was a furious dealmaker with God. I can still hear the guns. Day after day we watched American and Nazi airplanes fighting. We were boys. We'd jump on our bikes to see the wreckage of downed planes. I was the neighborhood specialist on war planes. I could identify them by the sound.

"One day a very big plane was shot down. It had four engines. I biked to the wreckage, and I couldn't believe my eyes. Was this a plane designed with a huge upright wing in the center? Then I realized this was only the tail section. The American tail section was as big as an entire German plane. I knew then that we would lose this war."

The years after the war were hungry years. "I would wake in the middle of the night and search the cupboards," he says. "There was no fat, no bread, no nothing. I licked spilled grain from the cupboard. We had friends from New York and they sent coffee that we could trade with farmers for grain. For this I have always been thankful.

"When I think of what the Nazis did to Germany, I remember that a fine soup cooked by 30 people can be spoiled by one man with a handful of salt."

Herr Jung takes me on a historic ramble through the back lanes of Bacharach. Like any good small-town teacher, he's known and admired by all.

Then we climb through the vineyards above town to a bluff overlooking a six-mile stretch of Rhine. "I came here often as a boy to count the ships," he says. "I once saw 30 in the river in front of Bacharach."

We look out over the town's slate rooftops. Picking up a stone, he carves the letters "Rick" into a slate step and tells me, "Now you are here, carved in stone . . . until the next rain."

Ever a teacher, he explains, "Slate is very soft. The Rhine River found this and carved out this gorge. Soil made from slate absorbs the heat of the sun. So, our vines stay warm at night. We grow a fine wine here on the Rhine.

"Today the vineyards are going back to the wild. Germans won't work for the small pay. The Polish come to do the work. During the Solidarity time I housed a guest worker. After 11 weeks in the fields, he drove home in a used Mercedes."

We pass under the fortified gate and walk back into town, cradled safely in half-timbered cuteness. My teacher can sense what I'm thinking: that Bacharach was never good for much more than inspiring a poem, selling a cuckoo clock, or docking a boat. Stopping at a bench, Herr Jung props his soft leather briefcase on his knee and fingers through a file of visual aids, each carefully hand-colored and preserved in plastic for rainy walks. He pulls out a sketch of Bacharach fortifications intact and busy with trade to show how in its heyday, from 1300 to 1600, the town was rich and politically important.

"Medieval Bacharach had 6,000 people. That was big in the 15th century," he says. "But the plagues, fires, and religious wars of the 17th century ended our powerful days. Bacharach became empty. It was called 'the cuckoo town.' Other people moved in the way a cuckoo takes over an empty nest. For 200 years now, our town has been only a village of a thousand."

In the mid-19th century, painters and poets like Victor Hugo were charmed by the Rhineland's romantic mix of past glory, present poverty, and rich legend. They put this part of the Rhine on the Grand Tour map. And the "Romantic Rhine" was born.

A ruined 15th-century chapel hangs like a locket under the castle and over the town. In 1842, Victor Hugo stood where Herr Jung and I now stand. Looking at the chapel, he wrote, "No doors, no roof or windows, a magnificent skeleton puts its silhouette against the sky. Above it, the ivy-covered castle ruins provide a fitting crown. This is Bacharach, land of fairy tales, covered with legends and sagas."

While military jets soar, Roman towers crumble. Herr Jung has since passed away. But the Lorelei still sings its siren song. Bacharach is a town with a story that I would never have known without a friend and a teacher like Herr Jung.

Bacharach (below its ruined chapel) on the Rhine River

Three Castles: Eltz, Rheinfels, and Neuschwanstein

GERMANY can overwhelm you with too many castles in too little time. My three favorites are the remote and beautifully preserved Burg Eltz, the ruined but powerful Rheinfels, and the 19th-century fantasy of Neuschwanstein.

Burg Eltz is my favorite castle in all of Europe. Lurking in a mysterious forest above the Mosel River, it's furnished throughout as it was 500 years ago. Thanks to smart diplomacy and clever marriages, Burg Eltz was never destroyed. It's been in the Eltz family for 850 years.

The first *burg* (castle) on the Eltz creek was built in the 12th century to protect a trade route. By about 1490, the castle looked like it does today: the homes of three big landlord families gathered around a small courtyard within one formidable fortification. Today, tours wind through two of those homes (the third is the caretaker's residence). The elderly countess of Eltz traces her roots back 33 generations. She enjoys flowers and has had the castle's public rooms adorned with grand floral arrangements every week for the last 40 years.

It was a comfortable castle for its day: 80 rooms made cozy by 40 fireplaces and wall-hanging tapestries. Many of its 20 toilets were automatically flushed by a rain drain. The delightful chapel is on a lower floor. Even though "no one should live above God," this chapel's placement was acceptable because its altar fills a bay window, which floods the delicate Gothic space with light as it protrudes out from the

Dreamy Burg Eltz hiding out above the Mosel

floor above. The three families met in the large "conference room" to work out common problems, as if sharing a condo. Colorfully painted carvings of a jester and a rose look down on the big table, reminding those who gathered that they were free to discuss anything ("fool's freedom"—jesters could say anything to the king), but nothing discussed could leave the room (the "rose of silence").

Rheinfels Castle, both much mightier and much more ruined, lords over its bend in the nearby Rhine River. It sits like a dead pit bull above the village of St. Goar. This most formidable of Rhine castles rumbles with ghosts from its hard-fought past. Burg Rheinfels was built in 1245 and withstood a siege of 28,000 French troops in 1692, the only Rhineland castle to withstand Louis XIV's assault. But in 1797, the French Revolutionary army destroyed it. Once the biggest castle on the Rhine, it spent the 19th century as a quarry. So today, while still mighty, it's only a small fraction of its original size, a hollow but evocative shell.

For centuries, the massive Rheinfels was self-sufficient and ready for a siege. During the age of sieging (which lasted until the advent of modern artillery), any proper castle was prepared to survive a six-month attack. Circling the central courtyard, you'd find a bakery, pharmacy, herb garden, brewery, well, and livestock. During peacetime, about 400 people lived here. During a siege, there could be as many as 4,000. Those 4,000 people required a lot of provisions. The count owned the surrounding farmland. In return for the lord's protection, farmers got to keep 20 percent of their production. Later, in more liberal feudal times, the nobility let them keep 40 percent. (Today, the German government leaves workers with 60 percent after taxes . . . and provides a few more services.)

Rheinfels, mighty even in ruins

I hike around the castle perimeter with the mindset of an invader. Noticing the smartly placed crossbow-arrow slit, I think, "*Thoop* . . . I'm dead." Lying there, I notice the fine stonework on the chutes high above. Uh-oh . . . boiling pitch . . . now I'm toast.

In about 1600, to protect their castle, Rheinfels troops cleverly booby-trapped the land just outside the walls by digging tunnels topped with thin slate roofs and packed with explosives. By detonating the explosives when under attack, they could kill hundreds of approaching invaders with a single blow. In 1626, a handful of Protestant Germans blew 300 Catholic Spaniards to (they assumed) hell.

I wander through a set of never-blown-up tunnels. It's pitch-dark, muddy, and claustrophobic, with confusing dead-ends. It's as much a crawl as a walk; the tunnel is never tall enough for me to stand higher than a deep crouch. Even with no wrong turns, it's a 200-yard-long adventure, aided by the flashlight I was given at the castle entrance.

A modern entryway blasted through the castle wall takes me to the small, barren dungeon. I walk through a door that prisoners only dreamed of 400 years ago. (They came and went through the little square hole in the ceiling.) The holes in the walls supported timbers that thoughtfully gave as many as 15 miserable residents something to sit on to keep them out of the filthy slop that gathered on the floor. Twice a day, they were given bread and water. Some prisoners actually survived for two years in this dark hole. While the town could torture and execute, the castle had permission only to imprison criminals in this dank dungeon. According to town records, the two men who spent the most time down here died within three weeks of regaining their freedom. Perhaps after a diet of bread and water, feasting on meat and wine was just too much. (Tour guides say that after months of prison darkness, the prisoners when freed were blinded instantly by the sunshine. It's a melodramatic story, tempting to repeat.)

Neuschwanstein is entirely different. It's the greatest of the fairy-tale castles of King Ludwig II, whose extravagance and Romanticism earned him the title "Mad" King Ludwig . . . and an early death.

While it's only about as old as the Eiffel Tower, Neuschwanstein Castle is a textbook example of 19th-century Romanticism. After the

Middle Ages ended, people disparagingly named that era "Gothic," or barbarian ("of the Goths"). Then, all of a sudden, in the 1800s, it was hip to be square, and a new Gothic style—or "Neo-Gothic"—became the rage. Throughout Europe, old castles were restored and new ones built, wallpapered with chivalry. King Ludwig II put his medieval fantasy on the hilltop not for defensive reasons, but simply because he liked the view.

Neuschwanstein, "Mad" King Ludwig's dream

The lavish, Wagner-inspired interior, covered with damsels in distress, dragons, and knights in gleaming armor, is enchanting. (A little knowledge of Richard Wagner's Romantic operas goes a long way in bringing these stories to life.) Ludwig had great taste . . . for a mad king. He was a political misfit: a poetic hippie king in the realpolitik age of Bismarck. After Bavarians complained about the money Ludwig spent on castles, his sanity was questioned. Shortly after that, the 40-year-old king was found dead in a lake under suspicious circumstances, ending work on his medieval fantasy-come-true. Ludwig almost bankrupted Bavaria building Neuschwanstein. But today, Germany is recouping its investment a hundredfold as huge crowds from all over the world pay to pack Europe's most popular castle.

Germany's history is long and many-faceted. Whether noble residences with flowers, feudal fortresses with rat-filled dungeons, or Romantic palaces fit for a king, its castles have become both amusement parks and classrooms.

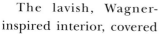

Baden-Baden: Getting Naked with Strangers

RELAXING at the spa resort of Baden-Baden in southern Germany's Black Forest, I see more naked people in two hours than many Americans see in their entire lives.

Ever since the Roman emperor Caracalla bathed in the mineral waters here, Baden-Baden has welcomed those in need of a good soak. In the 19th century, the town was Germany's ultimate spa resort, and even today, the name Baden-Baden is synonymous with relaxation in a land where the government still pays for its overworked citizens to take a little spa time. And since the beginning, the dress code has always been naked.

Americans who can't handle nudity don't know what they're missing. My first time was with some German friends—a classy, good-looking young couple. We were swept into the changing area with no explanation. Suddenly they were naked and I felt like the Road Runner just beyond the cliff's edge. Then—easing up, and stripping down—I realized it's not sexy . . . simply open and free.

For me, enjoying the Friedrichsbad Roman-Irish Baths in Baden-Baden is one of Europe's most elegant experiences. Traditional, stately, indoors, these baths are extremely relaxing . . . and not very social. It's just you, your body, and an unforgettable experience.

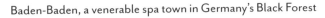

Baden-Baden, a venerable spa town in Germany's Black Forest

Wearing only the locker key strapped around my wrist, I start by weighing myself—92 kilos. The attendant leads me under the industrial-strength shower. This torrential kickoff pounds my head and shoulders and obliterates the rest of the world. He gives me plastic slippers and a towel, ushering me into a dry-heat room with fine wooden lounges—the slats too hot to sit on without the towel. Staring up at exotic tiles of herons and palms, I cook. After more hot rooms punctuated with showers, it's time for my massage.

An elegant pool

Like someone really drunk going for one more glass, I climb gingerly onto the marble slab and lay belly-up. The masseur holds up two mitts and asks, "Hard or soft?" In the spirit of wild abandon, I growl, "Hard," not even certain what that will mean for my skin. I get the coarse, Brillo-Pad scrub-down. Tenderized like a slab of meat, I feel entirely relaxed. The massage is over, and with a Teutonic spank, I'm sent off into the pools.

Nude, without my glasses, and not speaking the language, I bumble like Mr. Magoo in flip-flops through a series of steam rooms and cold plunges.

The steamy labyrinth leads to the mixed section. This is where the Americans get uptight. The parallel spa facilities intersect, bringing men and women together to share the finest three pools in Friedrichsbad. Here, all are welcome to drift under the exquisite domes in perfect silence, like aristocratic swans. A woman glides in front of me, on her back. Like a serene flotilla, her peaceful face and buoyant breasts glide by, creating barely a ripple. On my right, an Aryan Adonis, staring at

Extreme relaxation under tiled vaults of tradition

the ethereal dome, drapes himself over the lip of the pool. Germans are nonchalant, tuned in to their bodies and focused on solitary relaxation. Tourists are tentative, trying to be cool . . . but more aware of their nudity. I remind myself there's nothing sexy about it. Just vivid life in full flower.

The climax is the cold plunge. I'm usually not a fan of cold water—yet I absolutely love this. You must not wimp out on the cold plunge.

For my last stop, the attendant escorts me into the "quiet room" and asks when I'd like to be awakened. I tell him closing time. He wraps me in hot sheets and a brown blanket. Actually, I'm not wrapped . . . I'm swaddled: warm, flat on my back, among 20 hospital-type beds. Only one other bed is occupied; the guy in it is as still as a corpse. I stare up at the ceiling, losing track of time and myself. Sometime later, I'm jolted awake by my own snore.

As I leave, I weigh myself again: 91 kilos. I've shed two pounds of sweat. It would have been more if tension had mass. Stepping into the cool evening air, I'm thankful my hotel is a level, two-block stroll away.

Back in my room, I fall in slow motion onto my down comforter, the big pillow puffing around my head. Wonderfully naked under my clothes, I can only think, "Ahhh . . . Baden-Baden."

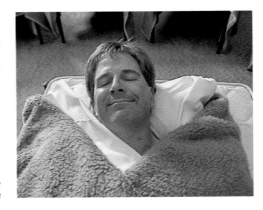

Swaddled, snoozy, and without a care

Rothenburg's Night Watchman

THE WALLED TOWN of Rothenburg, midway between Frankfurt and Munich, offers the best look possible at medieval Germany. And in this theme park of a town, the best ride is the night watchman's town walk. Each night through the tourist season, with his eyebrows frozen in a raised position, the night watchman listens to the clock tower clang nine times. Then he winks, picks up his *hellebarde* (long-poled axe), and lights his lantern. Welcoming the English-speaking group gathered in 15th-century Rothenburg, he looks believably medieval in his black robe, long curly hair, and scraggly beard. But the twinkle in his eyes admits, "I'm one of you."

With an insider's grin he begins: "It was a bad job, being medieval Rothenburg's night watchman— low esteem, low pay, dangerous work. Only two jobs were lower: the grave digger and the execu- tioner. Yes, this was a dangerous job. All the good people were off the streets early. He would sing the 'all's well' tune at the top of the hour through the night. You didn't want to hear the night watchman at three in the morning, but you were glad he was still alive.

The Night Watchman signals "All's well."

"These days, the job's more respectable: People take photos of me," he continues. "And it's no longer dangerous, because you're all com- ing with me." The night watchman's camera-toting flock of 30 tourists, already charmed, follows his bobbing lantern down the narrow, cobbled lane.

Stopping under a sign announcing *Kriminal Museum,* we watch the rusted old dunking cage swing in the breeze. The night watchman walks over to the stocks that stand empty next to the museum door and says,

"If you know what's good for you, tomorrow you'll visit our Kriminal Museum."

He opens the top half of the stocks then slams it shut, saying, "A naughty boy might be put in the stocks. We rub salt on his soles and bring the goats. But inside, you'll learn about more gruesome tools of torture and more embarrassing tools of humiliation."

Pausing to survey the group, he adds, "Like a metal gag for nags." He scans the group again. His eyes stop on me and he asks, "Are you from Rothenburg?"

"Nein," I say.

"Very good," he says. "Please come here."

As I move to the front he continues. "We were 6,000 here in Rothenburg. In those days, around here, only Nürnburg and Augsburg were bigger. The Kaiser made us a free Imperial City. Such a city was given special privileges. The top privilege: We had our own court of justice. Rothenburg's citizens must be tried by their own court."

Shaking his head sadly, he puts his robed arm on my shoulder. "And you are not protected by our court," he announces. "We get a half day off when there's a hanging. Do you know anything about Herr Baumann's missing beehive?"

Again I say, *"Nein."*

"You have no rights here, and we could use a half day off. You, my friend, have a problem. Local authorities might just allow a hanging."

In the good old days, death sentences started with your basic execution and then got worse. The legal concept of "cumulation" meant a criminal's punishments would multiply with his crimes. While that petty beehive thief might simply be hung, an adulterous beehive-thieving murderer could be dragged to the place of execution with painful stops along the way for pinching with red-hot tongs. If he were guilty of more crimes, he'd be tied to stakes over timbers so a big guy could bounce a wagon wheel on his arms and legs, breaking all his bones. Thoroughly "broken by the wheel," he would then be woven through the spokes of that wheel and hoisted high for all to see. Finally, his hanging could be fast or slow. It depended on the verdict.

Sometimes even death wasn't harsh enough. In cases when two capi-

The Night Watchman takes groups on his medieval rounds.

tal offenses were committed, a criminal's corpse would be "quartered" by four horses heading out in different directions.

A town's gallows, a medieval symbol of justice, was placed high for more spectacle. The most important criminals were hung on higher platforms in anticipation of greater crowds. Bodies of particularly dishonorable criminals were left out to rot. Some were left in a cage so birds could get to their bodies . . . but relatives couldn't.

Looking at me again, the night watchman says thoughtfully, "So, you're not from Rothenburg." Then, turning abruptly, he walks down the street. Mesmerized, we follow.

He stops under an old-fashioned streetlight and says, "It was a dirty time." Pointing with his boot to a gutter in the cobbles, he continues, "All the garbage—from the people and from the animals, too—it went into the road. They had this ditch in the middle of the street. People tried to hit the ditch. This was not a good system. Summer was stinking. The rich left for countryside homes. Back then it wasn't the Romantic Road. It was the Filthy Road. And this filth gave us the plague. The plague was a big killer. In one terrible year, in Rothenburg . . . one out of every three people died."

We follow him farther to the ramparts at the edge of town. Overlooking the valley, the watchman says, "Rothenburg was never conquered until 1631. There was a siege. The armory, which was along this wall, blew up. Double disaster: We had a hole in the wall and no ammunition to make a defense. To be looted by 40,000 mercenaries was no fun. They were Catholics, so it was even worse.

"Our town was broken. And for the rest of the Thirty Years' War, Rothenburg lay wide open, undefended. We were sacked many times. Between lootings we suffered plagues."

Popping from an alley back onto the main square, our hooded friend concludes, "From 1648—when the war and plagues stopped—time stood still in Rothenburg. Centuries of poverty . . . and nothing changed. Rothenburg's misfortune put the town into a deep sleep. And that is why you are here today. Now I must sing the 'all's well.'"

After finishing his short melody, he blows a long haunting tone on his horn. Then he ends by saying, "You, my friends, should hurry home. Bed is the best place for good people at this hour."

With Rothenburg's Night Watchman, the present meets the past.

After Hours at a German *Stammtisch*

IN EUROPE'S tourist towns, the best social moments combust after a long day of work, and after the guests say good night. After hours in an Irish pub in Galway, the door is locked and the musicians play on. On the Italian Riviera, the dishes are washed, the anchovies are eaten, and the guitars come out. And in small-town German hotels, the family and the hired help stow their workplace hierarchy with their aprons and take out a special bottle of wine.

During many visits to Rothenburg, Germany's ultimate medieval town, I've sat down hurriedly at the Golden Rose restaurant to update my guidebook listing, then dashed away. Tonight, I've decided to sit down and simply relax with the Favetta family. We gather around the *Stammtisch:* the table you'll find in most German bars and restaurants reserved for family, staff, and regulars. (An invitation to the *Stammtisch* is a good life goal.) Except for our candlelit table, the once noisy restaurant is empty and dark.

Well into our second glass of wine, we indulge in the sport many in the tourist business enjoy: cultural puzzles. The daughter, Henni, asks me, "Why can't Americans eat with a knife? You cut things with your fork."

Well-preserved Rothenburg welcomes visitors.

The friendly Favetta family, in the Golden Rose kitchen

I confess I know nothing about holding silverware. And just to hit a Yankee when he's down, she adds, "And you people love to drink plain water—we call this water the American Champagne. But you never eat liver or blood sausage. The Japanese love those."

I ask Henni if it's not dangerous to generalize about other cultures.

She says, "Even deaf people generalize."

When I ask how, she explains with the help of her hands. "In international sign language, 'Germany' is my finger pointing up from my head," she says, making a fist-and-finger Prussian helmet. 'France' is this wavy little mustache," she continues, wiggling a finger across her upper lip. "And 'Russia' is the Cossack dancer." Henni bounces on her chair and hooks her thumbs at her waist, while her index fingers do a jaunty little cancan dance.

"And what's the sign for America?" I ask.

"The fat cat," she says, propping up an imaginary big belly with her arms.

Her father, Rino, whose English is worse than my German, struggles to follow the animated discussion. Whenever the conversation reaches a spirited tempo, he jumps in, brings it to a screeching halt, and sends it in a completely new direction.

Pretending to add to Henni's thoughts, he leans over to me. As if a magician sharing a secret, he holds his hand palm down in front of my face. Stretching his thumb high and out, he forms a small bay in the top of his hand. Peppering in a little snuff tobacco, he announces, "Snoof tobak." With Henni's help, Rino clarifies. Struggling with the word, he says, "anatomical snuffbox," and snorts. With a quick sniff, I try it, and it works.

As noses wiggle, I ask Henni if living in a tourist fantasy-town gets old.

"I will live and die in Rothenburg," she answers. "Teenagers here dream of leaving Rothenburg. One by one they try the big city—Munich or Nürnberg—and they come home. Summer is action time. Winter is quiet. The tourists, they come like a big once-a-year flood. We Rothenburgers sit and wait for you to float by."

"Like barnacles," I add cheerfully, even though I figure that word is not in Henni's English vocabulary.

Henni looks at me like I just burped. "People who live here have magic vision," she says. "If we want to, we can see no tourists and only local people. Rothenburg is a village. We know everyone."

Henni's sister Fernanda bops in wearing fine new American hightop sneakers. Since she once had an American soldier for a boyfriend, her English is American. "Americans get fashion," she says. "But your really fat women wear shorts. I saw the biggest people in my life in the States."

As the family agrees, Henni says, "And they wear tight T-shirts!"

Rino empties his tall glass of beer, licks his foamy upper lip, and adds, "The big German women wear the *Ein-Mann-Zelt*."

I look to Henni, who translates, "One-man tent."

When I counter, "But fat German men have skinny legs," the entire family laughs.

"Beer bellies," Henni says. "German men say a man without a belly isn't a man. A German saying is, 'Better to have a big belly from drinking than a broken back from working.'"

The impromptu party continues as I learn that, even in the most touristy town in Germany, you can still make a genuine, cross-cultural connection. Sitting at the *Stammtisch* after hours, this conversation becomes my treasured souvenir.

Ghosts in Berlin

I HAVE A powerful image stuck in my mind of Hitler and his architect and right-hand man, Albert Speer, poring over plans for postwar Berlin . . . a metropolis super-sized in a way that makes Paris look quaint. Of course, by 1945, Berlin was in ruins, Hitler's charred corpse could be identified only by his dental records, and Speer was in jail writing his memoirs, *Inside the Third Reich* (which provided me with my most vivid impressions of the Nazi era).

Over my last few visits to the city, I can see the irony that in some ways, Speer's vision of a dynamic new Berlin dominating Europe could be coming true. For example, the massive Hauptbahnhof—the only train station in Europe with major lines merging at right angles—has a scale and grandeur that Hitler might have appreciated. Toss in 80 stores and local subway lines, and it's a city in itself.

But freedom, not Hitler, won. And the other strong feeling I get in Berlin is that it's a victory celebration for capitalism and its defeat of communism. Like ancient Romans keeping a few vanquished barbarians in cages for locals to spit at, capitalism and the West flaunt victory in Berlin. Slices of the Berlin Wall hang like scalps at the gate to the Sony Center, the audacious office park at Potsdamer Platz.

A sleek Radisson hotel now stands on the place where the old leading hotel of East Berlin once stood. I remember staying there during the Cold War, when a West German five-Mark coin changed on the black

Above: Memorial to the Murdered Jews
Left: Checkpoint Charlie

market would get me and my friends drinks all night. Now five euros barely buys me a beer, and the lobby of the Radisson hosts an exotic fish tank the size of a grain silo with an elevator right in the middle, zipping scenically up eight floors. Next door, the DDR Museum is filled mostly with East German tourists rummaging through the nostalgia on display from their parents' dreary lives under communism.

Across the street, statues of Marx and Lenin (nicknamed "the Pensioners" by locals) look wistfully at the huge TV tower East Berlin built under communism. It had a fancy bar on top, but the best thing East Berliners could say about it back then was, "It's so tall that if it falls, we'll have an elevator to freedom."

The victory party rages on at Checkpoint Charlie. With every visit, I remember my spooky first time there in 1971, when tour buses returning to the West were emptied at the border so mirrors could be rolled under the bus to see if anyone was trying to escape with us.

Now, a generation later, Checkpoint Charlie is a capitalist sideshow. Lowlife characters sell fake bits of the wall, WWII-vintage gas masks, and DDR medals. Two actors dressed as American soldiers stand between big American flags and among sandbags at the rebuilt checkpoint, making their living posing for tourists. Across the street at "Snack Point Charlie," someone sipping a Coke says to me, "When serious becomes kitsch, you know it's over."

Standing at the historic Brandenburg Gate, I face Berlin's fashionable new heart: Pariser Platz. Within about 100 yards of this square—once a vacant lot along the Berlin Wall, and now a festive gathering place that seems designed to celebrate freedom—is a poignant collection of sights.

There are many memorials, including one to the six million murdered Jews of Europe and another to the first victims of Hitler: 96 men, the German equivalent of congressmen, who spoke out in the name of democracy against his rule in the early 1930s. They were sent to concentration camps where they were eventually killed. Nearby is the American Embassy, famous for taking security concerns to new heights. Across from a very busy Starbucks is one of the "ghost" subway stations that went unused through the Cold War and now feels like a 1930s time warp. Above that is the hotel balcony where Michael Jackson famously dangled his baby (according to local guides, it's the sight of greatest interest for most American tourists). And the glass dome capping the bombed-out Reichstag is where, on the rooftop on May Day 1945, Russian troops quelled a furious Nazi last stand. The nearby hills were created entirely with the rubble of a city bombed nearly flat about 70 years ago. Considering all this, the clash of history and today's vibrant city is almost overwhelming.

Tucked away nearby is the Kennedys Museum, filled with JFK lore, including the handwritten note with the phonetics for his famous Berlin speech. Reading it, I can hear his voice: "eesh been ein Bear-lee-ner" ("I am a Berliner").

The amazing story of Berlin swirls through my head: Speer's vision, Hitler's burning body, the last stand on the rooftop . . . the communists, the heroic American airlift, when the Communists attempted to starve a free Berlin into submission . . . Kennedy's speech, followed 24 years later by Reagan's demand to "tear down this wall" . . . the euphoria-turned-challenge of Germany's reunification, and the gleaming city visitors marvel at today.

I wave down a cab and hop in. I use the opportunity to get a local's perspective and ask the driver if he is a Berliner. When he turns to me, I realize he's Turkish, which makes me feel a little foolish. Then, making me feel foolish for feeling foolish, he says, "I've lived here 31 years. If Kennedy, after one day, could say 'Ich bin ein Berliner,' then I guess I can say I am a Berliner, too."

Berlin's Brandenburg Gate, now a symbol of peace and reunification

Berlin's Reichstag: Teary-Eyed Germans and a Big Glass Dome

Y EARS AGO, when I got my history degree, I said to myself, "I'd better get a business degree, too, so I have something useful." But I've learned over the years that if more people knew more about history, our world would be a better place. History is constantly speaking to us. Travelers enjoy a privileged way to hear it—and sometimes an up-close chance to witness history in the making.

Whenever I see the restored Reichstag building in Berlin, I'm reminded of my visit in 1999, when it reopened to the public. For tourists unaware of history, it was just a new dome to climb, offering another vantage point on the city. But a knowledge of its past gives it far deeper meaning. It was in this building that the German Republic was proclaimed in 1918. In 1933, this symbol of democracy nearly burned down. While the Nazis blamed a communist plot, some believe that Hitler himself planned the fire. Whatever the case, he used the fire as a convenient excuse to frame the communists and grab total power.

After 1945, this historic home of the German parliament—which saw some of the last fighting of World War II on its rooftop—stood as an abandoned and bombed-out hulk overlooking the no-man's-land between East and West Berlin. After reunification, Germany's government returned from Bonn to Berlin. And, in good European fashion, the Germans didn't bulldoze their parliament building. They respected the building's cultural roots and renovated it.

They capped it with a glorious glass dome, incorporating modern architectural design into a late-19th-century icon, and opened it up to the people. The dome rises 50 yards above the ground. Inside, a cone of 360 mirrors reflects natural light into the legislative chamber below. Lit from inside at night, it gives Berlin a kind of lantern celebrating good governance.

The Reichstag dome is a powerful architectural symbol. German citizens climb its long spiral ramp to the very top and look down, literally over the shoulders of their legislators, to see what's on their desks.

Inside the dome of the Reichstag, Germany's parliament building

Jerked around too much by their politicians in the past century, Germans are determined to keep a closer eye on them from now on. And this dome is designed to let them do exactly that.

When the Reichstag first reopened, I climbed to the top of the dome and found myself surrounded by teary-eyed Germans. Anytime you're surrounded by teary-eyed Germans, something exceptional is going on. It occurred to me that most of these people were old enough to remember the difficult times after World War II, when their city lay in rubble. What an exciting moment for them: the opening of this grand building was the symbolic closing of a difficult chapter in the history of a great nation. No more division. No more communism. No more fascism. They had a united government entering a new century with a new capitol building, looking into a promising future.

It was a thrill to be there. I was caught up in it. As I looked around at the other tourists, it occurred to me that most of them didn't have a clue about what was going on. They were so preoccupied with trivialities—camera batteries, their Cokes, the air-conditioning—that they missed a once-in-a-lifetime opportunity to celebrate this great moment with the

German people. I thought, "I'm living in a dumbed-down society." And it saddened me. I don't want to live in a dumbed-down society.

Powerful forces find it convenient when we're dumbed down. As a society, we become easier to manipulate . . . easier to make money from. I vowed right there, in my work as a travel writer, that I would expect my readers to be engaged . . . and made smarter by their travels.

In mainstream tourism, we're often encouraged to be lighthearted and avoid the serious. Sure, fun in the sun, duty-free shopping, and bingo can be a big part of your vacation. I enjoy it, too. But all this can distract us from a more important reason to travel. Travel can broaden our perspective, enabling us to rise above the advertiser-driven info-tainment we call the news to see things as citizens of the world. By plugging directly into the present and getting the world's take on things firsthand, a traveler goes beyond traditional sightseeing. (And shortly after that inspirational Berlin visit, I wrote an entirely new kind of book that develops that notion, called *Travel as a Political Act*.)

When we travel, we have the opportunity to see history as it's unfolding. With knowledge of the past, we can better appreciate the significance of what's happening today. That's something a lot of travelers don't take advantage of . . . and it's never been more important.

The glass dome of the Reichstag promises transparency in government.

Dachau: Forgive, But Never Forget

E N ROUTE to Dachau's infamous concentration camp, I sit next to an old German woman on the city bus. I smile at her weakly as if to say, "I don't hold your people's genocidal atrocities against you."

She glances at me and sneers down at my camera. Suddenly, surprising me with her crusty but fluent English, she rips into me. "You tourists come here not to learn but to hate," she seethes.

Pulling the loose skin down from a long-ago strong upper arm, she shows me a two-sided scar. "When I was a girl, a bullet cut straight through my arm," she says. "Another bullet killed my father. The war took many good people. My father ran a *Grüss Gott* shop."

I'm stunned by her rage. But I sense a desperation on her part to simply unload her story on one of the hordes of tourists who tramp daily through her town to gawk at an icon of the Holocaust.

I ask, "What do you mean, a *Grüss Gott* shop?"

She explains that in Bavaria shopkeepers greet customers with a *"Grüss Gott"* ("Praise God"). During the Third Reich it was safer to change the greeting to *"Sieg Heil."* It was a hard choice. Each shopkeeper had to make it. As more and more shops became *Sieg Heil* shops, everyone in Dachau knew which shops remained *Grüss Gott* shops. Pausing, as if mustering the energy for one last sentence, she stands up and says, "My father's shop was the last *Grüss Gott* shop," then steps off the bus.

With big promises, bold lies, and charisma—empowered by an angry base—Hitler led a great nation astray.

By the end of the line there are only tourists and pilgrims on the bus. Together, in silence, we walk into the concentration camp.

Dachau, founded in 1933, was the first concentration camp, a model camp, and a training ground for wannabe camp commandants who studied such subjects as crowd control and torture. The camp at Dachau was built to hold 5,000, but on Liberation Day 30,000 were found packed inside its walls. Some 3,000 were so sick that they died after liberation. The number of Dachau deaths is estimated at 40,000, but the total will never be known. Thousands of Russian soldiers were brought here as prisoners. Not even registered, they were simply taken into the field and shot.

Since many Holocaust survivors refuse to re-enter Germany, the Dachau memorial headquarters is in Brussels. Some make the pilgrimage against the wishes of their parents. Others, refusing to spend a night in Germany, come after sunrise and leave before sunset.

I shuffle into the camp's memorial theater. It's filled with 300 people, mostly tourists who are pilgrims for the morning. They sit in silence, looking at black-and-white film clips of tangled bodies and ghostly faces of the dead. As the camera pans silently across the corpses, gasps emanate from the audience. A frothing Hitler stands high, his hand waving furiously at the adoring masses. Even on the scratchy newsreel clips, he seems strangely charismatic, not dead but only hiding.

After leaving the theater, I wander through the museum. It shows how, under Hitler, Germany's prison system overflowed. A network of concentration camps provided a solution. Standing before the chart of the camp system network, I see that fascist banality of evil, an integrated circuit of cruelty and misery. When you arrived, you passed under the *"Arbeit macht frei"* ("Work makes you free") sign. You traded your property, rights, and human dignity for a number, tattooed on your wrist. You would never hear your name again . . . only your number.

"Work makes you free."

No one had the right even to hope. During sick parade, the ill and infirm were beaten and ridiculed in public each evening. A photo shows a Jewish violinist forced to serenade the execution cart as his friend

A guide speaks to students as Germany is determined to learn from its hard history.

was paraded to his death. The eyes of the German guards are scratched out.

When one inmate escaped, all would suffer. For instance, after a successful escape one freezing February, the entire camp was forced to endure an all-night roll call. Inmates stood naked, at attention in long lines. Guards doused them with cold water. Catching a cold routinely led to death by pneumonia. Nazis could kill you without even touching you.

After the costly Battle of Stalingrad, the struggling German war machine pulled out all the stops. Able-bodied inmates were fed just enough to provide slave labor to keep Germany in armaments.

Toward the end of the war, inmates could hear the noise of the battlefront as the Allies closed in. The inmates took a deep breath. On the eve of liberation, 5,000 of the inmates who had survived the longest—considered the most damaging potential witnesses in war crimes trials—were marched out with the retreating soldiers. Nearly half of these dropped from exhaustion and were killed on the roadside.

The American soldiers found train cars filled with dead bodies. In

The crematorium at Dachau

"Forgive, but never forget."

the chaos of those last days, new arrivals to Dachau simply weren't unloaded. At the sight of this misery, battle-hardened American soldiers broke down and wept.

Wandering angrily through a gallery of inmate art leaves me with a jumbled collage of images: A sky filled with *Sieg Heil* arms mimics a field filled with tombstones. A bald man in rags stands at attention facing a brick wall. Behind the wall a man in shorts, shivering in a cell, pulls his knees tight to his chest in search of warmth. Outside, a skeleton bangs a drum while barking God-and-country slogans at a field of raised hands. And in the forest of howling wolves a man in white—eyes wide with terror—kneels on skulls and howls along. He figures it's that or death. In the distance, a bent old man paints a sea of crosses . . . anticipating many deaths.

Dachau is both a barbed-wire box of memories and an eternal flame for the future. The sound of hushed voices and sad feet on the pebbled walk seems to promise remembrance while the breeze whispers "never again" through trees that stand on the parade ground where inmates once stood. A statue, as big as the train cars that brought in the inmates, marks the middle of the camp. It's a black steel tangle of bodies—like the real ones found woven together at the gas-chamber door. At its base, in French, English, German, Russian, and Hebrew, is the wish of the survivors: Forgive, but never forget.

Italy

ITALY IS *"issimo"*—as in "over the top." It's talking with your hands through a mouthful of pizza, ignoring the catcalls coming from a speeding Vespa, and swooning before the greatest art of Western civilization. It's a land where prosciutto is sacred, coffee is an art form, and macho men are actually mama's boys.

Italy is a country I adore. Just strolling down an Italian street fills any writer's notebook with vivid impressions. The art is exquisite, the cuisine brings out the foodie in backpackers, and people-watching is more than a spectator sport. The corruption, cronyism, and bureaucracy are exasperating. But Italy is a package deal.

Travel in Italy—when done right—is a parade of great moments . . .

The euphoria that erupts in Siena with the finish of the Palio horse race, when the winning jockey is heaved onto the shoulders of local fans and into the sky. Gazing up at Michelangelo's *David* and suddenly better understanding the sweep of history as it leaped from medieval to modern. Strolling through a farm with a noblewoman who knows each of her sheep by name. Finding a parallel Venice blind to the crowds while gliding along canals in the boat of a local friend. Sharing a quiet moment visiting a loved one in a Cinque Terre cemetery. Watching the sunset glow in glasses of Aperol spritz with college students in Padua . . .

Years ago, as a budding tour guide, I had to take a member of my group to the hospital because of "Stendhal Syndrome." She was simply overcome by the richness of Italian culture. That's the kind of high you can only get in Italy.

The dome of ancient Rome's magnificent Pantheon

Swept Away in Rome

I'M HARD at work, writing in my hotel room. I've spent the whole after-noon splicing changes into the next edition of my Rome guidebook. It's time for just a quick little break, but stepping outside is hazardous. It's too easy to get swept away into a Roman sea of colorful—and fra-grant—distractions. The current out there is too strong. Still, promising to be back at my desk in a few minutes, I decide to take the risk and plunge in . . .

From my hotel, I flow downhill to the Pantheon's portico, where I wade into the surf of images. Designer shades and flowing hair are back-lit in the magic-hour sun, happy ice-cream lickers sit on a marble bench, and a fountain spritzes in the background under an obelisk exclamation point. Romanian accordion players stroll along entertaining passersby. The sunburned stains of a golden arch on a wall mark where a McDon-ald's once sold fast food.

As I let go of the Pantheon's columns, the current sweeps me past siren cafés, past TV crews covering something big in front of the parlia-ment building, and out into Via del Corso. On my swim through the city, this is the deep end: The crowd from the suburbs comes here for some cityscape elegance. Today they've gooped on a little extra hair product and have put on their best T-shirts, leggings, and heels.

Rome's Pantheon

Veering away from the busy pedestrian boulevard, I come upon Fausto, a mad artist standing proudly amid his installation of absurdities. He's the only street artist I've met who personally greets viewers. After surveying his tiny gallery of hand-scrawled and thought-provoking tidbits, I ask for a card. As he gives me a handmade piece of wallet-sized art, he directs me to the end of the curb and his "secretary"—a plastic piggy bank for tips.

I pass a homeless man, tattered but respectfully dressed, leaning against a wall. He's savoring a bottle of wine while studying the parade of Roman life as if trying to follow the plot. Next, I chat with twins from Kentucky, giddy about celebrating their 40th birthday together here in Rome. Their Doublemint smiles and high energy argue a good case for embracing the good life.

Moving on, I slip into a church just as the ushers close the doors for Mass. Inside, the white noise of Roman streets gives way to the incensed hum of a big church with a determined priest—and not enough people. I slip down the side aisle, hands folded as if here to worship, to catch a glimpse of a Caravaggio, that thriller of the early 17th century.

Slipping back outside, I find myself at the north entrance of the ancient city. Determined to swim to my hotel room to get back to work, I pass the same well-dressed bum with the wine buzz, still intently caught up in the city. I imagine being in his pickled head for just a moment.

Near him, guys from Somalia launch their plastic fluorescent whirlybirds high into the sky while their friends slam plastic doll heads into boards so hard the heads become spilled goop. Then the dolls creepily reconstitute themselves, ready for another brutal slam. Selling these street trinkets keeps undocumented African immigrants from starving. Seeing them today makes me think that if I had bought all the goofy things people tried to sell me on the streets of Rome over the years—from the flaming *Manneken-Pis* lighters and the five-foot-tall inflatable bouncing cigars to the twin magnets that jitter like crickets—I could have opened a kitschy museum.

Rome is a cauldron of urban life—mixing random bits from today, yesterday, and centuries gone by. It's high class and low class, sacred and profane, grandiose and fragile, stormy and tranquil all at once—a mix seemingly designed to give visitors from far away indelible memories.

I swim with a struggling stroke back to the stillness of my hotel, closing the door to keep out the Roman current. While taking a break from writing up my work, I wind up coming home with even more to write about. In Rome, one thing leads to another. For a travel writer trying to catch up on his notes, just going out can be dangerous.

Rome casts a spell at night.

A Romantic Breeze in Rome

A STATUE OF Giordano Bruno marks the center of Campo de' Fiori—my favorite square in Rome. Five centuries ago, Bruno challenged the Roman Church and was burned at the stake right here. With each visit, I make a quiet little pilgrimage, staring into the eyes of brooding Bruno, pondering the courage of those early heretics.

When in Rome, I use Bruno as a meeting point. (I like to say, "I'll be sitting under Bruno.") Tonight, I'm waiting for Stefano and Paola, who run one of my favorite hotels in Rome. With each visit, they take me on a quest for restaurants to recommend in my guidebook. They've promised to take me to a little restau-rant they deem perfect. When they arrive, I say *ciao* to Bruno and we walk down a narrow cobbled lane to a classic, crumpled little piazza filled with scooters. A stately but tiny Neoclassical white church is crammed into the corner. On the far side, a single eatery is all lit up. The sign above the door says *"Filetti di Baccalà."*

The heretic Giordano Bruno stands on the spot where he was burned.

"Stefano, you're right. This is perfect." I walk ahead, navigating the gridlock of abandoned scooters to get into the restaurant. A long line of tables, covered with white-paper tablecloths and crowded with locals, stretches to a neon-lit kitchen in the back. And there, two grease-splattered cooks are busy cranking out *filetti di baccalà* . . . Rome's answer to fish sticks.

There's one table open near the back, past an old man in a black suit playing the violin. We limbo by the violinist and grab it. Above our table a weathered sign reads *Specialità Filetti di Baccalà 60 lire*. The price has been revised over the years in response to the whims of the econ-omy, peaking at 4,000 lire. Today, it's €5. The harried waiter drops off

Paola enjoys a serenade and a sweet breeze.

a simple menu, listing a humble selection of appetizers and salads, but only one main course *(filetti di baccalà)* and, with his thumb hitchhiking into his mouth, asks, *"Da bere?"* ("To drink?").

Our fillet of cod is about what you'd expect at a top-notch London fish-and-chips joint. We enjoy it along with some breaded and fried zucchini, a salad of greens I'd never before encountered, and a carafe of white wine. Some people might think the meal is nothing special. But buried deep in the medieval center of the city, in a tarnished and varnished eatery without a tourist in sight, the ambience is intoxicating.

The violinist plays Sinatra's "My Way" to an appreciative crowd. Eventually he makes his way to our table, standing just beyond Paola's radiant face. It's a classic Roman moment. Her dark eyes, framed by little black glasses, are locked on Stefano's. Tiny rings of pearls set in gold swing from her ears. A gold necklace is the perfect complement to her smooth, olive complexion.

Like a hungry camera, my eyes compose the scene: carafe of golden white wine shimmering in the foreground, Paola's face looking lovingly at her husband in the middle, and the violinist—jaw tight on his instrument but still smiling—in the back. The happy chatter of dinner conversation rounds out the scene.

As if only for Paola, the musician plays a Roman anthem to the night. Paola whispers to me, "This is *Ponentino* . . . a special wind, a sweet . . . " brushing her hand gently along her cheek in search of the word, " . . . caressing Roman wind."

Then she and Stefano face the music, and with the entire room, sing the song:

Rome, don't be foolish tonight.
Give me the sweet wind to let her say yes.
Turn on all the stars that you have . . . the brightest ones.
Give me a small flash of the moon, only for us.
Let her feel that springtime is arriving.
Give me your very best crickets to sing to her.
Give me the Ponentino.
Be a partner with me.

Paola translates the rest of the song to me. In verse two, the woman answers: "Rome, give me a helping hand to tell him no," and so on. But, in the final verse, of course, they get together, creating the love triangle: a man, a woman . . . and Rome.

With the room still singing, the elegant older couple at the next table look over at us. Seeming pleased that the three of us—a generation behind hers—are enjoying this traditional Roman moment, the woman says, simply, *"Bella."*

Campo de' Fiori, romantic at night

Naples: *Bella* Chaos

S TROLLING THROUGH Naples, I remember my first visit to the city as a wide-eyed 18-year-old. My travel buddy and I had stepped off the train into vast Piazza Garibaldi. A man in a white surgeon's gown approached me and said, "Please, it is very important. We need blood for a dying baby." Naples was offering a dose of reality we weren't expecting on our Italian vacation. We immediately made a U-turn, stepped back into the station, and made a beeline for Greece.

While that delayed my first visit by several years, I've been back to Naples many times since. And today, even with its new affluence and stress on law and order, the city remains appalling and captivating at the same time. It's Italy's third-largest city, as well as its most polluted and crime-ridden. But this tangled urban mess still somehow manages to breathe, laugh, and sing with a joyful Italian accent. Naples offers the closest thing to "reality travel" in Western Europe: churning, fertile, and exuberant.

With more than two million people, Naples has almost no open spaces or parks, which makes its ranking as Europe's most densely populated city plenty evident. Watching the police try to enforce traffic sanity is almost comical. But Naples still surprises me with its impressive knack for living, eating, and raising children with good humor and decency. There's even a name for this love of life on the street: *basso* living.

In Naples, I spend more time in the local neighborhoods than the palaces and museums. Since ancient Greek times, the old city center has been split down the middle by a long, straight street called Spaccanapoli ("split Naples"). Just beyond it, the Spanish Quarter climbs into the hills. And behind the Archaeological Museum is perhaps the most colorful district of all, Sanità.

Walking through the Spaccanapoli neighborhood, I venture down narrow streets lined with tall apartment buildings, walk in the shade of wet laundry hung out to dry, and slip into time-warp courtyards. Couples artfully make love on Vespas while surrounded by more fights and smiles per cobblestone than anywhere else in Italy. Black-and-white death announcements add to the clutter on the walls of buildings. Widows sell cigarettes from plastic buckets.

I spy a woman overseeing the action from her balcony on the fifth floor. I buy two carrots as a gift and she lowers her bucket to pick them up. One wave populates six stories of balconies, each filling up with its own waving family. A contagious energy fills the air. I snap a photo and suddenly people in each window and balcony are vying for another. Mothers hold up babies, sisters pose arm in arm, a wild-haired pregnant woman stands on a fruit crate holding her bulging stomach, and an old, wrinkled woman fills her paint-starved window frame with a toothy grin.

On a nearby street I run across a small niche in the wall dedicated to Diego Maradona, the fabled soccer star who played for Naples in the 1980s. Locals consider soccer almost a religion, and this guy was practically a deity. This little Chapel of Maradona includes a "hair of Diego" and a teardrop from the city when he went to another team for more money. It's these little eccentric passions that make exploring Naples such fun.

Basso living (life on the street) in Naples

Three on a Vespa

Around the corner there's an entire street lined with shops selling tiny components of fantastic manger scenes, including figurines caricaturing politicians and local celebrities—should I want to add a Putin or a Berlusconi to my Nativity set.

The abundance of gold and silver shops here makes me think this is where stolen jewelry ends up. But I've learned that's not quite true. According to locals, thieves quickly sell their goods and the items are melted down immediately. New pieces go on sale as soon as they cool.

Paint a picture with these thoughts: Naples has the most intact ancient Roman street plan anywhere. Imagine life here in the days of Caesar, with street-side shop fronts that close up to become private homes after dark. Today is just one more page in a 2,000-year-old story of city activity: meetings, beatings, and cheatings; kisses, near misses, and little-boy pisses.

The only predictable elements of this Neapolitan mix are the boldness of mopeds—concerned residents will tug on their lower eyelid, warning you to be wary—and the friendliness of shopkeepers.

To cap my walk, I pop into a grocery and ask the man to make me his best ham-and-mozzarella sandwich. I watch, enthralled, as he turns sandwich-making into a show. After demonstrating the freshness of his rolls with a playful squeeze, he assembles the components, laying on a careful pavement of salami, bringing over a fluffy mozzarella ball as if performing a kidney transplant, slicing a tomato with rapid-fire machine precision, and lovingly pitting the olives

by hand. He then finishes it off with a celebratory drizzle of the best oil. Six euros and a smile later, I find the perfect bench upon which to enjoy my lunch while watching the Neapolitan parade of life.

An older man with a sloppy slice of pizza joins me. Moments later, a stylish couple on a bike rolls by—she sits on the handlebars, giggling as she faces her man, hands around his neck as he cranes to see where they're going.

I say, "*Bella* Italia."

My bench mate says, "No, *bella* Napoli."

I say, "Napoli . . . is both beautiful and a city of chaos."

He agrees, but insists, "*Bella* chaos."

"Tell me, what is Napoli in one word?" I ask.

Turning his head, he watches a woman stride by. Then, with a long string of mozzarella stretching between his mouth and what remains of his pizza, he chews for a moment, pauses, and says, "*Abbondante.*"

I agree. "Abundant."

Bella Napoli

Romantic Italy: Amalfi Coast and the Isle of Capri

A LONG THE HEIGHTS of the Amalfi Coast, every inch is terraced, connected by steep stony staircases that tempt visitors with twinkling but treacherous Mediterranean views. Climbing through terraced orchards of lemon trees, I'm hot and thirsty, fantasizing about fresh-squeezed lemonade.

And then, just like the fairy tale, I come upon the daughter of a farmer who seems to be waiting for a lost and parched American traveler. She welcomes me to her terrace to join her for a little slicing and squeezing. Then, as if teaching me a very important life skill, she demonstrates how you halve your lemon, stab it with a knife, and then—cupping the fruit with one hand—you wiggle the knife with the other, and watch the juice fill your glass. She adds lots of sugar, gives it a good stir, and hands me a glass of lemonade I'll never forget. As I drink, she quizzes me about my journey. It's one of those moments you travel for.

Lemons—fruit of the Amalfi Coast

I'm staying in Sorrento, a town wedged on a ledge between the mountains and the sea. An hour south of wild and crazy Naples, Sorrento feels like its opposite: calm and genteel.

Crowding onto the early bus for the ride along the Amalfi Coast, I sit on the right, primed for the big coastal views and bracing myself for one of the Italy's great thrill rides. The trip gives me respect for the engineers who built the road—and even more respect for the bus drivers who drive it. Maybe I'm just hyperventilating, but I'm struck by how the Mediterranean, a sheer 500-foot drop below, twinkles. Cantilevered garages, hotels, and villas cling to the vertical terrain. Exotic sandy coves tease from far below, out of reach. Traffic is so heavy that in the summer, locals are allowed to drive only every other day—even-numbered license plates one day, odd the next. Buses and tourists foolish enough to drive here are exempt from this system.

My first stop, the town of Positano, hangs halfway between Sorrento and Amalfi town on the most spectacular stretch of coastline. Most of the Amalfi Coast towns are pretty but touristy, congested, overpriced, and an exhausting daily hike from their tiny beaches. Specializing in scenery and sand, Positano is no exception. A three-star sight from a distance, Positano is a pleasant if pricey gathering of women's clothing stores and cafés, with an inviting beach. There's little to do here other than eat, shop, and enjoy the beach and views . . . and for most visitors, that's just fine.

For lunch, rather than paying resort prices in a restaurant, I find a *rosticceria*—a deli selling roasted meats and *antipasti*. Using one of my handier Italian phrases, I request my food *"da portare via"* ("for the road"), then take my meal down to the pebbly beach. Grabbing a nice perch, I munch while watching the scene as it unfolds. Colorful umbrellas fill the beach while boats shuttle visitors in and out. Young Romeos—inspired by the older boys working the beach—polish their girl-hustling craft. I ponder what to do the next day, though, for many, the choice seems obvious—repeat and enjoy.

Early the next morning, riding the 30-minute ferry from Sorrento, I head for the enchanting isle of Capri. I think of the rich and famous

Positano rises steeply from the Mediterranean.

who've headed to the same island over the centuries. Capri was the vacation hideaway of Roman emperors and centuries later became a favorite stop for Romantic Age aristocrats on their Grand Tour of Europe. Later, it was the safe haven of Europe's gay cultural elite—back when being openly gay often meant being dead.

Today, Capri is expensive and glitzy—and a world-class tourist trap. Landing on the island, I'm met with a greedy line of white convertible taxis, eager to sweep me away. Zigzagging up the cliff with the top down, I think that despite its crowds and commercialism, Capri is still flat-out gorgeous. Chalky white limestone cliffs rocket boldly from the shimmering blue and green surf. Strategically positioned gardens, villas, and viewpoints provide stunning vistas of the Sorrentine peninsula, Amalfi Coast, and Mt. Vesuvius.

To give my Capri visit an extra dimension, I take the scenic boat trip around the island. It's cheap and comes with good narration. Riding through the pounding waves, I work on my sunburn as we circle the island, marveling at a nonstop parade of staggering cliffs and listening to stories of celebrity-owned villas. There are also some quirky sights: a solar-powered lighthouse, statues atop desolate rocks, and caves in the cliffs with legends reaching back to the time of Emperor Tiberius.

Capri has attracted visitors since ancient times.

The last stop is the highlight: the fabled Blue Grotto, with its other-worldly azure water. At the mouth of the grotto, a covey of dinghies jockeys to pick up arriving tourists, who need to disembark from their larger transports. The grotto's entrance hole is small, so only these little rowboats can fit through. If the tide's too high or the chop too rough, dinghies can't get in, and visitors are turned back. Nervous that the waves will close it down, I gingerly climb into my dinghy and my raffish rower jostles his way to the tiny entry. He knows enough English to explain to me that if I don't scrunch down below the gunwales, I'll smash my skull on the rock and, as I've already paid, that was no concern of his. (I think this is intended as a joke.) Taking a moment to feel the rhythm of the swells and anticipating the instant when the dinghy reaches the low point, he pulls hard and fast on the old chain, and we squeeze—like birthing in reverse—into the grotto.

Inside, it takes my eyes a moment to adjust to the brilliant blue of the cave's water (an effect caused by sun reflecting off the limestone at the bottom). As my man rows me around, singing a little "O Sole Mio," I enjoy the iridescent magic of the moment.

Beaches, boutiques, blue grottos, and fresh-squeezed lemonade—it all combines to make clear why, for centuries, holiday-goers have chosen this corner of Italy to make their Mediterranean travel dreams come true.

Gliding through the Blue Grotto

My Dinner with Franklin

I LOVE THE way Italians enjoy their food. I'm sitting down for a meal with a friend at one of my favorite restaurants, Enoteca Can Grande in Verona. Eating in a little restaurant like this one, you have contact with the chef. We were here a year ago and chef Giuliano remembers us. Once we're comfortably seated, he consults with us. As is our tradition, we encourage him to bring us whatever he's most excited about today. Pleased with the freedom to dazzle us, he goes to work.

My friend and guide, Franklin, is a local. He knows the cuisine and gushes about the food incessantly. As the courses come and we eat, he shares his thoughts, which are sometimes impolite, but always come from the heart (perhaps with a side trip through the stomach).

With the first of many small plates, Franklin is delighted. "Raw Piedmont beef, *carne cruda*. It is like seeing the smile of a beautiful woman. Even after 10 years, you never forget her."

Our wine is Amarone della Valpolicella. Enjoying a sip, I ask, "*Sublime* is an Italian word, no?"

He says, "Yes, soo-blee-may . . . this is *sublime*."

Giuliano brings a plate of various cold cuts, glistening in a way that shows they're nothing but the best. We ponder, if you had to choose between salami and cheese in life, which would you choose? Giuliano and Franklin both agree that it would be a terrible choice . . . but they would have to go with the cheese. Then we nibble the mortadella with truffle, complicating that decision. Mortadella is the local baloney—not a high-end meat. But with the black truffle, it is exquisite. Imagine calling spam exquisite . . . just add truffle.

Franklin says, "I used to smoke, and I compared white wine and red like cigarettes and a good Cuban cigar. I enjoy my red wine like I enjoy my Cuban cigars." Then he gets distracted by the herb decorating the next little mozzarella dish. After tasting a sprig, he says, "Yes, fresh. It's normally served dried. The chef is a genius . . . fresh, brilliant with mozzarella."

Franklin's phone rings. It's his wife, who says, "Don't eat too much cheese or dessert." Franklin, who's not thin, surveys our table and sadly contemplates enjoying the enticing parade of food that has just begun with anything less than complete abandon. Then he sighs and tells me, "Many people live their entire lives and they do not have this experience."

Fresh mozzarella salad

I say, "That is a pity."

"Yes. It's like a man being born and being surrounded by beautiful women and never making love."

As we eat and drink, Franklin opens up about his passion for good eating. He says, "In Italy, you don't need to be high class to appreciate high culture, opera, cuisine. It's the only culture I know like this. Here in my country, a heart surgeon talks with a carpenter about cuisine. This is just how we are."

Next comes the polenta, the best I've ever tasted. This cornbread, typical of the Veneto region, comes in varieties, like bread ranges from whole grain to white. This is the darker *polenta integrale,* using all of the corn. And it comes with anchovies. "A good marriage," Franklin says. It's

The parade of food continues.

the simple things—the anchovies, the olive oil, the *polenta integrale,* and the proper matching of flavors—that bring the most joy to the table.

Noticing how Franklin polishes every plate, I say, "You even eat the crumbs."

He says, "Yes, I would feel like a sinner not to." Sipping his wine, he adds, "And to not finish the Amarone . . . Dante would have to create a new place in hell. Mortal sin."

As guides tend to do, especially after a little wine, Franklin mixes culture, history, and politics in with his commentary on cuisine. I find myself scribbling notes on the paper tablecloth.

Franklin is frustrated with how Italy's north subsidizes the south. He complains that the south is "corrupt, inefficient, lazy, no organization."

I remind him, "They say that here in the north—in regions like Veneto and Lombardi—you are like the Germans of Italy."

He says, "Even today, the south still has its organized crime. When fascism came to Italy, the Camorra went to the USA. Mussolini had zero tolerance. And he got things done. That's one reason why he was popular. And one reason why Mussolini is still popular. Then, after World War II, rather than tolerate communism, the government allowed the Camorra to reestablish itself in Italy."

I ask him if he enjoyed *The Godfather.*

To not finish the Amarone would be a mortal sin.

"I watched *The Godfather* with a certain pride because of the importance of food in that movie. Especially the scenes with tomatoes. Marlon Brando watched tomatoes ripen. When he said something like, 'Become red, you bastards,' to the yellow tomatoes, that took me back to Sicily and the home of my father."

We enjoy the conversation as much as the food.

Our conversation drifts to how modern societies mirror their ancient predecessors . . . or don't. Comparing the historic continuity between the ancient and modern civilizations of Rome, Greece, and Egypt, we agree that the biggest difference is in Egypt, a relatively ramshackle society today that feels a far cry from the grandiosity of the pharaohs and pyramids. Greece, which wrote the ancient book on aesthetics, developed an unfortunate appetite in modern times for poorly planned concrete sprawl. But Rome has the most continuity. Today's Romans, like their ancient ancestors, are still passionate about wine, food, and the conviviality offered by the public square. The piazza and good eating—in Italy those go back to Caesar.

Next comes the pumpkin ravioli. I hold the warm and happy tire of my full tummy and say, *"Basta."*

Giuliano comes by, sees my empty glass, and realizes we need another bottle. He warns us, "Next I bring you a small cheese course."

Contemplating the cheese platter, Franklin says, "I'm not so religious, but for this cheese, with Amarone . . . I fall on my knees."

I agree. "In cheese we trust."

He compliments my economy of words and repeats, "Yes, in cheese we trust."

"This cheese plate takes dessert to new heights."

Franklin, playing with the voluptuous little slices, says, "Even if we do not talk, with these cheeses we have a good conversation."

I support my heavy yet happy head with my hand as Franklin fills our

My dinner with Franklin: *Indimenticabale*

glasses from the second bottle and we move on to the parmesan and the gorgonzola. Sipping the wine, Franklin says, "If this was my only wine, I could be monogamous."

When Giuliano stops by again, I compliment him. He recalls that on our last visit, we sat at the same table. He serves thousands of people. I'm always impressed by people who care enough to remember their clients. It's the same in hotels. I don't remember which room I slept in last time, but often the proprietor greets me saying, "I put you in your room . . . number 510."

On my visit to Milan three years ago, I got a haircut. I remember really enjoying my barber. I needed a haircut on this trip, too, so when I was in Milan, I walked vaguely in the direction where I thought his shop was. Not sure whether I'd found the right place, I popped in on a barber. It seemed like the one, but I really didn't know. Ten minutes into my haircut, the barber—having gotten to know my hair—realized he remembered it and asked me if I hadn't been there before. He had a tactile memory not of me as a person . . . but as a head of hair he had cut that happened to be mine.

Giuliano asks if I'd like anything else.

I ask, *"Dov'è il letto?"* ("Where is a bed?")

Franklin agrees and says, "Yes, a good restaurant should come with a bed." It occurs to me that we must have tasted 30 different ingredients—all of them top quality and in harmonious combinations. Franklin again marvels at how Giuliano is creative and unpredictable without using garish combinations—no gorgonzola ice cream.

I have a feeling Giuliano will remember my table the next time I drop in. And I'll remember to invite my friend Franklin. Year after year, the experience is reliably *indimenticabale*. That's an Italian word I'm thankful is well-used in my tiny vocabulary: unforgettable.

The Italian Love of Eating

S PENDING A MONTH in Italy, the thought of eating anything other than Italian food never occurs to me. Other than France, I doubt there's another country in Europe that could hold my palate's interest so completely. One reason I don't tire of going local here is that this land of a thousand bell towers is also the land of a thousand regional cuisines. And I celebrate each region's forte.

Tuscany is proud of its beef, so I seek out a place to sink my teeth into a carnivore's dream. My favorite steakhouse is in Montepulciano. The scene in a stony cellar, under one long, rustic vault, is powered by an open fire in the far back. Flickering in front of the flames is a gurney, upon which lays a hunk of beef the size of a small human corpse. Like a blacksmith in hell, Giulio—a lanky, George Carlin look-alike in a T-shirt—hacks at the beef, lopping off a steak every few minutes. He gets an order and then it's *whop!* . . . leave it to cleaver.

In a kind of mouthwatering tango, he prances past boisterous tables of

"The best cuisine starts from the market."

Giulio shows raw steaks to customers.

eaters, holding above the commotion the raw slabs of beef on butcher paper. Giulio presents the slabs to my friends and me, telling us the weight and price and getting our permission to cook it. He then dances back to the inferno and cooks the slabs: seven minutes on one side, seven on the other. There's no asking how you'd like it done; *this* is the way it is done. Fifteen minutes later, we get our steaks.

In Italy, the cuisine is revered—and the quality of the ingredients is sacred. Italians like to say, *"La miglior cucina comincia dal mercato."* ("The best cuisine starts from the market.") They care deeply about what's in season.

One night in Florence, I'm dining with my friend Cincia at her favorite trattoria when the chef comes out to chat with her. They get into an animated debate about the ingredients: "Arugula is not yet in season. But oh, Signora Maria has more sun in her backyard, and her chickens give her a marvelous fertilizer."

Leave it to cleaver.

Then the topic changes to the cuisine turmoil caused by erratic weather. *Vignarola,* the beloved stew consisting of artichokes, peas, and fava beans, is on the menu before its normal season. Cincia, seeming traumatized, says, "*Vignarola,* how can it be

A happy customer with her steak

served so early? I've never seen it on a menu before Easter." The chef, who only makes it for a few weeks each spring during a perfect storm of seasonality when everything is bursting with flavor, has to convince her that the season has changed and it's on the menu because this is the new season.

Enjoying the commotion, I explain to Cincia that this is the kind of restaurant I seek out in Italy. It ticks all the boxes: It's personality-driven—a mom-and-pop place—and run by people enthusiastic about sharing their love of good cooking. It's a low-rent location, with lots of locals. The menu is small because they're selling everything they're cooking. It's in one language, Italian, because they cater to locals rather than tourists. And it's handwritten because it's shaped by what's fresh in the market today.

Cincia then takes control, telling me to put away my notepad and stop being a travel writer. She says, "Only a tourist would rush a *grappa* or pull the fat off the prosciutto. Tonight, we eat with no notes. We eat my way." Reviewing the options, she says to the chef simply, *"Mi faccia felice"* (Make me happy).

And he does.

"Make me happy."

Ciao Chow: Italians on American Food

WHEN ITALIANS sit down together for dinner, a special joy combusts from their mutual love of good eating: the flavors, the steam, the memories, the dreams . . . the edible heritage. Food is a favorite topic of conversation. And it seems every Italian has an opinion about American food.

During one long Italian meal, my friend Claudia says she loves American food. Her favorites include the BLT sandwich and "chili soup." She's charmed by our breakfast culture and that we "meet for breakfast." She says you would never see families going out for breakfast in Italy.

But she notes that in the US, size matters more than quality and dishes try too hard. She says that the average number of ingredients in an American restaurant salad or pasta is eight or ten—double the ingredients in the typical Italian salad or pasta. And she can't understand our heavily flavored salad dressings. "If your lettuce and tomato are good, why cover it up with a heavy dressing? We use only oil and vinegar," she says. When I try to defend the fancy dishes as complex, she says, "Perhaps 'jumbled' is a better translation."

My Tuscan friends laud the virtues of their regional cuisine. In Florence, I join my friend Manfredo and his girlfriend Diana for dinner. She sets a big plate of bruschetta in front of me. Each slice of toast

Bruschetta: It's best in Italy.

Manfredo talks up Tuscan food.

looks like a little brown ship, with a toothpick mast flying a garlic clove, as it sails over its oily deck. We hungrily destroy the tidy flotilla. Ripping off a mast and rubbing the sail on the crusty deck, I say, "My family eats bruschetta at home. But we all agree it's best in Italy."

"Real bruschetta needs real Tuscan bread," Manfredo says. "This is made with only flour, water, and yeast. No salt. It is great today. Hard like rock tomorrow."

Diana says, "Because the bread gets old quickly and we are a poor region, in Tuscany there are many dishes made with yesterday's bread."

In unison, they labor through a short list as if it were long: *"Minestrone di pane, ribollita, pappa al pomodoro."*

Manfredo explains, "*Ribollita* is for the poor. You cook and always stir together beans, cabbage, carrots, onions, old bread, and olive oil for at least two hours. Very filling. It is not good with fresh bread."

Manfredo picks up his knife, eyeing the lasagna on the big plate in front of him. "In America, a restaurant is not looking for what is good food. What is good is what sells." He sticks his knife through two steamy inches of lasagna. "Real lasagna is only this thick. In USA they make it twice this thick," he says, flipping another serving on top, "and they fill it with mozzarella." Then he says, "There is no mozzarella in lasagna."

The joy of eating in Italy

Diana chuckles in agreement.

After a swig of wine, Manfredo continues, "If you go to an American restaurant and say the food is bad, you get a coupon for a free

Service with a flourish

meal. More bad food. If you say the food is bad in a restaurant in Italy, you get kicked out. To get free food here, it is vice versa. You say, 'This is the best beefsteak I ever eat.' Chef will then say, 'You must try the dessert.' You say 'Oh no.' He says, 'Here. Please. Take it for free.'"

Diana says, "In a real Italian restaurant when you complain, the chef will tell you, 'I cooked this as a boy the way my grandmother cooked this.' It cannot be wrong."

I ask, "What do you think about French food?"

Manfredo, peppering a puddle of oil on a small plate, responds, "The French make fine sauces to help the taste of mediocre ingredients. With the French there are two things great: their wine and their art. Since the time of Napoleon, they think only of their wine and their art. In the south they are like the Italians. But from Paris and north, they are so proud they are boring."

Tearing off a piece of bread and dabbing it in the oil, Diana says, "For me, the French cheese, it is the Italian cheese with mold. If we have cheese that doesn't sell, it gets moldy. After some days, it is perfect for the French."

Raising my glass of wine, I offer a toast to Italian food: "To *cucina italiana!*"

Manfredo follows that, saying magnanimously, "To bacon and eggs!"

We all agree that American breakfasts are unbeatable.

"Omelets, hashbrowns . . . " Manfredo reminisces with a nostalgic sigh. "On my last visit to New York, I gain four kilos in three weeks."

Raising our glasses filled with fine *vino rosso,* we all say, "To American breakfasts!"

Florence: City of Art

AFTER MY first day in Florence, I remember thinking, "I've seen more great art in a few hours than many people see in a lifetime."

Geographically small but culturally rich, Florence is home to some of the finest art and architecture in the world. In that single day, I looked Michelangelo's *David* in the eyes, fell under the seductive sway of Botticelli's *Birth of Venus*, and climbed the first great dome of the Renaissance, which gracefully dominates the city's skyline today as it did 500 years ago.

After Rome fell in AD 476, Europe wallowed in centuries of relative darkness, with little learning, commerce, or travel. Then, around 1400, there was a Renaissance: a rebirth of the culture of ancient Greece and Rome. Starting in Florence, it swept across Europe. Wealthy merchant and banking families—like the Medici, who ruled Florence for generations—showed their civic pride by commissioning great art.

With the Renaissance, artists rediscovered the beauty of nature and the human body, expressing the optimism of this new age. The ultimate representation of this: Michelangelo's *David*. Poised confidently in the Accademia Gallery, *David* represents humankind stepping out of medieval darkness—the birth of our modern, humanist outlook. Standing

Florence skyline, with the cathedral's sublime dome

boldly, *David* sizes up the giant, as if to say, "I can take him." The statue was an apt symbol, inspiring Florentines to tackle their Goliaths.

Until 1873, *David* stood not in the Accademia, but outside Palazzo Vecchio, the former Medici palace and now Florence's City Hall. A replica *David* marks the spot where the original once stood. With goony eyes and a pigeon-dropping wig, this *David* seems dumbfounded, as tourists picnic at his feet and policemen clip-clop by on horseback.

Next door to the palace were the Medicis' offices, or *uffizi*. Now the Uffizi Gallery holds the finest collection of Italian paintings anywhere, sweeping through art history from the 12th through 17th centuries, with works by Botticelli, Raphael, Giotto, Titian, Leonardo, and Michelangelo. In the long, arcaded courtyard, a permanent line of tourists (who ignored my guidebook's advice to book reservations online in advance) waits to buy tickets.

For me, a highlight of the Uffizi is *Venus de' Medici*. Revered as the epitome of beauty, *Venus* is a Roman copy of a 2,000-year-old Greek statue that went missing. In the 18th and 19th centuries, wealthy children of Europe's aristocrats made the pilgrimage to the Uffizi to complete their classical education. They stood before the cold beauty of this goddess of love and swooned in ecstasy.

Classical statues like this clearly inspired Sandro Botticelli, my favorite Florentine painter. His greatest paintings, including the *Birth of Venus,* hang in this gallery. According to myth, Venus was born from the foam of a wave. This fragile Venus, a newborn beauty with flyaway hair, floats ashore on a clam shell while flowers tumble in slow motion.

Botticelli's *Birth of Venus*

For me, Botticelli's *Birth of Venus* represents the purest expression of Renaissance beauty.

In Florence, art treasures are everywhere you turn. The small, uncrowded Bargello Museum features the best collection of Florentine sculpture anywhere, including works by Michelangelo, Donatello, and Ghiberti. And hiding out at the underrated Duomo Museum, you'll see one of Michelangelo's *Pietà*s (which he designed as the centerpiece for his own tomb) and Ghiberti's *Gates of Paradise* panels. Revolutionary in their realism and three-dimensionality, these panels were created in response to a citywide competition in 1401 to build new doors for the Baptistery, an event that kicked off the Renaissance.

Across the street from the Duomo Museum towers Florence's famous cathedral. Boasting the first great dome built in Europe in more than a thousand years, the Duomo marked the start of the architectural Renaissance (later inspiring domes ranging from the Vatican's St. Peter's Basilica to the US Capitol). Designed by Filippo Brunelleschi, the immense dome is taller than a football field on end.

As if inspired by the centuries-old, greatest art of our civilization, Florence's artistic and artisan commmunity lives on today. To find it, I simply walk across the fabled bridge, Ponte Vecchio, and explore the Oltrarno neighborhood, home to small shops with handmade furniture, jewelry, leather items, shoes, and pottery. Craftsmen bind books and make marbled paper. Antique pieces are refurbished by people who've become curators of the dying techniques of gilding, engraving, etching, enameling, mosaics, and repoussé metalwork.

After a day filled with so much great art, I retreat to a stately former monastery and unwind in a Renaissance-era cell. It's my favorite Florentine hotel, Loggiato dei Serviti, and that cell is my bedroom.

Directly across from my window is the Accademia, filled with tourists clamoring to meet *David*. The peaceful courtyard in between is gravelly with broken columns and stones that students are carving like creative woodpeckers. I hear the happy chipping and chirping of their chisels gaining confidence, cutting through the stone. Five centuries later, it's comforting to know that the spirit of the Renaissance remains alive and well in Florence.

The Church of *David*

ENTERING Florence's Accademia Gallery is like entering the Church of *David*—a temple of humanism. At the high altar stands the perfect man, Michelangelo's colossal statue of *David*. Like a Renaissance Statue of Liberty, *David* declares, "Yes, I can."

This 500-year-old slingshot-toting giant-slayer is the symbol of Florence. The city's other treasures are largely ignored by the tourist hordes that roam the streets with one statue at the top of their sightseeing list. Each morning the line forms as tourists wait patiently to enter the temple. As at any pilgrimage site, the nearby streets are lined with shops selling *David* knickknacks.

Inside, smartly dressed ushers collect admission tickets. Dropping mine in the basket, I turn the corner and enter a large nave. Six unfinished statues called the *Prisoners*—brute bodies each fighting to free themselves from their rock—line the room leading to *David*. His feet are at a level just above the sea of tourists' heads. Round arches and a dome hover above him like architectural halos. People only whisper. Couples hold each other tighter in his presence, their eyes fixed on the statue.

The scene is black and white under a skylight. I don't miss the color. I wouldn't want color. *David* is beyond color, even beyond gender.

David is fundamentally human. Gathered with people from all nations, I look up to him. Tight-skirted girls who'd cause a commotion in the streets go unnoticed as macho men fold their hands. Students commune with Michelangelo on their sketchpads. Sightseers pause. Tired souls see the spirit in *David*'s eyes.

David is the god of human triumph. Clothed only in confidence, his toes gripping the pedestal, he seems both ready and determined to step out of the Dark Ages and into an exciting future.

When you look into the eyes of Michelangelo's *David,* you're looking into the eyes of Renaissance Man. This six-ton, 17-foot-tall symbol of divine victory over evil—completed in 1504—represents a new century and a new outlook. It's the age of Columbus and classicism, Galileo and

Gutenberg, Luther and Leonardo—of Florence and the Renaissance.

In 1501, Michelangelo Buonarroti, a 26-year-old Florentine, was commissioned to carve a large-scale work for Florence's cathedral. He was given a block of marble that other sculptors had rejected as too tall, shallow, and flawed to be of any value. But Michelangelo picked up his hammer and chisel, knocked a knot off what became *David's* heart, and started to work.

He depicted a story from the Bible, where a brave young shepherd boy challenges a mighty giant named Goliath. David turns down the armor of the day. Instead, he throws his sling over his left shoulder, gathers five smooth stones in his powerful right hand, and steps onto the field of battle to face Goliath.

Michelangelo's *David*

Michelangelo captures David as he's sizing up his enemy. He stands relaxed but alert. In his left hand, he fondles the handle of the sling, ready to fling a stone at the giant. His gaze is steady . . . confident. Michelangelo has caught the precise moment when David realizes he can win.

David is a symbol of Renaissance optimism. He's no brute. He's a civilized, thinking individual who can grapple with and overcome problems. He needs no armor, only his God-given physical strength and wits. Many complained that the right hand was too big and overdeveloped. But this was no mistake. It represents the hand of a man with the strength of God on his side. No mere boy could slay the giant. But David, powered by God, could . . . and did.

Renaissance Florentines identified with David. Like him, they considered themselves God-blessed underdogs fighting their city-state rivals.

In a deeper sense, they were civilized Renaissance people—on the cusp of our modern age—slaying the ugly giant of medieval superstition, pessimism, and oppression.

Gathered before the high altar of *David*, tourists share the pews with Michelangelo's unfinished stone *Prisoners*. Also known as the *Slaves*, they wade wearily through murky darkness, bending their heads under the hard truth of their mortality.

A passing tour guide says, "The *Prisoners* are struggling to come to life." But I see them dying—giving up the struggle, wearily accepting an inevitable defeat.

Michelangelo intended to show the soul imprisoned in the body. While the *Prisoners'* legs and heads disappear into the rock, their chests heave and their bellies shine. Talking through what I'm seeing, I say out loud, "Each belly is finished, as if it were Michelangelo's focus . . . the portal of the soul."

Without missing a beat, the woman next to me replies, "That's the epigastric area. When you die, this stays warm longest. It's where your soul exits your body."

I welcome this opportunity to get a new perspective on Michelangelo's work. She introduces herself as Carla and her friend as Anne-Marie. Both are nurses from Idaho. Carla turns from the *Prisoners* to *David*, raises her opera glasses, and continues, "And *David*'s antecubital space is perfectly correct."

"Anti-what?" I say, surprised by this clinical approach to *David*.

"That's the space inside the elbow. Look at those veins. They're perfect. He'd be a great IV start. And the sternocleidomastoid muscle—the big one here," she explains, running four slender fingers from her ear to the center of her Florence T-shirt, "it's just right."

Carla burrows back into the opera glasses for a slow head-to-toe pan and continues to narrate her discoveries. "You can still see the drill holes under his bangs. There's a tiny chip under his eye . . . sharp lips . . . *yeow*."

Her friend Anne-Marie muses, "They should make that pedestal revolve."

Carla, still working her way down *David*, dreams aloud. "Yeah, pop in a euro; get 360 slow-moving degrees of *David*. He is anatomically correct, anatomically really correct. Not as moving as the *Pièta*, but really real."

"He feels confident facing Goliath," I say.

Anne-Marie lowers her camera and says, "Well, he's standing there naked, so he must be pretty confident."

Turning to Carla, she observes, "The ears are ugly. The pubic hair's not quite right. And his right hand is huge. They always say to check out the fingers if you wonder about the other appendages. So what's the deal?"

"The guidebook says that's supposed to be the hand of God," Carla explains. "You can't measure the rest of *David* by 'the hand of God.'"

Settling back into a more worshipful frame of mind, Anne-Marie ponders aloud, "The Bible says he was like 12 or 14."

"This is no 14-year-old," says Carla, still lost in her opera glasses.

I ask, "What's *David* telling us?"

"He says God made people great," says Anne-Marie.

I say, "No, maybe it's *David* who's made in God's image, and *David* makes it clear that we—the rest of us—fall short."

Zipping her opera glasses into her day bag, Carla looks into the eyes of *David*. "No," she says. "I think we're each great. We're great. David's great. God's great. And Michelangelo's giving us a sneak preview of heaven . . . "

The guards begin to usher people out. I whisper, "I like that." Then, needing a few extra minutes to do my annual slow stroll around *David*, I say *"ciao"* and drift away from the nurses. I need more time to commune with this timeless symbol of a city that 500 years ago led Europe into a new age, a symbol that still challenges us to reach for all that we can be—to declare, "Yes, we can."

"Yes, we can," say the eyes of Renaissance Man.

Tuscany: "Here Begins Prosciutto"

I CHECKED INTO the farmhouse inn on the Gori family estate. This is Tuscany in the rough: a working farm, not a resort . . . no TV, no swimming pool, lots of real culture. My host, Signora Gori, is both old-money elegant and farmhouse tough. After I settle in, she takes me on a welcome stroll.

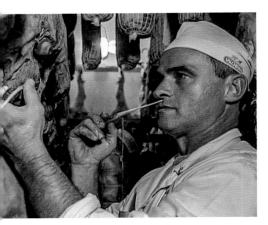

The meat is monitored.

Our first stop is a sty dominated by a giant pig. "We call him *Pastanetto*—the little pastry," Signora Gori says. While the scene through my camera's viewfinder is pristine and tranquil, the soundtrack is not. After a horrendous chorus of squeals, she says, "That is our little Beirut."

Hiking to the rustic slaughterhouse, we enter a room dominated by a stainless-steel table piled with red sides of pork. "Here begins prosciutto," Signora Gori says. Burly men in aprons squeeze the blood out of hunks of meat the size of dance partners. Then they cake the ham hocks in salt to begin the curing process, which takes months. While the salt helps cure the meat, a coating of pepper seals it.

In another room are towering racks of aging ham hocks. A man in a white coat tests each ham by sticking it with a bone needle and giving it a sniff. It smells heavenly.

Back outside, Signora Gori takes me into the next barn, where

The meat is served.

fluffy white lambs jump to attention, kicking up a sweet-smelling golden dust from beds of hay. Backlit by stray sunbeams, it's a dreamy, almost biblical scene. Picking up a baby lamb and giving it an Eskimo kiss, she explains, "We use unpasteurized milk in making the pecorino cheese. This is allowed, but with strict health safeguards. I must really know my sheep."

"I must really know my sheep."

This close-to-the-land-and-animals food production is part of Italy's Slow Food movement. Believing there's more to life than increasing profits and speeding up production people like the Gori family have committed to making and serving food in the time-honored way. It may be more labor-intensive and more expensive, but it's tastier. Because Italian foodies are happy to pay higher prices for higher quality, it's also good business.

Tuscany is trendy. Enticed by books like *Under the Tuscan Sun,* a persistent parade of visitors are hell-bent on sampling the Tuscan good life—and its prosciutto. The nearby town of Greve is happy to oblige. It's a facade of Tuscan clichés, with enough parking and toilets to handle all the tour buses, as well as a vast prosciutto emporium, with boastful newspaper clippings on its door and samples kept under glass. My stroll on the Gori farm reminds me how, especially here, it's critical to venture off the tourist track.

Walking down another lane, we observe the family's team of vintners. Signora Gori's brother empties a bucketful of purple grapes from a dump truck into a grinder, which munches through the bunches, spitting stems one way and juice with mangled grapes the other. Following pipes of this juice into a cellar, Signor Gori explains that winemaking is labor-intensive, "but right now, the grapes are doing most of the work."

As the new grapes ferment, we taste the finished product. A key word from my Tuscan travels is *corposo*—full-bodied. Lifting the elegant glass

Savoring dinner and camaraderie at the Gori family farm

to my lips, I sip the wine while enjoying the pride in the eyes of those who made it. Satisfied, I say, *"Corposo."*

"Si, bello," they reply.

That night at dinner, we're joined by the rest of the Gori family. The two sons dress and act like princes home on break from some Italian Oxford. We sit down to a classic Tuscan table, focused on simplicity, a sense of harmony, and the natural passage of time necessary for a good meal . . . each of us with a glass of good red wine. Dipping my bread in extra-virgin olive oil and savoring each slice of prosciutto, it's clear: Great wine goes best with simple food. I nod to my hosts, appreciating that I'm experiencing the true art of Tuscan cuisine.

Full and content, we sip port and enjoy a game of backgammon on a board that has provided after-dinner fun for 200 years in this very room. Surrounded by musty portraits that put faces on this family's long lineage, alongside a few guns used in Italy's 19th-century fight for independence, I realize this evening—so special for me—is just another night on the farm for the Gori family.

Corposo. That's how I like my wine . . . and my Tuscan travels.

Siena: Italy's Medieval Soul

STRETCHED ACROSS a Tuscan hill, Siena offers perhaps Italy's best medieval experience. Courtyards sport flower-decked wells, churches modestly share their art, and alleys dead-end into red-tiled rooftop panoramas. This is a city made for strolling. With its stony skyline and rustic brick lanes tumbling every which way, the town is an architectural time warp, where pedestrians rule and the present feels like the past.

Today, the self-assured Sienese remember their centuries-old accomplishments with pride. In the 1300s, Siena was one of Europe's largest cities and a major military force, in a class with Florence, Venice, and Genoa. But weakened by a disastrous plague and conquered by its Florentine rivals, Siena became a backwater—and it's been one ever since. Siena's loss became the traveler's gain as its political and economic irrelevance preserved its Gothic identity.

This is most notable in Il Campo, where I begin my stroll. At the center of town, this great shell-shaped piazza, featuring a sloped red-brick floor fanning out from the City Hall tower, is designed for people,

Siena's main square and gathering place, Il Campo

offering the perfect invitation to loiter. Il Campo immerses you in a world where troubadours stroke guitars, lovers stroke one another's hair, and bellies become pillows. It gets my vote for the finest piazza in all of Europe.

Most Italian cities have a church on their main square, but Il Campo gathers Siena's citizenry around its City Hall with its skyscraping municipal tower. Catching my breath after climbing to the dizzy top of the 100-yard-tall bell tower, I survey the view and think of the statement this campanile made. In Siena, kings and popes took a back seat to the people, as it was all about secular government, civic society, and humanism.

The public is welcome inside the City Hall where, for seven centuries, instructive frescoes have reminded all of the effects of good and bad government. One fresco shows a utopian republic, blissfully at peace; the other fresco depicts a city in ruins, overrun by greed and tyranny.

But the Church still has its place. If Il Campo is the heart of Siena, the Duomo is its soul—and my next destination. A few blocks off the main square, sitting atop Siena's highest point and visible for miles around, this white- and dark-green-striped cathedral is as ornate as Gothic gets. Inside and out, it's lavished with statues and mosaics. The stony heads of nearly 2,000 years of popes—that's over 170 so far—ring the interior, peering down from high above on all those who enter.

Great art, including statues carved by Michelangelo and Bernini, fills the church interior. Nicola Pisano carved the exquisite marble pulpit in 1268. It's crowded with delicate Gothic storytelling. I get up close to study the scenes from the life of Christ and the Last Judgment.

Trying to escape the crowds in the cathedral and on the main square, I venture away from the city center. I get lost on purpose in Siena's intriguing back streets, studded with iron rings for tethering horses and lined with colorful flags. Those flags represent the city's *contrade* (neighborhoods), whose fierce loyalties are on vivid display twice each summer during the Palio, a wild bareback horse race that turns Il Campo into a thrilling and people-packed racetrack.

Wandering further into the far reaches of the city, I'm tempted by Sienese specialties in the shops along the way: gourmet pasta, vintage Chianti, boar prosciutto, and the city's favorite treat: *panforte*.

Panforte is Siena's claim to caloric fame. This rich, chewy concoction of nuts, honey, and candied fruits impresses even fruitcake haters. Local bakeries claim their recipe dates back to the 13th century. Some even force employees to sign nondisclosure agreements to ensure they won't reveal the special spice blend that flavors their version of this beloved—and very dense—cake.

A key to enjoying Siena is to imagine it in its 14th-century heyday while taking advantage of today's modern scene. After chewing on a chunk of that *panforte,* I decide to linger here into the evening, after the tour groups have boarded their buses and left town.

I duck into a bar for *aperitivo* (happy hour), which includes a free buffet—a light dinner for the cost of a cocktail. Now I'm primed and ready to join the *passeggiata*—an evening stroll. I time my arrival back at Il Campo to savor that beautiful twilight moment when the sky is a rich blue dome, no brighter than the proud Siena towers that seem to hold it high.

Il Campo at twilight

Siena's Palio: 90 Seconds of Sheer Medieval Madness

"**F**OR THE SIENESE life story: You're born . . . there's the Palio . . . and then you die."

That's how my friend Roberto explains the importance of the world-famous horse race, the Palio di Siena, which takes place twice every summer on July 2 and August 16. The city's residents hurl themselves into the traditional revelry of the event with abandon. This year, I'm watching the race in person for the first time ever.

Siena is divided into 17 neighborhoods, or *contrade,* of which 10 are selected by a drawing to vie for the coveted Palio banner—and all-important bragging rights. Each competing *contrada*'s horse is chosen randomly by lottery. The neighborhood then adopts it, showering it with love, washing and grooming it, and keeping it in a five-star stable. The *contrade*—each with its own parish church, fountain, and square—are staunch rivals. Each *contrada* is represented by a mascot (porcupine, unicorn, she-wolf, and so on) and a distinctive flag. Its colors are worn and flown all year long, but omnipresent as the race nears.

While the race itself lasts just 90 seconds, it's preceded by days of festivities. As the big day approaches, processions break out across the city, including one in which the famed and treasured Palio banner—featuring the Virgin Mary, to whom the race is dedicated—is held high as it's paraded to the cathedral. Locals belt out passionate good-luck choruses. With the waving flags and pounding drums, it all harkens back to medieval times, when these rituals boosted morale before battle.

The day before the race, I joined a crowd in the main square, Il Campo, to see the jockeys—mostly hired hands from out of town—get to know their horses in a practice run called the "charge of the *carabinieri.*" At midnight, the streets were filled with eating, drinking, singing, and camaraderie, as neighborhoods gathered to pump themselves up.

On race day, bets are placed on which *contrada* will win . . . and lose. Despite the shady behind-the-scenes dealing, the horses are taken into their *contrada*'s church to be blessed. "Go and return victorious," says the priest. It's considered a sign of luck if a horse leaves droppings in the church.

Meanwhile, Il Campo has been converted into a racetrack. Clay is brought in and packed down to create the surface while mattresses pad the walls of surrounding buildings. The most treacherous spots are the sharp corners, where many a rider has bitten the dust.

The horses line up.

The entire city of Siena packs into Il Campo. Bleacher and balcony seats are expensive, but it's free to join the masses in the square. The well-connected get to watch from the comfort of an apartment window. Roberto's friend, Franco, shares his apartment overlooking the racecourse . . . and we enjoy the best seats in town. From this vantage point, we watch as the square fills, with pageantry unfolding, flags waving, and excitement building.

Pageantry and people at Siena's Palio

Finally, it's time. A cart pulled by oxen carries the Palio banner into the arena. The crowd goes wild. As the starting places are announced, 10 snorting horses and their nervous riders line up to await the start. Silence takes over. And then . . .

They're off! Once the rope drops, there's one basic rule: There are no rules. The jockeys ride bareback while spectators go berserk. Life stops for these frantic three laps. Up in the apartment, Roberto and Franco hold their breath . . .

And then, it's over. The winner: Lupa, the she-wolf district! We zip out into the street to join the ecstatic mobs coursing toward the cathedral. The happy "Lupa-Lupa-Lupa!" horde thunders through town, weeping with joy. At the cathedral, the crowd packs in, and the winning *contrada* receives the beloved banner. They are champions . . . until the next race.

Seeing euphoria overcome members of the winning *contrada*—it's Lupa's first win in 27 years—reminds me that it's impossible for a tourist to really understand what this ritual race means to the people of Siena.

Carrying their coveted Palio banner high and hoisting their jockey to their shoulders, the Lupa contingent tumbles out of the cathedral and back into the streets, where the celebration continues into the wee hours—500 years of proud tradition, still going strong.

The blessed Palio banner will be awarded to the winner.

Civita di Bagnoregio: Italy's Dead Town

O F ALL the Italian hill towns, Civita di Bagnoregio was my favorite. But then it died.

During 30 years of visits, I watched it wither. Its young people left, lured away by the dazzle of the city. Its elderly grew frail and moved into apartments in nearby Bagnoregio. Today, Civita (dubbed *La città che muore*) is being bought up by rich, big-city Italians for their country escapes. And, just like I had a lemonade stand when I was little, their kids sell bruschetta to a steady stream of gawking tourists.

As I enjoy the picture-perfect panorama of Civita from across the canyon, I get nostalgic recalling this precious chip of Italy when it was a traffic-free community with a grow-it-in-the-valley economy.

Civita teeters atop a pinnacle in a vast canyon ruled by wind and erosion. The saddle that once connected Civita to its bigger and busier sister town, Bagnoregio, eroded away, replaced by only a narrow bridge. On my early visits, a man with a donkey ferried the town's goods up and down this umbilical cord connecting Civita with the rest of Italy. His son inherited the responsibility, doing the same thing, using a Vespa rather than a donkey.

Entering the town through a cut in the rock made by Etruscans 2,500 years ago and heading under a 12th-century Romanesque arch, I feel

Civita, perched on a pinnacle

Civita's main (and only) square, with the church

like I'm walking into history on the smooth, hubcap-sized cobblestones under my feet. This was once the main Etruscan road leading to the Tiber Valley and Rome, just 60 miles to the south, which feel a world away. Those searching for arcade tourism won't find it here: There are no lists of attractions, orientation tours, or museum hours.

The charms of Civita are subtle. It's just a lovingly crafted stone shell, a corpse of a town. Yet it's also an artist's dream. Each lane and footpath holds a surprise. The warm stone walls glow, and each stairway is dessert to a sketchpad or camera.

The basic grid street plan of the ancient town survives—but its centerpiece, a holy place of worship, rotated with the cultures: first an Etruscan temple, then a Roman temple, and today a church. The round tops of ancient pillars that stand like bar stools in the square once decorated the pre-Christian temple.

I step into the humble church, the heartbeat and pride of the village for centuries. This was where festivals and processions started. Sitting for a cool, quiet moment in a pew, I see faded paintings by students of famous artists, relics of the hometown-boy Saint Bonaventure, and a dried floral decoration spread across the floor.

Where the grapes were pressed, the visitors now drink.

Just around the corner from the church, on the main street, is Bruschette con Prodotti Locali, Rossana and Antonio's cool and friendly wine cellar. I pull up a stump and let them serve me panini, bruschetta, fresh white wine, and a cake called *ciambella*. After eating, I ask to see the cellar with its traditional winemaking gear and provisions for rolling huge kegs up the stairs. Grabbing the stick, I tap on the kegs . . . *thimp, thimp, thomp* . . . to measure their fullness.

The ground below Civita is honeycombed with ancient cellars like this one (for keeping wine at the same temperature all year) and cisterns (for collecting rainwater, since there was no well in town). Many of these date from Etruscan times.

Behind the church, at Antico Frantoio Bruschetteria, an olive press—the latest in a 2,000-year line of olive presses—fills an ancient Etruscan cave. Brothers Sandro and Felice sell bruschetta to visitors. Bread is toasted on an open fire, drizzled with the finest oil, rubbed with garlic, and topped with chopped tomatoes. These edible souvenirs stay on my breath for hours and in my memory forever.

As I walk back to my car to re-enter the modern world, I stop under a lamp on the donkey path and just listen. I listen to the canyon . . . distant voices . . . animals on humble farms . . . *fortissimo* crickets . . . the same sounds villagers heard here when their town was still alive.

Communicating in Italy

I AM TERRIBLE AT foreign languages. Despite traveling around Europe four months a year since I was a kid, I can barely put a sentence together anywhere east or south of England. But with some creative communication, I manage just well enough to write guidebooks, produce TV shows, and enjoy Europe on vacation. And nowhere do I have more fun communicating than in Italy.

Auntie Pasta says, *"Mangia!"*

Because Italians are so outgoing and their language is such fun, interactions are a pleasure. Italians have an endearing habit of speaking Italian to foreigners, even if they know they don't speak their language. If a local starts chattering at you in Italian, don't resist. Go with it. You may find you understand more than you'd expect. Italians want to connect and try harder than any other Europeans. Play along.

I find Italian beautiful, almost melodic. It's fun to listen to and even more fun to speak. It has a pleasing rhythm and flow, from *buon giorno* and *buona sera* ("good day" and "good evening"), *ciao* ("goodbye") and *per favore* ("please") to *bellissima* and *La Serenissima* (Venice's nicknames). Two of my favorite phrases—and sentiments—are *la dolce vita* ("the sweet life") and *il dolce far niente* ("the sweetness of doing nothing").

Watch it!

Italians are animated and dramatic, communicating as much with their bodies as with their mouths. You may think two people are arguing, when in reality, they're agreeing enthusiastically. When I'm in Italy, I make it a point to be just as melodramatic and exuberant. Don't just say, *"Mamma mia."* Say, *"MAMMA MIA!"* with arms open wide and hands up in the air. It feels liberating to be so uninhibited. Self-consciousness kills communication.

Hands are part of the conversation.

In Italy, hand gestures can say as much as words. For instance, the cheek screw (pressing a forefinger into the cheek and rotating it) is used to mean cute or delicious. A chin flick with the fingers means, "I'm not interested; you bore me." The hand purse (fingers and thumb bunched together and pointed upward) is a gesture for a question, such as, "What do you want?" or, "What are you doing?" It can also be used as an insult to say, "You fool."

The Italian version of the rude middle finger is to clench the right fist and jerk the forearm up, slapping the bicep with the left hand. This jumbo version of "flipping the bird" says, "I'm superior." If Italians get frustrated, they might say, *"Mi sono cadute le braccia!"* ("I throw my arms down!")—sometimes literally thrusting their arms toward the floor to say, "I give up!"

Italians appreciate sensuality, which can be heard in their language. Rather than differentiating among the five senses to describe what they're hearing, smelling, or tasting, Italians talk about sensing *(sentire):*

"Did you sense the ambience as you walked by?"

"Wow, sense this wine."

"Oh, sense these flowers."

Instead of asking, "Are you listening?" an Italian will ask, "Do you sense me?"

One of the best ways to observe Italians communicating—and to communicate with them—is to participate in the *passeggiata.* This ritual promenade takes place in the early evenings, when shoppers, families,

Join the *passeggiata*, Italy's ritual evening promenade.

and young flirts on the prowl all join the scene to stroll arm in arm, spreading their colorful feathers like peacocks. In a genteel small town, the *passeggiata* comes with sweet whispers of *"bella"* (pretty) and *"bello"* (handsome). In Rome, the *passeggiata* is a cruder, big-city version called the *struscio* (meaning "to rub"). Younger participants utter the words *"buona"* and *"buono"*—meaning, roughly, "tasty." As my Italian friends explained, "*Bella* is a woman you admire—without touching. *Buona* is something you want, something . . . consumable. *Bella* is too kind for this *struscio*."

To really immerse yourself in the culture, it's important to take risks in conversation. Italians appreciate your attempts. Miscommunication can happen on both sides, but it's part of the fun.

One night my waiter declared in English, "The cook is in the chicken." Later, when I ordered a tonic water, he asked me, "You want lice?"

On another trip I was eating at a restaurant in Assisi with a guide named Giuseppe and his wife, Anna. Anna greeted each plate with unbridled enthusiasm. Suddenly, Giuseppe looked at me and said in English, "My wife's a good fork."

Shocked, I thought I must have misheard him.

Giuseppe explained, "*Una buona forchetta* . . . a good fork. That's what we call someone who loves to eat."

The Italian Alps: Lounging in the Dolomites

L EANING BACK in my lounge chair, I enjoy the heat of the sun on my skin. A vibrant sea spreads out before me, but it's a sea of wild-flowers. I'm not at the beach, I'm on a farm, looking out on Europe's largest high alpine meadow, manicured by munching goats and cows. In the distance, stark snow-dusted peaks tower boldly against the blue sky. These are Italy's Alps, the Dolomites.

My soundtrack is the happy laughter of Italian children enjoying a petting zoo filled with alpine critters. A few yards away, their parents sip wine on the veranda of their chalet guesthouse—thoroughly enjoying that *dolce far niente* (sweetness of doing nothing) . . . like me.

The sky-high meadow called the Alpe di Siusi (or "Seiser Alm" in Ger-man) seems to float high above the city of Bolzano, separating two of the most famous Dolomite ski-resort valleys, Val di Fassa and Val Gardena. Measuring three miles by seven miles, and soaring 6,500 feet high, Alpe di Siusi is dotted with farm huts and happy hikers enjoying gentle trails. These mountains differ from the rest of the Alps because of their dominant rock type—limestone—which forms sheer vertical walls

The Dolomites, ideal for hiking . . . or thinking about hiking

of white, gray, and pale pink rising abruptly from green valleys and meadows.

At the head of the meadow, the Sasso Lungo mountains provide a storybook Dolomite backdrop. And opposite, the bold, spooky Mt. Schlern stands gazing into the haze of the Italian peninsula. Not surprisingly, the Schlern gave ancient peoples enough willies to spawn legends of supernatural forces. Fear of the Schlern witch, today's tourist-brochure mascot, was the cause of many a medieval townswoman's fiery death.

As a nature preserve, the alpine meadow cradled by the peaks is virtually car-free. A cable car whisks visitors up to the park from the valley below. Within the park, buses shuttle hikers to and from key points along the tiny road all the way to the foot of the picturesque Sasso peaks. Meadow walks are ideal for wildflower strolls, while chairlifts serve as springboards for more dramatic and demanding hikes. Mountain bikes are easy to rent, welcome on many lifts, and permitted on the meadow's country lanes.

The Alpe di Siusi is my favorite stop in the Dolomites because of its quintessential views, but also its easy accessibility and the variety of walks and hikes. There's also the charm of the neighboring village of Castelrotto (population: 2,000), which I use as my home base.

The village of Castelrotto makes a good home base.

Mount Schlern, home to a legendary witch

Castelrotto is also a fun dollop of Germanic culture in Italy: There's yogurt and yodeling for breakfast . . . wiener schnitzel and strudel for dinner. The region has long faced north, first as part of the Holy Roman Empire and then firmly in the Austrian Habsburg realm. After Austria lost World War I, its "Südtirol" (South Tirol) became Italy's "Alto Adige." Mussolini did what he could to Italianize the region, including giving each town an Italian name (like Castelrotto, also known as Kastelruth).

This hard-fought history has left this northeastern corner of Italy bicultural as well as bilingual. Signs and literature in the autonomous province are in both languages, but there's an emphasis on *der Deutsch.* It still feels Austrian, culturally as much as geographically. Germanic color survives in a blue-aproned, ruddy-faced, lederhosen-wearing way. Most locals still speak German first and many feel a closer bond with their Germanic ancestors than with their Italian countrymen. While most have a working knowledge of Italian, they watch German-language TV, read newspapers *auf Deutsch,* and live in Tirolean-looking villages. The government has wooed cranky German-speaking locals with economic breaks that make this one of Italy's richest areas.

I love coming home to Castelrotto after a hike in the meadow. It was built for farmers rather than skiers, so it has more character than any town around. Popping into the church, I enjoy the choir practicing. Then, stepping outside the church at 3 p.m., the bells peal as I witness the happy parade of parents bringing home their preschoolers. These idyllic moments may seem like cultural clichés, but they're authentic, not performances for tourists. It's moments like these that make it easy to enjoy this high-altitude Germanic eddy in the whirlpool of Italy.

Venice: Piero's Boat

DESCENDING the Rialto Bridge, I shuffle slowly, spinning my wheels in a human traffic jam congesting one of the biggest shopping streets in Venice. Finally breaking free, I turn down a dank and empty lane, reach the big black door of my hotel, and push a bronze lion's nose. This security buzzer brings Piero to the second-floor window. He welcomes me with a *"Ciao,* Reek!" and buzzes the door open. I climb the steps, eager to settle in.

Piero, who runs the Venetian hotel I call home, shaved his head five years ago. His girlfriend wanted him to look like Michael Jordan. With his operatic voice, he reminds me more of Yul Brynner. He often says, "My voice is guilty of my love for opera."

Proud of the improvements in his place since my last visit, Piero shows me around. While remodeling the hotel, he discovered 17th-century frescoes on the walls of several rooms. The place was a convent back then. An antique wooden prayer kneeler, found in the attic and unused for generations, decorates a corner of my room. The whitewash is partially peeled away, revealing peaceful aqua, ochre, and lavender floral patterns. In Venice, behind the old, the really old peeks through.

The breakfast room is decorated with traditional Venetian knick-knacks—green and red decorative glass, prints of canal scenes, and sequined masks reminiscent of Carnival indiscretions. The room is strewn with antiques. Everything is old. "It's kitsch," Piero admits, "but only the best kitsch." I sit down. As Piero brings me red orange juice—made from blood oranges—he reports on his work and the latest Venice news. While the sounds of Don Giovanni fill the air, guests prepare for their day.

Piero's cell phone rings and he apologizes with operatic eyes. "In Italy, this is success." He answers it and talks as if overwhelmed with work: *"Si, si, si, va bene* ("that's fine"), *va bene, va bene . . . certo* ("exactly"), *certo . . . bello, bello, bello* ("beautiful," in descending pitch) *. . . OK, ciao, ciao, ciao."* He hangs up and explains, "That was the night manager. Always problems. I call him my nightmare manager."

Venice's Grand Canal

In my early travels, hotel night managers were a sorry lot. Generally speaking only the local language, they worked at night when the most complicated guest problems hit. When a tourist in a bind came to them, communication was impossible, so things just got worse. On a good night, they'd spend their time carefully ripping the paper napkins neatly in two so they'd go twice as far at the breakfast table.

Opera continues to fill the air as Piero dashes to help some French guests heading out for the day. He pours coffee for both of us, then sits back down and says, "In hotels all the people are different. The French don't use the shower. Young Americans are most messy but use the shower very much. I don't understand this. Americans ask, 'What is this bidet for?' I cannot tell them. It is for washing more than the feet. In it we wash the parts . . . that rub together when you walk. The Japanese think the bidet is very funny."

"The tourists have taken over your city," I say sadly.

Walking me to the window and tossing open the decrepit blind, Piero answers, "But Venice survives."

As my gaze moves from the red-tiled roofs to the marketplace commotion filling the street below, I see his point. Tourists cannot take over Venice.

"Venice is a little city," he says. "Only a village, really. About 55,000 people live on this island. Not Italian—we are just one century Italian. I am Venetian in my blood. I cannot work in another town. Venice is boring for young people—no disco, no nightlife. It is only beautiful. Venetian people are travelers. Remember Marco Polo? He was Venetian. But when we come home we know this place is the most beautiful. Venice. It is a philosophy to live here . . . the philosophy of beauty.

Cruising with Piero

"The life here is with no cars . . . only boats. To live properly in Venice, you must have a boat. With a boat you live in Venice in another dimension—with no tourists. You cruise under bridges and see the tourists walking in their dimension but you are in the Venice of no tourists. The boat is my alternative Venice."

"To live properly in Venice, you must have a boat."

Venice's *Cicchetti* Crawl

V ENICE ENTERTAINS millions of visitors each year. On a recent trip, a Venetian friend told me that these days almost every restaurant caters to the tourists. Then, with a sly smile, he added, "But there are still the *cicchetti* bars."

Cicchetti (pronounced chi-KET-tee) are the local appetizers that line the counters of little pubs all over Venice at the end of each workday. My favorite meal is what I call "The Stand-Up Progressive Venetian Pub-Crawl Dinner." In a town with canals and no cars, pub-crawling is easy and safe—perhaps

Sampling *cicchetti* on a pub crawl

safer if you know how to swim. Tonight I'll visit a series of these characteristic hole-in-the-wall pubs, eating ugly-looking morsels on toothpicks, and washing it all down with little glasses of wine. I look forward to the local characters I'll meet along the way. *Cicchetti* bars have a social standup zone with a cozy gaggle of tables. In some of the more popular places, the crowds spill happily into the street.

Venetians call this pub crawl the *giro d'ombra*. *Giro* means "stroll," and *ombra*—slang for a glass of wine—means "shade." It dates back to the old days, when a portable wine bar scooted with the shadow of the Campanile bell tower across St. Mark's Square. That wine bar is long gone, but the *cicchetti* bars remain, tucked away in the perpetual shade of the back streets.

While Venice is, it seems, sinking in tourist crowds, I'd bet 90 percent of those tourists gather along the glitzy shopping streets between the Rialto Bridge and St. Mark's Square. To find a characteristic *cicchetti* bar, you have to wander. I don't worry about getting lost—in fact, I get

Drinks are affordable.

as lost as I can. I remind myself, "I'm on an island and I can't get off." Even though there generally aren't street names, when I want to find my way, I simply look for small signs on the corners directing me to the nearest landmark (e.g., "per Rialto").

The *cicchetti* selection is best early, so I start my evening at 6 p.m. It's in the far reaches of Venice that I bump into the thriving little *bacari* (as the local pubs are called). I ask for *"un piatto classico di cicchetti misti da otto euro"* and get a classic plate of assorted appetizers for €8. I sample deep-fried mozzarella cheese, gorgonzola, calamari, and artichoke hearts. *Crostini* (small pieces of toasted bread with a topping) are also a favorite, as are marinated seafood, olives, and prosciutto with melon. Meat and fish *(pesce)* munchies can be expensive, but veggies *(verdure)* are cheap. Bread sticks *(grissini)* are free for the asking.

Part of the attraction is the funky decor. There are photos of neighborhood friends here for a family party; St. Mark's Square the morning

At *cicchetti* bars, you can assemble a meal.

after a wild Pink Floyd concert; Carnevale masks evoking a more mysterious past; and of old-time Venice, proving that people may change but the buildings remain essentially the same.

Venetians kick off the experience with an *aperitivo*, a before-dinner drink. Know your options. A blackboard usually lists several fine wines that are uncorked and available by the glass. Most nights, I get a small glass of house red or white wine *(ombra rosso* or *ombra bianco).* Tonight, I'm in the mood for an Aperol spritz—it makes me feel more local.

A man asks me, *"Le dispiace se mi siedo qui?"* (Do you mind if I sit here?) before sitting down next to me. It occurs to me that's a handy, polite phrase for making new friends. He orders a drink and food. When his plate of fish arrives, he picks up one of the tiny fish, delicately tied in a loop. Holding it by the toothpick that harpoons it, he looks at it lovingly, says, *"Sei il mio piu bel ricordo"* ("You are my most beautiful souvenir"), and pops it happily into his mouth. Pushing over his plate, he offers one of the fish to me.

Connecting with people makes a pub crawl more fun: You can meet an Italian, learn some Italian, eat better . . . and collect your own beautiful souvenirs.

Salute! Cheers!

Italian Boys: Macho or *Mammone*?

AT SUNSET I meet my Venetian hotelier friend, Piero, and we head for his friend's restaurant.

"Such a long line just to enter St. Mark's Basilica today," I tell him, "Even the back alleys were clogged with people. It's a zoo."

Piero leans toward me. "Yes! Zoo, zoo, zoo! Is a problem. In Venice the people come every day like a wave. There is no high season, no low season. Every morning we are invaded. But at six o'clock, the tourists go away."

As if in command of the city, Piero waves a hand across the empty market square, grandly saying, "And now Venice lives. Really, Venice is a fine place in the night. Sleep in Venice and you see the quiet Venice. When you see a *menu turistico*, go away. When you see old men speaking Italian in a restaurant . . . this is a good place. I take you now to Bepi's."

Greeting old friends as we walk, Piero explains how in Venice, if you open a restaurant you must decide if you want to attract tourists or Venetians. "To make a tourist restaurant is no problem," he says. "You see the people only one time. Even talking to them is not necessary. One-time visitors, it means bad food."

We arrive at Trattoria da Bepi and Piero kisses the cheeks of the waiter before he continues. "For me, a good restaurant is like home. Mama is cooking."

Sitting down at an outdoor table, Piero points out Bepi. He stands as if carved into his *cicchetti* bar, surrounded by toothpick munchies on trays and well-fed neighbors.

"We are maniacs about fish in the North Adriatic," Piero says, before introducing me to Bepi's son, Loris. "Loris is a nightmare in the fish market.

Macho or *mammone*?

He knows what is no good . . . what is okay . . . always finds the best. His mama is a Venetian mama, Delfina. I ask her to tell me how she cooks the fish. She puts her hand on her heart and says, 'There is no recipe. It is from here.'"

Loris and Piero work up a dinner plan on a scratch pad as if putting together the guest list for a very special evening. They discuss each plate like it's an old friend.

Soon plates start to arrive. Piero goes immediately for the polenta with cod saying, "In the south they call the people of Venice 'polenta eaters.'"

Piero splashes a hunk of bread into the broth under a pile of empty mussel shells and says, "You can feel the sea here."

The conversation stops as a girl in a short wispy skirt prances by on the arm of a local Romeo. Piero says, "Is incredeeble. Look at this one! This is Venice. I am sorry. I am Italian. I watch the girls."

As another lovely Italian woman struts by, Piero observes, "Giorgione, he is a good artist—yes—but this . . . this is better. Oh, *Dio*. I have a beautiful girlfriend. She is a model. But I cannot be married. It is impossee—"

I interrupt Piero by pretending to notice a woman over his shoulder. He stops mid-sentence to see what distracts me. It's nothing—but I make my point: The default switch in his mind is set on girl-watching.

Loris brings a plate of six crawfish with tails peeled and ready to bite. As I peer skeptically at the strange-looking creatures, Piero says, "More aliens."

As I pick one up and bite off the tail, I notice how cold and limp it feels. I ask, "Is this raw?"

"Yes . . . Italian sushi."

A bit later, Loris returns. "Now we have the pasta with crab sauce." He serves Piero and puts the big bowl in front of me.

"Ahhh," Piero says, "For the peasant family, this was the biggest honor . . . to get the original bowl."

Later, watching the heads of five Italian boys turn in unison as another girl walks by, I ask, "Do the Italian girls watch the boys?"

"No, the boys watch the girls. Teenage Venetian boys go to San Marco to make an experience with American girls. Their first words in English are, 'My name ees _____ . You are pretty girl. Where you sleep tonight?'"

Nibbling on an artichoke heart, I say, "For many American girls, Italian boys are nice."

Piero's feet do a little tap dance. Like a giddy teenager, with bouncing eyebrows sending happy wrinkles to the top of his bald head, he adds, "Yes, and for Italian boys, American girls are very nice. It is international public relations. I am sorry," admits 42-year-old Piero, "I am too old now."

"It is very dangerous because if Venetian girls see the boys on San Marco, they are jealous. The girls, they don't look for boys. They are . . . " and he does a couple of quick stuffy sniffs while scratching the underside of his nose with a proud knuckle. "And Venetian girls are not open. They are like a clam. This is typical in the Italian south. Venice is like the south in this way. We say Venice is like the Naples of the north. We sing, we talk with our hands, and our women . . . they are like clams."

I'm concerned that I'm not getting the female side of this story.

Antonella, the daughter of Alessandro the barber, waves to Piero as her dog drags her down the lane. We're just finishing up our meal, but I invite her over. Pouring her a glass of Bepi's famous licorice liqueur, I say, "Please, Antonella, help me. We are talking about Italian living, but Piero is giving me only the macho side."

"What is macho? There are no macho men in Venice," she says, stepping over her dog's leash and grabbing a seat. Antonella is no longer the temptress I knew when she was in her twenties. Now she's a businesswoman used to dealing with Italian men. She's small and tough, more savvy than sweet, with a thick head of long black hair. When she talks, her direct eyes and busy hands give an intensity to her words. "They are mama's boys. We call this *mammone.*"

Piero, as if he's heard the complaint a thousand times, cries, "Ahhh, *mammone.*" Pulling an imaginary umbilical cord from his belly and petting it rather than cutting it, he says, "It is true. I cannot cut the *cordone ombelicale.* I love my mama. And she loves me even more."

Antonella sips her liqueur. "The Italian boys, 95 percent stay at home until they find a wife to be their new mother," she says. "At 30, 35

Venetian gondolier

years old they are still with their mothers. Even if they move out, they come home for the cooking and laundry. This is not macho . . . this is ridiculous.

"And . . . " she continues, lighting a cigarette, "they want a wife exactly like their mother. If they find a woman like me, independent, with some money, perhaps beautiful, this is a problem."

Piero nods like a scolded puppy. "Yes, this is true."

Antonella says, "If I make my hair special and wear strong makeup, they will take me to dinner and take me to bed. But they will not look at me to make a family. They want to be sure their wife won't leave them. A woman like me . . . it is too risky."

We pay and promise Loris we'll be back soon. Antonella unties her dog and, together, the three of us walk through the quiet and romantic alleys of Venice.

I tell Antonella, "I could not finish a sentence with Piero. Always looking at the girls."

Piero raises his eyebrows and his hands as if to mount a defense and just sighs.

Antonella says, "I was in England for two years. No boys looked at me. When I came home, in five minutes I was being stared at. I like this. It feels good to be home."

"But why are the Italian boys always thinking about the girls?"

Antonella says, "In Venice, I think part of the reason is because the American tourist girls come here looking for the boys. They like the Italian boys very much."

Walking over a marble veneered bridge, we pass a gondolier. He's dashing in his straight-brimmed, red-sashed straw hat, obviously well-built under his striped shirt and black pants.

"The gondoliers, they get the girls."

As the gondolier hollers a hopeful hello to a cute passing tourist, Piero says, "He hopes to be so-sess-full."

"Successful," Antonella says.

He tries again, looking at her. "This word, it is difficult, so . . . "

Antonella interrupts, "No, suc . . . "

"Suc-*sex*-ful," says Piero. As we turn the corner, Piero giggles. "The gondoliers, they get the girls."

Bouncing happily, waving his hands melodramatically, he plays the gondolier on the prowl, singing, "The moon. Me and you and the lagoon. Oh my, I feel romantic today. I don't know why. My heart is going *boing boing*. May I offer you a small special ride for free later on? Here, grab my oar." Grabbing Antonella from behind around the waist as if she's about to fall from a gondola, he says, "Be careful, you can fall."

Pushing Piero away, Antonella says, "Gondoliers are the worst. Here, if a woman marries a gondolier and expects him to be true, we say she has hams over her eyes."

Piero, with suddenly sad eyes, says, "This is true."

Antonella adds, "But I think any Italian woman who trusts her husband has hams over her eyes. The newspaper said 97 percent of Italian men cheat. I believe this. It is easy for them because for them, sex is for the body and not for the mind. When a woman falls in love with someone else, she can leave her husband in five minutes. A man can have many affairs and never think about leaving his family. For him, sex is only the body."

We walk to moonlit St. Mark's Square, where the orchestra plays as if refusing to go home. The vast, nearly empty square has been claimed by two seniors, waltzing like they did 50 years ago. They twirl gracefully round and round. The woman smiles with her eyes closed. In Venice, love is a threesome: you, your partner, and the city.

Stendhal Syndrome

CASANOVA'S DEFENSE could have been simply, "It was Venice." One night, I was with a tour group of older American women gazing at the Bridge of Sighs. We were talking about Casanova, the famous Italian author and lover who was sentenced for spying in the Doge's Palace. He crossed that saddest of bridges, casting one last look at Venice, before descending into the prison.

My tour group and I were absorbed in Venice. Suddenly, as if stepping out of an old movie, a debonair Italian man walked up, embraced a woman from my group, and gave her a deep and passionate kiss. Her glasses nearly tumbled into the canal. Five other women lined up and took their turn.

The man walked back into his movie. We all stood there in stunned silence—surprised at the man, but just as surprised at the women. Then Dave, my assistant guide, took off his shoes, stripped to his boxers, and dove into the canal. Venice is a seductress. She tempts people to do things they don't normally do.

Romantic Venice with the Rialto Bridge

For some, the beauty of Venice can be too much. The 19th-century French novelist and art critic Stendhal became physically ill in Italy, overcome by trying to absorb it all. He gave his name to a syndrome all travelers risk.

Arlene had a classic case of Stendhal Syndrome. Many years ago, she was on one of our tours a day ahead of the tour I was leading. Throughout the trip from Amsterdam to the Rhine to the castles of Bavaria, she left me notes and messages describing her enjoyment, which approached ecstasy. In the Tirol, she left me a postcard—which I still keep on my office wall—of hang gliders soaring through the Alps past King Ludwig's fairy-tale castle of Neuschwanstein. She circled a distant glider and marked it, "This is me!"

Arlene's tour arrived in Venice, followed by my group the next day. As usual, we got off the vaporetto at the Rialto Bridge stop and I marched quickly ahead of the group to the hotel to arrange room assignments so the road-weary gang could go immediately to their rooms and relax. As I approached the hotel, a chill filled the alley. The boys at the corner gelato stand looked at me in horror, as if I were about to be gunned down.

Then, from the dark end of the alley, I saw her. Sprinting at me was an American, hair flying like a Botticelli maiden, barefoot, shirt half off, greeting me as if she was a drunk bride waiting for her groom. It was Arlene.

I climbed with her up the long stairway to the hotel lobby, humoring her as she babbled about how she loved Venice and she loved me and life was so wonderful. My friend Sergio, who ran the hotel, said simply, "Okay, Rick, now she is yours."

Arlene had flipped out the day before. Her tour guide opted to leave her in Venice and let me handle the problem. Sergio had watched her all day long. Taking me to her room, an exhausted Sergio explained, "She threw her passport and room key from the breakfast room into the Grand Canal. Look at this room." She had been given the small room normally reserved for bus drivers. Strewn with dainties and cute knickknacks, it looked like a wind chime sounds.

Sergio said if she continued to run half-naked through the streets,

Venice is awash with beauty.

she'd be arrested. A doctor on the tour sedated her the best he could. My assistant guide, role-playing the happy groom, took Arlene by ambulance boat to the hospital while I carried on with the tour. A sensitive and creative person, Arlene had thrown away her regulatory drugs and overdosed on Venice.

Later, while waiting for her husband to call from the States, I packed up her things. Underwear was draped from old-time Venice prints on the wall. Tiny touristy souvenirs—a doll in a dirndl, a miniature glass bear with a red nose, a cow creamer, three shiny Mozart chocolate balls—were lined up on the windowsill.

Arlene's husband flew over and checked her out of the hospital. With the help of her medication, she recovered and went on to continue her love affair with Italy.

When I returned to my office after the tour, Arlene had flowers waiting for me with a thank you and an apology.

I understood. It was Venice.

Padua: Students, Saints, and *Scarpette*

NICKNAMED "the Brain of Veneto," Padua is home to the prestigious university (founded in 1222) that hosted Galileo, Copernicus, Dante, and Petrarch. Pilgrims know this city for the Basilica of St. Anthony, where the faithful assemble to touch his tomb and marvel at his holy relics. It's a great place to experience Italy: to make some new friends, get chummy with the winds of its past, and connect with the delights of its now.

I start my visit with a ramble around the old town center. It's a colonnaded, time-travel experience through some of Italy's most inviting squares, perfect for lingering over an *aperitivo*. But it's not stodgy—this university town has 60,000 students and a youthful spirit. No wonder Galileo called his 18 years on the faculty in Padua the best of his life. I see young people—apparently without a lot of private space in their apartments—hanging out, kissing, and cuddling in public. Students are making themselves at home with their heritage, lounging literally under a medieval tomb that stands atop ornate columns.

Since the students can graduate whenever they defend their thesis, little graduation parties erupt on the streets throughout the year. Graduates are given a green laurel wreath. Then formal group photos are taken. It's a sweet, multigenerational scene with familial love and pride busting out all over.

Then, once grandma goes home, the craziness takes over. Sober, scholarly clothing is replaced by raunchy wear as gangs of friends gather around the new grad in front of the university, and the roast begins. A giant butcher-paper poster with a caricature of the student—generally obscene—and a litany of "This Is Your Life" photos is presented to the new graduate. The happy grad reads

A grad celebrates.

the funny text out loud while various embarrassing pranks are pulled. The poster is then taped to the university wall for 24 hours for all to see.

Friends roast a graduate.

During the roast, the friends sing a catchy but crude local university anthem, reminding their newly esteemed friend to keep his or her feet on the ground. Once I hear this song, I just can't stop singing it. The melody is infectious, starting like an Olympic Games fanfare and ending with *oom-pah-pahs* like a German cartoon. It becomes even more endearing when a student translates the lyrics for me: "You're a doc . . . tor, you're a doc . . . tor, but you're still just an asshole. You're a doc . . . tor, you're a doc . . . tor, but you're still just an asshole. *Oom-pah-pah, oom-oom-pah-pah.*"

Eventually I stop humming this profane ditty to seek out Padua's sacred sights: the Basilica of St. Anthony and the Scrovegni Chapel. Buried in the basilica is Friar Anthony of Padua, patron saint of travelers, amputees, donkeys, pregnant women, barren women, flight attendants, and pig farmers. Construction of this impressive Romanesque/Gothic church, with its Byzantine-style domes, started immediately after Anthony's death in 1231. As a mark of his universal appeal and importance in the medieval Church, he was sainted within a year of his death. And for nearly 800 years, his remains and this glorious church have attracted a steady stream of pilgrims.

Going with the flow of the pilgrim groups, I enter the church. Gazing through the incense haze, I see Donatello's glorious crucifix rising from the altar, a masterpiece appropriate for one of the most important pilgrimage sites in Christendom. Following the pilgrims into the Chapel of the Reliquaries, I stand before the basilica's most prized relic: Anthony's tongue. When the saint's remains were exhumed 32 years after his death, his body had decayed to dust, but his tongue was found miraculously unspoiled, still red in color. How appropriate for the great preacher who, so full of the Spirit, couldn't stop talking about God.

My next stop is across town at the glorious Scrovegni Chapel. It's

Giotto's glorious Scrovegni Chapel

wallpapered with Giotto's beautiful cycle of nearly 40 frescoes depicting the lives of Jesus and Mary. Painted by Giotto and his assistants from 1303 to 1305, it's considered to be the first piece of "modern" (as opposed to medieval) art. This work makes it clear: Europe was breaking out of the Middle Ages and heading into the Renaissance. Giotto placed real people in real scenes, expressing real human emotions. These frescoes were radical not only for their three-dimensional effects, lively colors, and light sources, but also for their humanism.

In the early evening, after the museums and churches have closed, Padua's squares become open-air student parties, dotted with drinks of rosy *spritzes* that glow with the light of the setting sun. I cap my day by joining the festivities. Reminding myself that I'm as interesting to these young Italians as they are to me, I befriend a table of college students and buy a round of drinks. Diving headlong into a vigorous political discussion, I partake in the Italian ritual of the bread and oil. I pour some fine olive oil on a dish, season it with salt and pepper, rip a long strip from our bread, dip it, and bite. A student, nodding with approval, explains that I am making the *scarpette:* "the little shoes."

Soaking up the oil along with the conversation, I'm still thinking about my day, witnessing the sacred and the profane here in Padua. I realize that travelers can become human *scarpette*—sopping up culture—wherever we venture.

Appreciating Milano

THEY SAY that for every church in Rome, there's a bank in Milan. Indeed, the economic success of postwar Italy can be attributed, at least in part, to this second city of bankers, publicists, and pasta power-lunchers. While overshadowed by Venice, Florence, and Rome in the minds of travelers, Milan still has plenty to offer anyone who visits.

The importance of Milan is nothing new. Ancient Romans called this place Mediolanum, or "the central place." By the fourth century AD, it was the capital of the western half of the Roman Empire. After struggling through the early Middle Ages, Milan rose to prominence under the powerful Visconti and Sforza families. By the time the Renaissance hit, Leonardo had moved here and the city was called "the New Athens."

Milan's cathedral, the city's centerpiece, is the third-largest church in Europe. It's massive: 480 feet long and 280 feet wide, forested with 52 sequoia-sized pillars and populated by 2,000 statues. The place can seat 10,000 worshippers. Climbing the tight spiral stairs designed for the laborers who built the church, I emerge onto the rooftop in a forest

Milan's main square and cathedral

Exploring the roof of Milan's cathedral

of stony spires. Crowds pack the rooftop for great views of the city, the square, and, on clear days, the Italian Alps. But it's the architectural details of the church that grab my attention. Marveling at countless ornaments carved more than five centuries ago in marble—each flower, each gargoyle, each saint's face different—I realize the public was never intended to see this art. An expensive labor of love, it was meant for God's eyes only.

The cathedral sits on Piazza del Duomo, Milan's main square. It's a classic European scene. Professionals scurry, fashionista kids loiter, and young thieves peruse.

The grand glass-domed arcade on the square marks the late-19th-century mall, Galleria Vittorio Emanuele. Built around 1870, during the heady days of Italian unification, it was the first building in town with electric lighting. Its art is joyful propaganda, celebrating the establishment of Italy as an independent country. Its stylish boutiques, restaurants, and cafés reflect Milan's status as Italy's fashion capital.

I make the scene under those glassy domes, slowly sipping a glass of the traditional Italian liqueur, Campari, first served in the late 1800s at a bar in this very gallery. Some of Europe's hottest people-watching turns my pricey drink into a good value. While enjoying the parade, I notice some fun-loving commotion around the bull in the floor's zodiac mosaic. For good luck, locals step on the testicles of Taurus. Two girls tell me that it's even better if you twirl.

Twirling for luck

It's evening, and I see people in formal wear twirling on that poor bull. They're on their way to the nearby home of what is quite possibly the world's most prestigious opera house: La Scala. Like other great opera houses in Europe, La Scala makes sure that impoverished music lovers can get standing-room tickets or nose-bleed seats that go on sale the day of the performance. And the La Scala Museum has an extensive collection of items that are practically objects of worship for opera devotees: original scores, busts, portraits, and death masks of great composers and musicians.

Shoppers in Milan's Galleria Vittorio Emanuele

Leonardo's faded but still masterful *Last Supper* enthralls visitors.

Imagine: Verdi's top hat, Rossini's eyeglasses, Toscanini's baton . . . even Fettucini's pesto.

The next morning is the highlight of my visit: Leonardo's ill-fated *The Last Supper,* painted right onto the refectory wall of the Church of Santa Maria delle Grazie. Leonardo was hired to decorate the monks' dining room and this was an appropriate scene. Suffering from Leonardo's experimental use of oil, the masterpiece began deteriorating within six years of its completion. The church was bombed in World War II, but—miraculously, it seems—the wall holding *The Last Supper* remained standing.

Today, to preserve it as much as possible, the humidity in the room is carefully regulated—only 30 people are allowed in every 15 minutes, and visitors must dehumidify in a waiting chamber before entering. I jockey with the other visitors, like horses at the starting gate. We all booked our timed entry weeks ago. Knowing that when the door opens we get exactly 15 minutes to enjoy the *Ultima Cena,* we're determined to maximize the experience. I've studied up, but waiting to enter I review my notes, like cramming for a test. I want to get the most out of every second in the presence of Leonardo's masterpiece.

The door opens and we enter. There it is . . . filling the far wall in a big, vacant, whitewashed room: faded pastels, not a crisp edge, much of it looking look like an old film negative.

To give my 15 minutes an extra punch, I decide to enter the room as if I was one of the monks for whom *The Last Supper* was painted some 500 years ago . . . I imagine eating here, in my robe and sandals, pleased that the wall in my dining room, which for so long has been under some type of construction, is finally done.

It's a big day—the unveiling. The painting is big and realistic. Jesus and the 12 apostles are sitting at a table just like the three big tables we monks share here in our dining room. It's as if we were just blessed with more brothers. The table in the painting is even set like ours—right down to the stiffly starched and ironed white tablecloth.

The scene now gracing our refectory is a fitting one. The Last Supper was the first Eucharist—a ritual we celebrate daily as monks. The disciples sit with Jesus in the center. Jesus seems to know he'll die—his face is sad, all-knowing, accepting. His feet are crossed one atop the other, as if ready for the nail.

While we eat in silence, I meditate on the painting. It shows the moment when the Lord says, "One of you will betray me." The apostles huddle in small groups, wondering, "Lord, is it I?" Some are concerned. Others are confused. Only Judas—that's him clutching his bag of silver—is not shocked.

Again and again, my eyes return to Christ. He's calm despite the turmoil he must feel over the ultimate sacrifice he must make.

But then, my modern-day sensibility intrudes. I can't help it. I want to tell the monk that Leonardo cleverly used lines of perspective that converge on Christ, reinforcing the idea that everything does indeed center on him. But I suspect the monk wouldn't care, since he already understands the artist's intent.

Suddenly, two doors burst open—abruptly ending my musings. My group and I are sternly ushered out one door and a new group of 30 enters the room through the other. On a bench in front of the church, I sit down for a moment to settle back into the 21st century.

Lago di Como: Where Italians Honeymoon

Stretched over two chairs atop the skinny passenger deck of a 10-car ferry as it shuttles across Lago di Como, I look south into the haze of Italy. I'm savoring the best of my favorite country with none of the chaos and intensity that's generally part of the Italian experience. Looking north, into a crisp alpine breeze, I see snowcapped Alps.

I'm just minutes from Switzerland . . . but it's clear I'm in Italy. The ferry workers are Italian, with that annoying yet endearing and playful knack for underachieving. Precision seems limited to the pasta: exactly al dente. Rather than banks and public clocks (which inundate nearby Swiss lake resorts, such as Lugano), the lanes that tumble into this lake come with lazy cafés and hole-in-the-wall shops, brimming with juicy fruits and crunchy greens.

In this romantic Lakes District in the shadow of the Alps, wistful 19th-century villas are seductively overgrown with old vines that seem to ache with stories to tell. Stunted palm trees look as if held against their will in this northern location. And vistas are made to order for poets. In fact, it was Romantic-age nature lovers who wrote and painted here that put this region on the tourism map in the 1800s.

The million-euro question: Which lake to see? Little Orta has an offbeat, less-developed charm. Maggiore has garden islands and Stresa, a popular resort town. Garda is a hit with German windsurfers. But for the best mix of scenery, old aristocratic romance, and wisteria charm, my choice is Como.

Sleepy Lago di Como, just an hour north of Milan by convenient train, is a good place to take a break from the obligatory turnstile culture of Italy. It seems half the travelers I meet have tossed their itineraries into the lake and are actually relaxing.

Today, the hazy lazy lake's only serious industry is tourism. Many lakeside residents travel daily to nearby Lugano, in Switzerland, to find work. The area's isolation and flat economy have left it pretty much the way those 19th-century Romantics painted it.

The self-proclaimed "Pearl of the Lake," Bellagio is the leading Lago di Como resort, a classy combination of prim tidiness and Old World elegance. If you don't mind feeling like a "tramp in the palace," it's a fine place to surround yourself with the more adventurous of the posh travelers. Arcades facing the lake are lined with shops. The heavy curtains hanging between the arches keep VIP visitors and their poodles from sweating. While the fancy ties and jewelry sell best at lake level, the locals shop up the hill.

Lago di Como is famous among Italians for its shape: like a stick figure of a man with two legs striding out. Bellagio is located where the two legs come together (which makes it the subject of funny, if crude, local rhymes you can learn when you visit). I wander from the town right on out to the crotch, following the view of the lake. At Punta Spartivento (literally "the point that divides the wind"), I find a Renoir atmosphere, perfect for a picnic while gazing north and contemplating the place where Italy is welded to the Swiss Alps.

I head to the town of Varenna (another 10-minute hop on the ferry), which is my home base. Narrow stepped lanes climb almost invisibly from

The village of Varenna, jutting into Lago di Como

Lago di Como, with snowcapped Alps

the harbor to the ancient arterial road that runs parallel to the lake along the top of town. Varenna packs its 800 residents into a compact townscape—tight as 50 oysters overloading a too-small rock. Individual homes are defined only by their pastel colors.

With Varenna's dwellings crowding the lake, the delightful *passerella* (boardwalk) arcs from the ferry dock to the tiny harbor past private villas guarded by wrought iron and wisteria. Two centuries ago, the harborfront was busy with coopers expertly fitting their chestnut and oak staves into barrels, stoneworkers carving and shipping prized black marble, and characteristic wooden boats heading out to catch the lake's unique *missoltino*—freshwater "sardines" still proudly served by local chefs. Today, the harbor's commerce is little more than the rental of paddleboats and a *gelateria* run by a guy named Eros.

Other than watch the ferries come and go, there's wonderfully little to do in Varenna. At night, it whispers *luna di miele*—honeymoon. And strolling its *passerella*, passing by those wisteria-drenched villas where caryatid lovers are pressed silently against each other, I'm reminded of the importance of choosing the right travel partner.

Romantic lakeside dining

The Cinque Terre: Italy's Riviera

I CAP the best day imaginable on the Cinque Terre with a glass of *sciacchetrà* dessert wine on the breakwater. It's midnight and the Mediterranean is darker than the sky. I scan the horizon for the bobbing lanterns of old-school fishermen seducing anchovies into their nets. But I see none.

During 40 years of visits, I've nursed a drink on this breakwater and seen the number of bobbing lanterns dwindle. The lanterns are gone now, as are many of the traditions . . . lost to the rising tide of modernity. But the weekly street markets still roll in, with the wives of fishermen selling their catch. And, after all these years, I'm thankful for this fragile yet surviving bit of the old Riviera and the community that keeps it vital.

The buzz I'm savoring is not from the wine, but from enjoying this world of ancient terraced vineyards, little pastel ports, rustic cuisine, and twinkling vistas. (OK, it's also from the wine.)

Resting between Genoa and Pisa, the Cinque Terre is the most dream-worthy stretch of Italy's Riviera. Leaving the nearest big city, La Spezia, the train lumbers into a mountain. Ten minutes later, bursting into the sunlight, it arrives at the first of the five towns. Rolling from

Riomaggiore, aglow at night

town to town, the train nips in and out of the hills, teasing you with a series of Mediterranean views. Each moment is grander than the last: azure blue tinseled in sunbeams, frothy waves hitting desolate rocks . . . interrupted only by the occasional topless sunbather camped out like a lone limpet.

The Cinque Terre (pronounced CHINK-weh TAY-reh) means "five lands." This quintet of pint-sized port towns clings to this most inaccessible stretch of coastline. Each is a well-whittled pastel jumble of homes filling a gully like crusty sea creatures in a tide pool.

These rugged ports, founded by Dark Age locals hiding out from marauding pirates, were cut off from the modern world until the arrival of the train. Today, the once foreboding castles protect only glorious views and the train brings hordes of hikers. To preserve this land, the government has declared the Cinque Terre a national park, collecting a small fee from each visitor. (The fees are intended to protect the flora and fauna and maintain the trails, but I've seen little evidence of that.)

Beyond the towns, vineyards with their many terraces blanket the mountainside. Someone—probably after too much local wine—calculated that the roughly 3,000 miles of terrace walls have the same amount of stonework as the Great Wall of China. Wine production is down nowadays, as younger residents choose less physical work. But many locals still maintain their tiny family plots and proudly serve their grandfather's wine.

The government, recognizing how wonderfully preserved these towns are, has long prohibited anyone from constructing any new buildings. That's why the region has no big, modern resort hotels—something I appreciate. The lack of comfortable accommodations leaves the towns to the more rugged travelers—those content to rent a room in a private home or simple *pensione*—and we enjoy a land where the villagers still go about their business as if this was the very edge of the Earth.

I always eat well in the Cinque Terre. This is the home of pesto. Basil, which loves the region's temperate climate, is mixed with cheese (half parmigiano cow cheese and half pecorino sheep cheese), garlic, olive oil, and pine nuts, then poured over pasta. And the *vino delle Cinque Terre* flows cheap and easy. The sweet, sherry-like *sciacchetrà* wine is served with a cookie. While 10 kilos of grapes yield 7 liters of wine, 10 kilos of grapes make only 2 liters of *sciacchetrà,* which is made from near-raisins. *Sciacchetrà* is much stronger than regular wine, something to keep in mind if your room is up a lot of steps.

Hikers taking a scenic break near Manarola

Of the five towns, Vernazza, overseen by a ruined castle and with the closest thing to a natural harbor, is the jewel. The occasional train popping in and out of the mountain tunnels is the only reminder that the modern world is still out there somewhere. It's a tough community long living off the sea . . . and, in the last generation, living off travelers who love the sea. The church bells dictate a relaxed tempo. Yellow webs of fishing nets, tables bedecked with umbrellas, kids with plastic shovels, and a flotilla of gritty little boats tethered to buoys provide splashes of color. And accompanying the scene is the mesmerizing white noise of children at play, happy diners, and the washboard rhythm of the waves.

Vernazza's one street connects the harbor with the train station before melting into the vineyards. Like veins on a grape leaf, paths and stairways reach from the main street up into this watercolor huddle of houses that eventually dissolve into the vines high above. A rainbow of laundry flaps as if to keep the flies off the fat grandmothers who clog ancient doorways.

At the top end of town, Vernazza's scrawny access road hits a post. No cars enter this community of 600 people. Like the breakwater holds off the waves at the bottom of town, the post holds back the modern storm at the top. But the town's ruined castle no longer says, "Keep out." The breakwater is a broad, inviting sidewalk edged with boulders—reaching out into the sea like a finger beckoning the distant excursion boats.

While Vernazza's fishing fleet is down to just a couple of boats, locals are still more likely to own a boat than a car. Boats are tethered to

Vernazza, the jewel of the Cinque Terre

buoys, except in winter or when the red storm flag indicates bad seas. In that case they're pulled up onto the little harborfront square, usually reserved for restaurant tables.

The humble town gathers around its pebbled cove, where well-worn locals enjoy some shade on benches and tourists sunbathe on the rocks. From end to end, everything's painted in one of the "Ligurian pastels," as regulated by a commissioner of good taste in the regional government. High above, the castle—now just a tower, some broken stone walls, and a grassy park—served as the town's lookout back in pirate days. Below the castle, an interior arcade connected houses—ideal for fleeing attacks. In front of the church, a mini piazza decorated with a river rock mosaic is a popular hangout. It's where the town's old ladies soak up the day's last bit of sun and kids enjoy a rare patch of level ball field.

My evenings in Vernazza are spent sitting on a bench and people-watching, either with gelato or a glass of local white wine (I usually borrow the glass from a bar; they don't mind). During the *passeggiata* (evening stroll), locals meander lazily up and down the main street doing their *vasche* (laps). Sometimes I join in, becoming part of the slow-motion parade. Gelato in hand, I gaze up at the people looking out the windows of the faded pastel buildings like a gallery of portraits hanging on ancient walls.

Traditions ring through the Cinque Terre as persistently as its beloved church bells—which remind residents of the days before tourism. The fishermen out at sea could hear the bells; the workers in the vineyards high on the mountain could hear them, too. In one town, the hoteliers tried to stop the bells for the tourists who couldn't sleep. But the community nearly revolted, and the bells ring on.

Vernazza: Lorenzo's View

VERNAZZA'S STROLLABLE breakwater creates a little harbor, rare on this rugged Riviera coastline. Grabbing a comfortable hollow in a boulder on the tip, I study the arrangement man and nature have carved out here over the last thousand years. Crumpled hills come with topographical lines: a terraced, green bouquet of cactus, grapevines, and olive trees.

With a closer look, I notice that the hills silently seethe with activity. Locals tend their vines and hikers work up a thirst for the white wine these hills produce. The single silver rail line runs perpendicular to the terraces, scaling the hillside like a rock climber's rope. It's autumn and the grape pickers' tiny train—the *trenino*—is busy ferrying grapes down into town from the highest terraces.

Below my rocky perch, a fisherman cleans his nets. The cool mist that follows each crashing wave reminds me how easily this breakwater is conquered during winter storms. High above the breakwater, at the base of the castle, is a restaurant called Il Castello. This pricey place was my private little splurge back when I stretched my money by choosing popsicles over gelato.

Vernazza feels populated by descendants of the pirates who plundered

The village cemetery, high above Vernazza

With Monica, Lorenzo's daughter

this coast. But Lorenzo, who ran Il Castello, was a rare Vernazzan who didn't take advantage of tourists held captive by his town's beauty. He'd sit me down under an umbrella with the most commanding view in town. And with the love of a small-town priest, he'd put a cookie next to my glass of cool, sweet *sciacchetrà* wine, and say, "Rest here. The view is nice."

Cancer took Lorenzo quickly one winter. Now he's king of the Vernazza mountain. He's resting and enjoying the best view of all from a different kind of hotel, booked out by locals for years . . . the hilltop cemetery.

Leaving the harborfront, I climb the steep, stony staircase up to Il Castello. Monica, Lorenzo's daughter who runs the place now with her husband Massimo, greets me warmly. Her dark hair backlit by the sun, she seems to have an aura. Her penetrating eyes seem to really see me. She has Barbra Streisand lips and a bony nose. In her caring face I see Lorenzo, as if he were still standing there with a nice bottle of *sciacchetrà*.

I tell Monica that I've been thinking about her father and she suggests we visit the cemetery. Hiking through narrow back alleys that smell of damp cats, we reach the lane that leads uphill to the cemetery. After a funeral Mass, the entire village spills out of the church and trudges darkly up this same route.

At the top of the lane, a black iron gate is open. Inside, the cemetery is fragrant with fresh flowers. Quiet pathways separate marble walls of niches, stacked five high. Walking down a lane closest to the sea, Monica explains that coffins are not put into the ground but slid into a *loculo*. Squinting at a wall of niches, reflecting bright white in the late-afternoon sun, I review names and dates carved into the marble. Each niche is wired with a minuscule light and comes with a built-in vase. And next to each vase is an inset oval window filled with a black-and-white portrait.

Stepping around a rolling ladder—left out for loved ones with flowers for those resting on the top row—Monica arrives at her father's *loculo*. She leaves me long enough to cross herself. Then, turning toward the sea, Monica sits on a flat rock just big enough for two. Patting the other half of her perch, she invites me to sit down. She doesn't know it, but it's as if to say, "Rest here. The view is nice."

We ignore the red tiles, flapping laundry, and tourists lounging on the breakwater below. From here, enjoying what we call "Lorenzo's view," the world is peaceful green and reassuring blue, blending the sea and sky. To the left and right, I pick out each of the Cinque Terre towns along the coast. Each is alone in the world—seemingly oblivious to the march of time. I wonder what could possibly improve the setting. Then the church bells ring.

Lorenzo's view

Scandinavia
and the Baltics

T RAVEL IN Northern Europe and the Nordic Europe region challenges any American's ethnocentricity in an enjoyable way—like
the slap of birch twigs on hot ruddy skin in a neighborhood sauna.

In Norway, where city halls are treated like churches, I'm evange-
lized by people who believe in the goodness of big government and
proudly reject a materialistic Big Gulp world. At a hippie commune
in Copenhagen, I hang with people whose mantra is "Only dead fish
swim with the current."

This peace-loving region celebrates the power of music. In Helsinki,
visiting choirs from around Finland invade the bar scene—bringing
choral music to the pubs. And across the Baltic Sea in Tallinn, Estonians won their freedom not with guns but with singing.

Majestic fjords of mountainous Norway

Ærø: Denmark's Ship-in-a-Bottle Island

Few visitors to Scandinavia even notice Ærø, a sleepy little island on the southern edge of Denmark. It's a peaceful and homey isle, where baskets of strawberries sit in front of farmhouses—for sale on the honor system. Its tombstones are carved with such sentiments as: "Here lies Christian Hansen at anchor with his wife. He'll not weigh until he stands before God."

The island's statistics: 22 miles by 6 miles, 7,000 residents, 350 deer, no crosswalks, seven pastors, three police officers, and a pervasive passion for the environment. Along with sleek modern windmills hard at work, Ærø has one of the world's largest solar power plants.

Ærø's main town, Ærøskøbing, makes a fine home base for exploring the isle. Many Danes agree, washing up on the cobbled main drag in waves with the landing of each ferry.

With lanes right out of the 1680s, the town was the wealthy home port to more than 100 windjammers. The post office dates to 1749 and cast-iron gaslights still shine each evening. Windjammers gone, the harbor now caters to German and Danish holiday yachts. On midnight low tides, you can almost hear the crabs playing cards.

Beach bungalows at Ærøskøbing

The town's sights, while humble, are endearing. The Hammerich House, full of old junk, is a 1920s garage sale of a museum. Around the corner, the Bottle Peter Museum is a fascinating house with a fleet of more than 750 different bottled ships. Old Peter Jacobsen devoted a lifetime to his miniature shipyard before he died in 1960 (probably buried in a glass bottle). Squinting and marveling at his enthralling little cre-

For sale on the honor system

ations, it occurs to me that Ærø itself is a ship-in-a-bottle kind of place.

Taking a 15-mile bike ride, I piece together the best of Ærø's salty charms. Just outside of town, I see the first of many U-shaped farmhouses, so typical of Denmark. The three sides block the wind to create a sheltered little courtyard and house cows, hay, and people. I bike along a dike built in the 1800s to make swampland farmable. While the weak soil is good for hay and little else, they get the most out of it. Each winter farmers flood their land to let the saltwater nourish the soil and grass, in the belief that this causes their cows to produce fattier milk and meat.

Struggling uphill, I reach the island's 2,700-inch-high summit. It's a "peak" called Synneshøj, pronounced "Seems High" (and after this pedal, I agree).

Rolling through the town of Bregninge, I notice how it lies in a gully. I imagine pirates, centuries ago, trolling along the coast looking for church spires marking unfortified villages. Ærø's 16 villages are built low, in gullies like this one, to make them invisible from the sea—their stubby church spires carefully designed not to be viewable from potentially threatening ships.

A lane leads me downhill, dead-ending at a rugged bluff called Vodrup Klint. If I were a pagan, I'd worship here—the sea, the wind, and

Bicycling is a breezy way to explore Ærø.

the chilling view. The land steps in sloppy slabs down to the sea. The giant terraces are a clear reminder that when saturated with water, the massive slabs of clay that make up the land here get slick, and entire chunks can slip and slide.

While the wind at the top seems hell-bent on blowing me off my bike, the beach below is peaceful, ideal for sunbathing. I can't see Germany, which is just across the water, but I do see a big stone which commemorates the return of the island to Denmark from Germany in 1750.

Back up on the road, I pedal down a tree-lined lane toward a fine 12th-century church. As they often do all over Europe, this church marks a pre-Christian holy site. In a field adjacent to the church stands the Langdyssen Tingstedet—a 6,000-year-old dolmen, an early Neolithic burial place. While Ærø once had more than 200 of these prehistoric tombs, only 13 survive.

The name "Tingstedet" indicates that this was also a Viking assembly spot. This raised mound, roughly the shape and length of a Viking ship, evokes the scene when chiefs gathered here around their ancestors' tombs a thousand years ago. The stones were considered fertility stones. For centuries, locals in need of a little extra virility chipped off bits and took them home.

I enter the church. Like town churches throughout the island, a

A church on Ærø

centuries-old paint job gives the simple stonework a crude outline of the fine Gothic features this humble community wished it could afford. Little ships hang in the nave, perhaps as memorials to lost sailors. A portrait of Martin Luther hangs in the stern making sure everything's theologically shipshape. The long list adjacent allows today's pastor to trace her pastoral lineage back to Dr. Luther himself. The current pastor, Janet, is the first woman on the five-centuries-long list. A pole with an offering bag comes equipped with a ting-a-ling bell to wake those nodding off.

From the church, it's all downhill back to Ærøskøbing. The sun is low in the sky, so I coast right on through town to the sunset beach—where a row of tiny huts lines the strand and where so many locals enjoyed a first kiss. The huts are little more than a picnic table with walls and a roof, but each is lovingly painted and carved—stained with generations of family fun, memories of pickled herring on rye bread, and sunsets. It's a perfectly Danish scene—like Ærø itself—where small is beautiful, sustainability is just common sense, and a favorite local word, *hyggelig*, takes "cozy" to delightful extremes.

Enjoying the beach at sunset

Norway: The Old Country and a New Outlook

I'LL NEVER FORGET my first trip to Europe. I was a gangly 14-year-old, dragged to the old country by a conspiracy of grandparents and parents solely to visit strangers who happened to be Norwegian relatives. I didn't want to go. It just made no sense.

Jet lag wasn't the problem. It was teen culture shock: No Fanta. No hamburgers. Far beyond the reach of my favorite radio station. Their "Top 40" had nothing to do with my "Top 40." But after a few days I was wild about Solo (Norway's orange pop), addicted to the long and skinny *pølse* wieners, and enjoying new music. Noticing stunning women . . . with hairy armpits . . . I began to realize that our world is intriguing and exploring it can be endlessly entertaining.

Visiting the house where my great-grandmother was born, I imagined the courage it must have taken to leave Norway and her entire family for America a century ago.

Sitting with my cousins on their living room floor in 1969 to watch the Apollo moon landing, I began to see the world differently. Hearing them

Norway's timeless beauty

Oslo's Vigeland Park

translate Neil Armstrong's words *("Ett lite skritt for et menneske, ett stort skritt for menneskeheten"),* it dawned on me: That first big step was more than just an American celebration. It was a human accomplishment.

In Oslo's Vigeland Park, I was grossed out by the nude statues by sculptor Gustav Vigeland. But I also experienced an important revelation in that same park that I share every chance I get: As I watched towheaded kids splashing with their parents in a fountain, I realized those parents loved their kids as much as mine loved me. This planet is home to billions of equally precious children of God. Travel was causing me to think bigger. And it was prying open my hometown blinders.

The next time we visited Norway, we looked up our ancestral roots. My grandfather, famous in the 1930s in Leavenworth, Washington, as a rowdy ski jumper, was a Romstad. So although my last name is Steves (after a step-grandfather), my blood is Romstad. That branch of my family comes from a scenic valley called Gudbrandsdalen.

These days, I don't visit Norway just to read my family name on tombstones. The roots I seek are also cultural. It's stimulating to learn about different social systems (many of which confound Americans). A friend in Oslo introduced me to the ideas of Norwegian philosopher Erik Dammann, who in the 1970s started a movement called "The Future in Our Hands." His book by the same name lit a political fire in my belly that burns to this day. Dammann argued that a successful society can rise above materialism and that being content with your material wealth is a virtue. Dammann (and Norway) helped me imagine a society where consumption was not the goal. Norwegians are almost evangelical about their belief in organizing society for the benefit of all. City halls here are as grandly and lovingly decorated as churches.

Norwegians are talented linguists. I speak only English. Of all the places in Europe that I've traveled and worked, Norway has

A flag-flying perch above Bergen

been the easiest place to communicate. Not long ago, I was at a cousin's dinner party with a dozen people in Oslo. Out of deference to me, it was agreed: Everyone would speak English.

The topics were fascinating. One man, an author who had just written a book on Franklin D. Roosevelt, talked with me about the intricacies of American post-WWII politics. Two new parents gently debated the various ways to split their paid maternal and paternal leave (standard in Scandinavia where, for the father, it's use it or lose it). People seemed very content. It was a house full of chatty Norwegians just loving their salmon, shrimp, and goat cheese.

Sure, Norway is an oasis of warmth and love because I've got family there. But I also appreciate the chance to rein in my Ameri-centricity. I admire a smart and creative land where well-being is not preceded by the word "material."

Family time in Norway

Charming, Challenging Oslo

I'VE BEEN VISITING Oslo since I was a kid, thinking about it as both the home of my forefathers and as a model modern city that I wish could inspire my hometown.

I'm at the harborfront dock, where my old haunt, a Hurtigruten steamer, was once moored. In its prime, the romantic old postal boat linked Oslo with remote communities along the fjords and islands all the way north to the Arctic. Later it became a hotel. My favorite room was its "writer's cabin," the only room on that old ship that lacked plumbing and was, therefore, affordable to me. This same dock also marks the spot where my grandparents embarked for the US. They traded the old country for a new one, hoping to swap a dead-end economy for a land of promise.

Standing here today, I survey the modern, people-friendly promenade and think about how life has changed. I can now afford a room with a shower, but the ship is gone. And the relatives who stayed behind in Norway are now living better than many of the ones who left.

I'm surrounded by the white noise of pedestrian bliss. I can hear people talking and laughing, the birds, the breeze—but no cars. A popular "congestion fee" keeps most cars from the center of town. An efficient

Oslo's people-friendly harborfront

tunnel diverts nearly all the traffic under the city. The old train station facing the fjord boat dock has become the Nobel Peace Prize Center, thanks to a visionary man who dedicated the wealth he earned inventing dynamite to celebrate peacemakers. And towering high above the harbor action is Oslo's stately brick City Hall—where Nobel's prize is awarded. It stands like a cathedral to good civic values, decorated inside and out with statues and murals featuring stoic Norwegians who seem more than willing to pay their steep taxes.

Oslo's City Hall, with stirring murals and art that depict Norway's history

Every time I come to Norway, I'm fascinated by the way they've chosen to organize their society. And then, when I get home, I routinely challenge my fellow Americans by telling tales of a land where the desired alternative to big, bad government is not small, good government—but big, good government. While I certainly wouldn't want to run my business in heavily regulated Europe, I'm challenged and inspired by the Norwegian way of organizing their society.

Discussions with relatives and new friends alike often lead to comparisons of our two very affluent but very different societies. For example, even though North Sea oil is plentiful and a big part of Norway's economy, the government understands that the world is warming and knows it's only ethical to have policies to help counteract climate change. To encourage clean electric cars, the government underwrites

Disposable grills

Dessert with family

car charging, parking, tolls, and taxes—making even a luxury Tesla an affordable ride. As Norway steadily reduces its use of gasoline-powered cars, it has become Tesla's second-biggest market.

Norway is expensive for tourists—and also for Norwegians. The society is designed in a way that encourages people to consume less, to chew more slowly, and to sip rather than gulp. A glass of beer costs $12. A cup of coffee can cost $8—and free refills are unheard of. I think Norwegians know they could make more money if they embraced the "big gulp" and started supersizing. But the collective decision is not based purely on what would be good for the economy. A big-box economy would just not be Norwegian.

In Scandinavia, tourists are sometimes put off by the many young beer-drinking revelers they see out on the streets, canalside, and littering the parks. But alcohol consumption is no greater here than it is farther south. It's just that while pubs in Britain and beer halls in Germany are affordable, Scandinavia's bars come with extremely high alcohol taxes. So people start their evening with a drink at home or a friend's house before hitting a bar. Or they just B.Y.O.B.—buying cheap beers at a convenience store, then finding a pleasant perch outside for an impromptu gathering. For young Norwegians, "going out" means literally "going outside." Norwegians cope with the high cost of dining out by using "one-time grills." On balmy evenings, the city is perfumed with the smell of these disposable foil grills being fired up for dinners in the parks.

Revisiting family
and memories in Oslo

Walking through a light mist along the new harborfront development, I stop by a shrimp boat to buy a small bag of shrimp, pulled out of the fjord by a weather-beaten fisherman just hours ago. It's been my happy ritual at this very spot since my mom first brought me to this little boat when I was a kid.

The commotion of a festive celebration draws me farther along the harborfront. A hundred Norwegians are swing-dancing on the sturdy boardwalk, which glistens as if pleased to be the city's dance floor. Sometimes, good-looking, self-assured Norwegians annoy me with their perfection. But these strike me as extremely normal people—a little overweight, a little wrinkled, dancing in content twosomes in front of yacht club bars and restaurants most of them likely can't afford. It's mostly American-style two-step to recorded oldies—familiar tunes with unfamiliar Norwegian lyrics—like a line dance without cowboy hats or much of a line. Girls look up at their tall guys with big smiles.

Walking back to where my "writer's cabin" used to be, I get nostalgic for the long-ago joy of settling into my humble stateroom, gathering the experiences of the day, and weaving them into an article—hoping to share new insights into this capital city—a city that still charms and challenges me all at once.

Copenhagen's Christiania:
No Cars, Corporations, or Dead Fish

I'M STROLLING through the commotion of downtown Copenhagen, past chain restaurants dressed up to look old, and under towering hotels that seem to be part of a different international chain each year. Then, as if from another age, a man pedals by with his wife on a "Christiania Bike"—two wheels pushing a big utilitarian rounded bucket. You'd call them "granola" in the US. They look as out of place here in Copenhagen as an Amish couple in Manhattan.

I pause to watch the parade that follows them: ragtag soldiers-against-conformity dressed in black making their way through the bustling, modern downtown. They walk solemnly behind a WWII vintage truck blasting Pink Floyd's "Another Brick in The Wall." I've never really listened to the words until now. These "soldiers" are fighting a rising tide of conformity. They want to raise their children to be free spirits, not cogs. Painted onto their banner—an old sheet—is a slogan you see in their Christiania squatter community: *"Lev livet kunstnerisk! Kun døde fisk flyder med strømmen."* ("Live life artistically! Only dead fish swim with

Christiania, an experiment in alternative living

Nonconforming housing is the norm.

the current.") They fly the Christiania flag: an orange background with three yellow dots for the three "i"s in "Christiania" (or, some claim, for the "o"s in "Love Love Love").

In 1971, the original 700 Christianians established squatters' rights in an abandoned military barracks, just a 10-minute walk from the Danish parliament building. Half a century later, this "free city" still stands—a human mishmash of idealists, hippies, potheads, non-materialists, and free-spirited children. The population includes 900 people, 200 cats, 200 dogs, 17 horses, and 2 parrots. Over 100 of the original squatters, seniors with Willie Nelson's fashion sense, still live here. When someone moves out, the community decides who will be invited in to replace that person. Most residents are employed: A third of the adult population works on the outside, a third works on the inside, and a third doesn't work much at all.

Christiania sprawls just behind the spiral tower of Our Savior's Church in the trendy district of Christianshavn. Welcoming visitors and even offering daily tours in summer, it's become the second-most-visited sightseeing stop in Copenhagen (move over, *Little Mermaid*). Tourists react in very different ways to this place. Some see a haven of peace and freedom. Others see dogs, dirt, and dazed people. Some see no taboos. Others see too many tattoos.

Entering the community, I pass under the sign announcing that I am leaving the European Union. The main drag is nicknamed "Pusher Street" for the marijuana-selling stands that line it. (Residents preemptively destroyed the stalls in 2004 to reduce the risk of Christiania being disbanded by the government, but that didn't last.) While the laws here are always in flux, I notice the

Concert in Christiania

small, sweet-smelling stretch of Pusher Street, dubbed the "Green Light District," where pot is openly sold, is back. Signs, while acknowledging that this activity is still illegal, announce: "1. Have fun; 2. No photos; and 3. No running—'because it makes people nervous.'"

As I walk down Pusher Street, I see Nemoland, a kind of food circus. At the end of the street, a huge warehouse called Den Grønne Hal ("The Green Hall") does triple-duty as a recycling center, a craft center for kids, and an evening concert hall. Behind it, climbable ramparts overlook an idyllic lake and a forest that's dotted with cozy if ramshackle cottages.

From Den Grønne Hal, a lane leads to a pleasant café, and beyond that, to the Morgenstedet vegetarian restaurant—a great place for a simple, friendly meal. A former barracks near the entrance of Chris-

No hard drugs are allowed.

tiania now houses Spiseloppen, a classy restaurant serving up gourmet anarchy by candlelight. Away from Pusher Street, I find myself lost in truly untouristed, residential Christiania, where the old folks sit out on the front stoop watching kids chasing ducks and flying with delight down homemade ziplines.

The free community has nine

rules: no cars, no hard drugs, no guns, no explosives, and so on. While exploring this idealistic world, I realize that, except for the bottled beer being sold, there's not a hint of any corporate entity. Everything is hand-made. Nothing is packaged. That rejection of corporate values is part of what makes this community's survival so tenuous.

Christiania has long faced government attempts to shut the place down. Back when real estate was much cheaper in Copenhagen, city officials looked the other way. But as the surrounding neighborhood gentrified, developers began eyeing the land Christiania's hippies were squatting on. A certain intense breed of capitalist has a tough time allowing something that could be privatized and profitable stay public. The people of Christiania have learned to live with uncertainty.

Recently, I received an email from some readers who'd visited. They said: "We're not prudes, but Christiania was creepy. It was too much for our family. Don't take kids there or go after dark." I agree that a free city is not always pretty. But perhaps those parents were as threatened as much by Christiania's non-materialism as they were by its grittiness. Watching parents raise their children with Christiania values, I've come to believe very strongly in this social experiment. Certainly our world, so driven by aggressive corporate and materialist values, can afford to let people with alternative viewpoints have a place to be alternative. Christiania is a social flower that deserves a chance to bloom.

For Christiania's residents, the experiment is working.

Helsinki: "Relax . . . I Wash You Twice"

I'M IN HELSINKI, surveying the city from its fanciest rooftop restaurant. The setting sun glints off the cruise ships in the harbor as fish merchants are taking down their stalls in the market. But a fleshier scene on the rooftop below me steals my attention.

It's six bankers wrapped in white towels enjoying a sauna. In all proper Finnish office buildings—whether banks, insurance companies, or research institutes—a rooftop sauna is an essential part of the design. Free snacks and drinks at the sauna after work is almost an expected perk. One rotund fellow is so pink from the heat that—with his white towel wrapped around his waist—he reminds me of a billiard ball.

As a tourist, I'm not invited to join the bankers on the rooftop and the few remaining public saunas in Helsinki are in gritty neighborhoods. In this affluent city, most people have private saunas in their homes or cabins. Rough working-class neighborhoods are most likely to need—and therefore have—a public sauna. So I get on the subway and head for Kotiharjun Sauna in the scruffy Sörnäinen district. At first glance, it's clear that this place is the local hangout—and rarely sees a tourist. Outside, a vertical neon sign in simple red letters reads: *SAUNA*. Under it, a gang of big Finnish guys wrapped only in small towels fills a clutter of white plastic chairs. They are expertly relaxing.

As there isn't a word of English anywhere, I rely on the young attendant at the window for instructions. He explains the process: Pay seven euros, grab a towel, strip, stow everything in an old wooden locker, wear the key like a bracelet, shower, enter the sauna . . . and reeeelax.

"Is it mixed?" I ask.

"No, there's a sauna upstairs for women."

"What about getting a scrub?"

Pointing to an aproned woman, he says, "Talk directly with her . . . six euros extra."

The sauna is far from the sleek, cedar pre-fab den of steam I expected. Six crude concrete steps with dark wooden railings and rustic walls create a barn-like amphitheater of steam and heat. The clientele is tough

A rustic sauna in a workaday Helsinki neighborhood

and working class. A huge iron door closes off the wood stove (which is busy burning through its daily cubic meter of firewood). The third step up is all the heat I can take. Everyone else is twice as high, sitting on the top level for maximum steam and maximum heat. Towel in hand, I'd wondered whether it'd be used for hygiene or modesty. Now inside, the answer is clear . . . neither.

The entire scene is three colors: gray concrete, dark wood, and ruddy flesh. Naked with their hair wet and stringy, people look both more timeless and more ethnic. There's virtually no indication of what century we're in. But looking at their faces, it's clear to me: This is Finland.

Each guy has a tin bucket between his legs for splashing cool water on his face. I ask about the bin of birch twigs that sits on the bottom step. Slapping your skin with these, one man explains, enhances your circulation. The roughed-up leaves emit a refreshing birch aroma as well as chlorophyll, which opens the sinuses.

Part two of a good sauna is the scrub down. The woman in the apron scrubs men one at a time all day long. She's finishing up with a guy sitting on a plastic chair, dousing him with water. After his work-over, he looks like a lifeless Viking Gumby.

Awkwardly I ask, "Me next?"

She welcomes me to her table. She reminds me of a Stalin-era Soviet tractor driver.

I ask, "Up or down?"

She pushes me flat . . . belly up . . . and says, "This is good. Now, I wash you twice."

Lying there naked, I feel like a salmon on a cleaning table, ready for gutting. With sudsy mitts, she works me over. Then she hoses me off, which makes me feel even more like a salmon. It's extremely relaxing. Moving from deep in my scalp to between my toes, she washes me a second time.

Stepping back out into the gritty Helsinki neighborhood, I'm clean, relaxed, and assured that—for bankers, laborers, and tourists, too—the sauna is the great equalizer.

800 Finnish Singers March into Battle

T HERE'S A definite energy on the streets of Helsinki tonight. My friend Hanne explains, "We call Wednesday our 'little Friday.'"

People are filling up the city's main boulevard, named Boulevardi. (It was given that grandiose title 200 years ago, when the concept of a grand boulevard in Helsinki, then Europe's newest capital, was somewhere between wishful thinking and absurdity. But the name stuck.)

There are so many people that I wonder if it's some kind of demonstration. Then I see their robes and sheets of music and realize that these are choral groups, each represented by a placard. From all corners of the country, some 800 singers converge on the massive steps of the Lutheran Cathedral, overlooking the Neoclassical Senate Square. Crowds gather, enthusiastic to hear this annual massing of the choirs.

The crowd quiets and the singers begin a rousing series of hymns. While I can't understand a word, the songs are sung with such a stirring air that I imagine they tell both of their hard-fought history, their solid faith, and their gratitude to be who they are—the people of Finland. As the last hymn ends, balloons are freed, and the singers

Choirs gather to sing on the steps of Helsinki's Lutheran Cathedral.

disperse, kicking off a festive initiative called "Art Goes to the Pubs." The city's watering holes are about to be filled with song.

Leaving the square, Hanne and I pass a poster of a demonic-looking rock band. "Hell froze over that year," she explains. Europe's biggest TV event is the annual Eurovision Song Contest, most famous as the event that launched ABBA in 1974 with their breakout song, "Waterloo." Perennial losers in the event, Finns have long said, "Hell will freeze over before Finland wins the Eurovision Song Contest." In 2006, Finland's Kiss-inspired heavy-metal band Lordi won with a rocking, gravelly voiced number called "Hard Rock Hallelujah."

At the curb, there's no traffic, so I jaywalk across the street. I get halfway across Boulevardi before looking back for Hanne, who is still waiting for a walk signal. In defeat, I return to the curb. She says, "In Finland, we wait. It can be two in the morning and not a car in sight, but we wait."

I note that Germans respect authority, too.

Hanne says it's different in Finland. "We buck authority. But we follow the laws . . . even little ones. That's why we have such low crime."

Hanne points out an elegant restaurant with a dining hall that was perfectly preserved from the 1930s. Its Alvar Aalto-designed Functionalism is the kind of straight design and practical elegance Finns love. A private office party is raging—specifically, a crayfish party. Crayfish are in season, but at $10 each, they are hardly a budget meal. But all over town Finns are doing the crayfish tango: Suck and savor a red minilobster, throw down a glass of schnapps, sing a song, and do it again. The "99 Bottles of Beer" repetition just gets more fun with each round.

Hanne shows me the table where Gustaf Emil Mannerheim always sat. He was the heroic George Washington of modern Finland, who led the feisty resistance against the USSR. Many Finns consider him personally responsible for keeping their country free during and after World War II. No Finnish military leader will ever again hold Mannerheim's rank of "Field Marshal." But anyone can sit at his favorite table . . . and suck a crayfish.

We continue walking, ending up back on the grand Senate Square. The city seems a tale of two cultures. The late-setting sun gleams on both the

Helsinki's Russian Orthodox Church

Lutheran Cathedral and the golden onion domes of the Russian Orthodox Church. They seem to face off, symbolizing how east and west have long confronted each other here in Finland. Europe's second-mightiest sea fortress—after Gibraltar—fills an island in the harbor . . . which allowed the village of Helsinki to grow into a booming capital.

Finns have a fun-loving confidence and seem to live well. I ask how Nordic Europe can be so prosperous when only Norway has oil.

Hanne responds, "Norway has oil—Finland has Nokia. It's like Microsoft for you in Seattle."

"So what's Sweden's trick?" I ask.

Hanne sighs, showing the standard Scandinavian envy of the regional powerhouse. "They never get in a war. They're always rich . . . just collecting money all the time. The Swedes are like our big brother. They always win. Like in ice hockey. We won only once . . . back in the 1990s. The Swedes—assuming they'd win—had already written their victory song. But we won. We Finns still sing this song to give the Swedes a hard time. It's the only song Finns know in Swedish and every Finn can sing it . . . even today."

Our conversation is interrupted by a different song—a rousing hymn. Across the square is a church choir, marching to yet another pub, joyfully, as if going to battle in a war for music.

Helsinki's Lutheran Cathedral

Estonia: The Song of Freedom

IN TALLINN, my guide Mati suggests that we visit the cemetery just outside of town. As we arrive and step out of his beat-up Soviet-made car, I realize this is no ordinary cemetery. The lovingly tended tombs are scattered throughout a dense pine forest.

"Estonia is a thickly forested country," Mati explains. "Many Estonians see trees as spiritual. Since ancient pagan times, we have buried our loved ones with the trees. We are people of the trees. This is one way we are still connected with our pagan past . . . still uniquely Estonian." Walking under these towering trees makes me think about the Estonians' connection to their land and heritage.

It's amazing what a stretch of water can do. The Baltic Sea separates Estonia from Sweden and Finland. The struggles of the last couple of generations couldn't be more different on these opposite shores. When I visited the Baltic states back in the 1980s, times were very tough. Labor was cheaper than light bulbs. While I was touring museums, an old babushka would actually walk through the museum with me, turning the lights on and off as we went from room to room.

Estonia's Forest Cemetery

Tallinn's Alexander Nevsky Cathedral

Those days are long gone. Estonia's busy capital, Tallinn, is like a petri dish of capitalism. Since winning its freedom in 1991, the country has blossomed. Mati brags that Estonia has the strongest economy, most freedom, and highest standard of living of any republic that was part of the USSR. He says that by some measures, Estonians are now one of the freest people on Earth.

Mati points out the great irony of Russia's communist experiment. Russia, once the supposed champion of radical equality—as far as Leninism and Marxism were concerned—is now infamous for having the worst inequality. In the dirty derby of unequal wealth distribution, Russia is one of only a few countries to actually beat the US. Estonians are better off today than Russians not because they have more money per capita (they don't), but because the wealth in this country is distributed much more evenly. Mati, who's spent half his life under communism and half under capitalism, says, "Politics. It's all about the distribution of wealth."

Mati drives us back into Tallinn to explore the Old Town. Strolling the street in need of a coffee break, we step into a courtyard. At the entry the landlord has hung a photo of the place back in 2000. It looked like a war had hit it. Today, while it looks much the same, it's inhabited by thriving businesses.

The courtyard's trendy little café has wicker chairs rocking on the rough cobbles. The first seat I eye seems empty, but it has a vest hanging on it. So I look for another empty spot . . . it has a vest, too. I really, really need coffee. Then I realize that on the back of every chair hangs a different vest. They're not saving anyone's seat, they're just decor. Noticing my confusion, Mati explains, "Estonian chic."

Over coffee, I ask Mati more about the USSR. Mati spent time in the USSR military, driving Soviet officers around the Crimea. Estonian boys got this plum assignment because they were considered smarter (and therefore safer drivers) than village boys from the interior of Russia.

With Finland within distance of rabbit-ear antennas, Estonians were the only people in the USSR who got Western TV during the Cold War. Mati remembers when the soft-porn flick *Emmanuelle* aired. No one

Café in Tallinn

here had seen anything remotely like it. With that single broadcast, there was a historic migration of Estonians from the south of the country to Tallinn, where they could receive Finnish TV. He said, "Nine months later, we Estonians experienced a spike in births."

In Mati's youth, the entire USSR—one-sixth of the world—was theoretically open to him, but he had no way to get a plane ticket or a hotel room, so in practice travel was not possible. The other five-sixths of the world was simply off-limits. In 1950s and 1960s, the USSR ordered all Estonian recreational boats destroyed because they were considered potential "escape vehicles." It was an era in which Estonia was virtually a prison.

When Mati was young and asked his grandmother where his grandfather had gone, she said, "He's a tourist in Siberia." Because loved ones were routinely imprisoned in the far east of the Soviet Union, that was the standard answer to shield kids from knowing about the hell their family members were living in. After Estonia's independence, Mati learned that his grandma had a bag packed under her bed for the surprise visit from the local police that she both dreaded and expected.

In the early 1990s, after the fall of the USSR, a kind of Wild West capitalism swept the country. The country's first millionaire was a clever entrepreneur who dismantled the physical trappings of Soviet control and sold it as scrap metal. Mati and five friends made good money by importing classic American cars and selling them to rich Russians. But one day, four of Mati's friends went to Russia to collect payment on a car and were killed—riddled with machine-gun bullets. Mati decided to drop his car business and become a tour guide.

Mati says, "The Russian mob makes Sicily's mob look like a church choir. Putin directed the KGB back then. If you think Putin doesn't understand how to hold on to power, forgive me, but you are a fool or you are blind."

Mati and I visit Tallinn's huge Song Festival Grounds, which looks like an oversized Hollywood Bowl. Overlooking the grassy expanse, with the huge stage tiny in the distance, Mati explains that in 1988, when Estonia was breaking away from the USSR, over 300,000 people—a third of the country—gathered here to sing patriotic songs.

Mati says, "Stuck between Russia and Germany, we were almost invisible. Our national songfest was a political statement. We are so few in number that we must emphasize that we exist. We had no weapons. All we could do was be together and sing. This was our power."

Their Singing Revolution, peaceful and nonviolent, persisted for several years, and in the end, Estonians gained their freedom in 1991. The Song Festival Grounds, still used for concerts today, is a national monument for the compelling role it played in this small country's fight for independence. Traveling with Mati through Estonia, I'm reminded that I simply inherited freedom. For many, freedom has to be earned.

The Song Festival Grounds, where Estonians sang for their independence

BOHU
VLAST1
UMĚNÍ KE
BANKA

KU CHVÁLE
K SLÁVĚ
CTI VĚNUJE
SLÁVIE

Eastern Europe

NO CORNER of Europe has changed more dramatically in my lifetime of travel than Eastern Europe. Poland, Hungary, and the Czech Republic were devastated in World War II and then downtrodden under Soviet control. To the south, much of what had been Yugoslavia found itself mired in a bloody breakup. Thankfully, in this century, the explosions have generally been happy ones: booms of development and rocketing progress.

There's a new vitality in the former Eastern Bloc, where the tumult of the 20th century is just one more thread in the weave of history that provides a rich backdrop for today's travels. A new affluence—amped up by a thriving tourism industry—has reinvigorated each country.

Prague is well-established as the leading tourist destination of the region, while Kraków is called "the next Prague," and Budapest seems to be the sophisticate's choice. Dubrovnik, the coveted "Pearl of the Adriatic," is the darling of the cruise industry, which makes often-overlooked, offbeat destinations nearby—Bosnia's Mostar and Montenegro's Bay of Kotor—particularly appealing.

Alphonse Mucha's stained-glass window in Prague's St. Vitus Cathedral

Czech Out Prague

IT SEEMS when my Czech friends take me around Prague, the capital of the Czech Republic, we see the sights and then invariably end up in a pub, where my lessons on the country continue over a few mugs of their beloved pilsner.

Pivo (beer) is a frothy hit with tourists, too. After all, the Czechs invented Pilsner-style lager in nearby Plzeň, and the result, Pilsner Urquell, is on tap in many pubs. In Czech restaurants, a beer hits your table like a glass of water does in the US. I've learned to be careful—it's stronger than the beer back home. *Pivo* for lunch has me sightseeing for the rest of the day on what I call "Czech knees."

Honza—a young yet professorial guide I've known for years—has hair I've always envied. I always thought it was Albrecht Dürer hair. Then one evening, realizing it was Jim Morrison hair, I got Honza to take off his shirt and stretch out his arms. He looked just like a Doors album cover.

Honza teaches more emphatically after a couple of beers. I'll never forget how he slammed his glass mug down on a sticky beer-hall table to announce "Czechs are the world's most enthusiastic beer drinkers—adults drink an average of 150 liters a year! We couldn't imagine living without this beer . . . the Czech pilsner."

I think the hardest I've ever laughed in Europe was when Honza explained the three kinds of Czech drunks. "There's the sleeper," he said, putting his head down on the table. "There's the entertainer," he exclaimed, while flapping his arms in my face. "And there's 'at the dentist,'" he demonstrated, reclining way back on his bar chair with his eyes closed and his mouth wide open.

The joy of having a good time in Prague seems heightened by my physical surroundings and by the heaviness of the country's recent history. Prague is "the golden city of a hundred spires." Because this vibrant Baroque capital escaped the bombs of the last century's wars, it's remarkably well-preserved. But it didn't avoid the heavy, deadening economic and political blanket of communism.

It's hard for today's visitors to imagine the gray and bleak Prague of the communist era. Before 1989, the city was a wistful jumble of lost opportunities. Sooty, crusty buildings shadowed cobbled lanes. Thick, dark timbers bridging narrow streets kept decrepit buildings from crumbling. Consumer goods were plain and uniform, stacked like bricks on thin shelves in shops where customers waited in line for a beat-up cabbage, tin of ham, or bottle of ersatz Coke. The Charles Bridge was as sooty as its statues, with a few shady characters trying to change money. Hotels had two-tiered pricing: one for people of the Warsaw Pact nations and another for capitalists. This made the run-down Soviet-style hotels as expensive for most tourists as fine hotels in Western Europe. At the train station, frightened but desperate characters would meet arriving foreigners to rent them a room in their flat. They were scrambling to get enough hard Western cash to buy batteries or Levis at one of the hard-currency stores.

Today, that's all ancient history. The people of Prague are as free and capitalistic as any other citizens of the European Union. They wear their Levis oblivious to how they were once the pants of dreams. The

Prague's Old Town Square

city is fun—slinky with sumptuous Art Nouveau facades, offering tons of cheap Mozart and Vivaldi, and still brewing some of the best beer in Europe.

With every visit, to get oriented, I head for the vast Old Town Square. It's ringed with colorful pastel buildings and dotted with Baroque towers, steeples, and statues. Street performers provide a jaunty soundtrack. Segways dodge horse-drawn carriages crisscrossing the square. At the top of the hour, tourists gather around the towering 15th-century astronomical clock to see a mechanical show of moving figures. With Turks, Jews, bishops, a grim reaper with an hourglass, and a cock crowing, the fears and frustrations of the Middle Ages are on parade every 60 minutes. It must have been an absolute wonder to country folk visiting the big city 500 years ago.

In those days, people were executed for disagreeing with the Catholic Church. The square's focal point, the Jan Hus Memorial, was unveiled in 1915, 500 years after Hus was burned at the stake for heresy. The statue of the Czech reformer stands tall, as he did against both the pope in Rome and the Habsburgs in Vienna. He has become a symbol of the long struggle for Czech freedom.

I continue a few blocks past the Old Town Square to the centerpiece

Prague's pedestrian-only Charles Bridge, crossing the Vltava River

Prague at night

of modern Prague: Wenceslas Square. Looking around, I realize that the most dramatic moments in modern Czech history played out on this stage. The Czechoslovak state was proclaimed here in 1918. In 1969, this is where Jan Palach set himself on fire to protest the puppet Soviet government. And it was here that massive demonstrations led to the overthrow of the communist government in 1989. Czechs filled the square night after night, 100,000 strong, calling for independence. One night, their message was finally heard and the next morning, they woke up a free nation.

After crossing the much-loved Charles Bridge, which spans the Vltava River and links the Old Town and Castle Quarter, I give it my vote for Europe's most pleasant quarter-mile stroll. Commissioned by the Holy Roman Emperor Charles IV in the 1350s, the bridge is a chorus line of time-blackened Baroque statues mixing it up with street vendors and buskers.

Buskers play at Prague Castle.

High above, the hill-topping Prague Castle looks out over the city. The highlight of the castle complex is the cathedral, where locals honor Wenceslas, patron saint of the Czechs, who's buried here. This "good king" of Christmas-carol fame was not a king at all, but a wise, benevolent Duke

Wenceslas Square, where the history of the Czech people plays out

of Bohemia—and another beloved symbol of Czech nationalism for this country that's both new and old.

Every evening, Prague offers tempting reasons to be out and about. Black Light Theater, a combination of illusion, pantomime, puppetry, and modern dance that has no language barrier, is uniquely entertaining. Much like the work of hometown writer Franz Kafka—and, many would say, like the city of Prague itself—Black Light Theater fuses realism, the fantastic, and the absurd. I've capped other evenings with live opera, classical, jazz, and pop music. Crowd-pleasing concerts are hosted nightly in the city's ornate Old Town halls and historic churches, featuring all the greatest hits of Vivaldi, Mozart, and local boys Anton Dvořák and Bedřich Smetana.

What to do after a concert? My Czech friends and I always finish our evening with another mug of that local beer. While I haven't picked up many Czech words, *"Na zdraví!"* ("To your health!") is a must. I always remember it by saying, "Nice driving!" My pronunciation isn't perfect, but that's OK. After raising their mugs a few too many times, I've heard fun-loving Czechs bellowing *"Nádraží!"* (which means "Train station!"). Good to know that tipsy Czechs stumble on their words, too.

A Czech Mud Bath in Třeboň

SUBMERGED IN a mucky peat brine, it occurs to me that this must be the strangest bath I have ever taken.

I'm in the well-preserved Czech spa town of Třeboň. I've decided to supplement my intense time in touristy Prague by venturing south, deeper into the Czech countryside. Třeboň's biosphere of artificial lakes dates back to the 14th century. Over the years, people have transformed what was a flooding marshland into a clever combination of lakes, oak-lined dikes, wild meadows, Baroque villages, peat bogs, and pine woods. Rather than unprofitable wet fields, they wanted ponds that swarmed with fish—and today Třeboň remains the fish-raising capital of the Czech Republic.

People come from near and far to soak in Třeboň's black, smelly peat sludge, thought to cure aching joints and spines. Envisioning the elegance of the baths I've experienced in Germany's Baden-Baden, I decided to give it a whirl. I'm filming a show on the Czech Republic and suspect it will make good TV.

My attendant doesn't understand why I have an entourage (which includes my local guide, Honza, and our two-person TV crew), but she also doesn't pay them much attention. She points to my room and mimes undressing. With the crew here working, I decide to keep my swimsuit on. She shakes her head, disappointed. The camera equipment takes some time to set up. The masseuse is impatient, anxious to get started because the peat muck only flows at the top of the hour. I climb into the stainless-steel tub, she pulls a plug, and I quickly disappear under a

My toes poking out of the mucky bath

rising sea of gurgling sawdust soup. My toes look cute poking out of the hot brown muck.

Filming takes a long time—and this is one of the quirkiest sequences we've ever done for the show. The attendant wants to hurry things along. She acts like I'll overdose if I stay in the tub too long. When we finish shooting, I stand up in the tub and she showers off the sludge, then ushers me into the massage room, where she has me lie face down. It feels like a nurse's office with a pile of dirty sheets stacked in the corner. Honza translates what I'm about to experience as a "hand massage." That sounds redundant at best . . . kinky at worst. He explains that's literally what massages are called in Czech *(ruční masáž)*.

We just want to film my shoulders. But she insists on ignoring the camera's needs and giving me a hand massage from my shoulders to just about where I don't want the camera to go. When the crew gets what they need, they leave. I try to go, too, but my earnest masseuse won't let me. She insists on the full body massage that every patient at the Třeboň spa expects.

After finally being set free, I get dressed. Alone and still covered in greasy oil, I head out to meet my crew at dinner. When you come to Třeboň, you have to try the fish. We order all the appetizers on the menu—a good trick when trying to sample another culture's cuisine.

In Třeboň, you must try the fish.

There's "soused" (which must mean "pickled") herring, fried loach, "stuffed carp sailor fashion," cod liver, pike caviar, and something Honza translates as "fried carp sperm." As we eat, I notice that the writing on my beer glass says, "Bohemia Regent anno 1379." It occurs to me that I'm consuming exactly what people have been eating here for 600 years: fried carp sperm from the nearby reservoir, washed down with the local brew.

Dinner comes with a lively band. They play everything from Bach and Smetana to Czech folk favorites and 1930s anti-fascism blues. The string bass player grooves like a white Satchmo, his long and forceful bow sliding in and out between diners. The bandleader plays a 100-year-old black wood flute. During a break, I run my finger along its smooth mouthpiece—worn down like an ancient marble relic by countless nights of musicmaking. The flutist sports a big bushy mustache just like Emperor Franz Josef, who looks down at us from a yellowed poster.

Above the quartet is a high window. The heads of teenagers bob into sight—they're straining on tiptoes and craning to look in. Each time a song ends, glass mugs of golden beer rattle on rough wood tables as the roaring crowd claps and cheers for more. As the night wears on, there are fewer tourists snapping photos and more locals singing along as the quartet sways together like seaweed in a nostalgic musical tide.

I compliment our server on the beer. He says, "These days, many Poles and Hungarians are going west to France and Germany to get jobs. But not the Czechs. We can't find good enough beer anywhere but here. Our love of Czech beer keeps us from going abroad for better jobs."

The quartet rouses the pub with a mix of spirited tunes.

The wooden flute

Back in my hotel, I climb to my attic room—careful not to bean myself on a thick medieval timber. I lean out my tiny dormer window, the sound of the boisterous bar small in the distance. The new, sturdy roof tiles around me are slick and gleaming with a light rain. The street, wet and shiny, is as clean as a model railroad town. Cars, while not expensive, are new and parked as tidy as can be. Cheap yellow lampposts light the scene. After 40 bleak years of communism, the lampposts seem to be intentionally cheery, decorating the line of pastel facades arcing into the distance. They seem to proclaim a society on track for a brighter future.

Yellow lampposts brighten a street in Třeboň.

Poland's Historic, Captivating Kraków

MY FIRST IMPRESSION of Kraków is that it feels like it must have been really important a long time ago. In fact, it was Poland's capital from the 11th through the 16th century. Within its medieval walls, I wander the Old Town, which converges on the Main Market Square, lined with cafés and gorgeous architecture.

Vast as it is, the square has a folksy intimacy. It bustles with street musicians, cotton-candy vendors, and the lusty coos of pigeons. A folk band, swaggering in colorful peasant costumes, gives me a private concert. Feeling flush—not unusual with the low prices in Poland—I tip them royally. Perhaps too royally. That big tip gets me "The Star-Spangled Banner."

Moments after the band moves on, I hear a bugle call. Glancing around, I pan up to see a trumpet poking out of the tallest tower of the hulking, red-brick St. Mary's Church. Just as I spot the sun glinting off the trumpet's bell, the song stops abruptly and the crowd below applauds appreciatively. I learn that this tune, which is performed every

Kraków's Main Market Square, with St. Mary's Church

A vodka tasting at a bar

hour on the hour, comes with a legend. During the 1241 Tatar invasion, a watchman saw the enemy approaching and sounded the alarm. Before he could finish, an arrow pierced his throat—which is why even today, the music stops, a bloody *subito,* partway through.

This is just one example of Kraków's long history. With the city's power waning, the capital was moved to more centrally located Warsaw in the late 1500s. In the 1800s, Poland was partitioned by neighboring powers. Warsaw ended up as a satellite of oppressive Moscow, the capital of imperial Russia, while Kraków became a poor provincial backwater of Vienna. Austria's comparatively liberal climate helped Kraków become a haven for intellectuals and progressives—including a young Russian revolutionary named Vladimir Lenin.

Kraków emerged from World War II virtually unscathed. But when the communists took over, they decided to give intellectual—and therefore potentially dissident—Kraków an injection of good Soviet values in the form of heavy industry. They built Nowa Huta, an enormous steelworks on the city's outskirts, dooming it to decades of smog.

I'm thankful that Kraków is now much cleaner—and freer—than it was a generation ago. But I'm also thankful that one charming souvenir of communist times does survive: the milk bar *(bar mleczny).* And that's my next stop. The communist government subsidized the food at these cafeterias to provide working-class Poles with an affordable meal out. The tradition continues today, as capitalist Poland still subsidizes milk-bar meals. I head to the counter, point to what I want, and get a quick, hearty, and very cheap meal. The soup is just a dollar. I'm happy to discover that while communist-era fare was gristle and gruel, today's milk-bar cuisine—while still extremely cheap—is much tastier.

Needing something with a little more kick, I wander into Staropolskie Trunki ("Old Polish Drinks"), a friendly little place with a long bar and countless local vodkas—each one open and ready to be sampled. For $5, I get a complete vodka education from a cheery bartender who talks me through five different tastes.

After my private vodka tour, which makes me uncharacteristically giddy so early in the day, I continue walking and end up on Wawel Hill, considered sacred ground as a symbol of Polish royalty and independence. I step into Wawel Cathedral, a stony jungle of memorials that houses the tombs of the country's greatest rulers and historic figures. (While I keep thinking "this is like the Westminster Abbey of Poland," I'm also struck by the ethnocentricity of my Western orientation. I recognize lots of names on the tombs in England and almost none here in Poland.)

Beyond Wawel Hill, I eventually wander into Kazimierz, the city's historic Jewish Quarter. At one time, most of Europe's Jews lived in Poland. Kraków was their social and political base. This is where the big events of World War II intersected with ordinary, everyday lives. Businessman Oskar Schindler ran his factory here, saving the lives of more than a thousand of his Jewish workers. Now his building houses an excellent museum that tells the story of Schindler's list and the painful era of Nazi occupation.

While most travelers come to see Kazimierz's historic museums and synagogues during the day, I stay long enough to see how the neighborhood changes after the sun sets. Throngs of young clubgoers and an ever-changing array of bohemian-chic food trucks and restaurants bring the streets to life after dark.

Reflecting on my day, I think of the ten million Americans who trace their roots to Poland. Those who visit their ancestral homeland must feel at home right away. But today, I realized that you don't have to be Polish to fall in love with Kraków.

Cold War Memories in Budapest

B ACK IN THE 1980s, on a train heading for Budapest, I stood in the aisle with my elbows on the edge of an open window, enjoying the moonlit countryside rushing by. I was soon joined by a Czech woman who was doing the same thing. She told me she was on her first trip out of her country. I asked her if she was excited about visiting Budapest. She said she was most excited about eating a McDonald's hamburger. The buzz throughout Eastern Europe was that Hungary had just opened a branch of the American chain.

If communism was a religion during the Cold War, Budapest was Eastern Europe's sin city, offering tourists from communist countries a taste of the decadent West: rock concerts, Adidas sports gear, and the first McDonald's east of the Iron Curtain. Back then, eating a Big Mac was an act of defiance. There was nothing fast or cheap about Western "fast food." A Happy Meal was a splurge. People traveling from other communist countries to Hungary waited in lines that stretched around the block for a burger, fries, and a Coke. Ronald McDonald stood on the street corner like a heretic prophet, cheering on the downtrodden proletariat, while across the street, wannabe capitalists drooled over window displays featuring running shoes that cost two months' wages.

Communist statues corralled at Memento Park

Budapest's House of Terror

As I visit Budapest today, it's clear that the younger generation of Eastern Europeans has no memory of the communist era. Enough time has passed that former Warsaw Pact nations can take an honest look at the period.

My first stop on this trip is the House of Terror, long the headquarters of communist Hungary's secret police. When the Communists moved into Budapest after World War II, their secret police took over the Nazis' secret police headquarters. It was here that Hungarians suspected of being "enemies of the state" were given sham trials, tortured, and routinely executed. The museum's atrium features a Soviet tank and a vast wall plastered with portraits of victims. Exhibits cover gulag life, Social Realist art, and propaganda. A labyrinth built of pork-fat bricks reminds old-timers of the harsh conditions in the 1950s, when lard on bread was the standard dinner.

I enter the elevator to continue into the museum. As it slowly descends, a guard on video explains the execution process. When the door opens, I step into the basement chambers of torture and death. In 1956, the blood was hosed away and this cellar was made a clubhouse for the local communist

Portraits of victims of the communists

A statue at Memento Park runs
nowhere.

youth club. In the museum today,
it has been restored to its con-
dition circa 1955, with chilling
prison cells instead of ping-pong
tables and chess sets.

In the museum's poignant
finale, the "walls of victimizers"
are lined with the photos and
biographical information of
members and supporters of both
the Nazi and communist secret
police—many of whom are still
living and were never brought to
justice. The House of Terror must be a particularly powerful experience
for elderly Hungarians who actually knew many of the victims of the
secret police . . . and who remain neighbors of the victimizers.

When regimes fall, so do their monuments. Across Eastern Europe,
statues of Stalin, Lenin, and their local counterparts came crashing to
the ground. In Budapest, these stony reminders of communist tyranny
are collected in Memento Park, where tourists flock to get a taste of the
communist era. I head over for a lesson in Social Realism, the art of
communist Europe. Under the communists, art wasn't just censored. It
was acceptable only if it furthered the goals of the state. Aside from a
few important figureheads, individuals didn't matter. Statues featured
the generic working man or working woman. Everyone was a cog in the
machine—unquestioning servants of the nation.

Wandering through Memento Park, I'm entertained by the jumbled
collection of once fearsome and now almost comical statues. While
they seem to preach their ideology to each other, locals and tourists
take funny photos mocking them. The gift shop hawks a fun parade of
communist kitsch. I pick up a Stalin vodka flask and a CD featuring 20
patriotic songs—The Greatest Hits of Communism. It occurs to me that
Stalin—whose estate gets no royalties for all the merchandise featuring
his dour mug—must be spinning in his communist grave.

Walking Dubrovnik's City Walls

JOSTLED BY the crowds, I walk toward the still-stout medieval wall encircling Dubrovnik, deservedly known as the "Pearl of the Adriatic." It's an unforgettable mile-long stroll above the city. While constructed over many centuries, today's impressive fortifications date from the 1400s, when they were beefed up to defend against the Ottoman Turks.

I jockey my way between cruise-excursion groups that have descended upon the town (in good times about 800,000 cruisers stop here each year) and climb the steep steps to the top of the mighty wall. As I begin a slow, circular walk around the fortified perimeter, I'm bombarded with ever-changing views. On one side is a sea of red rooftops; on the other side, the actual sea.

As I approach the wall's formidable gate—the walled city's front door—I pause to enjoy a sweeping view of the Stradun, the 300-yard-long promenade that runs through the heart of the Old Town. In the Middle Ages, merchants lined this drag; before that, it was a canal. Today, it's the city's pedestrian boulevard: an Old World shopping mall by day and sprawling cocktail party after dark.

Strolling atop the wall overlooking Dubrovnik

Dubrovnik's inviting Buža bar, with a seaview terrace

Farther along on my rampart ramble, I look down and see a peaceful stone terrace perched above the sea, clinging like a barnacle to the outside of the city wall. Generously shaded by white umbrellas, this is my favorite Dubrovnik escape, a rustic outdoor tavern called Buža. The name means "hole in the wall"—and that's exactly what customers have to climb through to get there. Filled with mellow bartenders and tourists, Buža comes with castaway views and Frank Sinatra ambience.

Looking inland from my rampart perch, my eyes fall on a random arrangement of bright- and dark-toned red roof tiles. In this complex and once-troubled corner of Europe, even a tranquil stroll comes with a poignant history lesson. After Croatia declared independence from Yugoslavia in 1991, the Yugoslav National Army laid siege to this town and lobbed mortars from the hilltop above. Today, the new, brighter-colored tiles mark houses that were hit and have been rebuilt. At a glance, it's clear that more than two-thirds of the Old Town's buildings suffered bomb damage.

Locals are often willing to talk openly about the bombing, offering a rare opportunity to grasp the realities of war from a survivor's perspective. As I survey the rooftops, my thoughts turn to Pero, my B&B host, who spent years after the war turning the bombed-out remains of his Old Town home into a fine guesthouse.

When I arrived last night, Pero uncorked a bottle of *orahovica,* the local walnut liqueur. Hoping to write that evening with a clear head, I tried to refuse the drink. But this is a Slavic land. Remembering times when new friends force-fed me vodka in Russia, I knew turning Pero down was hopeless. My host had made this hooch himself, with green walnuts. As he slugged down a shot, he handed me a glass, wheezing, "Walnut grappa—it recovers your energy."

Pero reached under the counter and held up the mangled tail of a mortar shell, describing how the gorgeous stone and knotty-wood building he grew up in suffered a direct hit in the siege. He put the mortar in my hands. Just as I don't enjoy holding a gun, I didn't enjoy touching the twisted remains of that mortar. Pero explained that he gets a monthly retirement check for being wounded in the war, but he got bored and didn't want to live on the tiny government stipend, so he went to work rebuilding his guesthouse.

I asked Pero to hold up the mortar for a photograph. As he held up the mortar, he smiled. I didn't want him to smile, but that's what he did. He seemed determined to smile—as if it signified a personal victory over the destruction the mortar had wrought.

Pero holds the mortar . . . and smiles.

It's impressive how people can weather tragedy, rebuild, and move on. In spite of the terrors of war just a couple of decades ago, life here is once again very good—and, as far as Pero is concerned, filled with promise.

The Back Road to Mostar: Off the Beaten Path in Bosnia-Herzegovina

Looking for a change of pace from Croatia's touristic Dalmatian Coast, I'm driving from Dubrovnik east to the city of Mostar, in Bosnia-Herzegovina. Almost everyone making this trip takes the scenic coastal route. But with a spirit of adventure, I take the back road instead: inland first, then looping north through the Serbian part of Herzegovina.

Bosnia-Herzegovina's three main ethnic groups—Serbs, Croats, and Bosniaks—are descended from the same ancestors and speak closely related languages. The key distinction is that they practice different religions: Orthodox Christianity (Serbs), Roman Catholicism (Croats), and Islam (Bosniaks). For the most part, there's no way that a casual visitor can determine the religion or loyalties of the people just by looking at them. Studying the complex demographics of the former Yugoslavia, I gain a grudging respect for the communist-era dictator Tito—the one man who was able to hold this "union of the South Slavs" together peacefully.

Bosnia-Herzegovina is one nation, historically divided into two regions: Bosnia and Herzegovina. But the 1995 Dayton Peace Accords gerrymandered the country along sectarian lines, giving a degree of autonomy to the area where Orthodox Serbs predominate. This "Republika Srpska" rings the core of Bosnia on three sides. When asked for driving tips, Croats—who, because of ongoing tensions with the Serbs, avoid this territory—insist that the road I want to take through their country doesn't even exist. From the main Croatian coastal road just south of Dubrovnik, directional signs would send me to a tiny Croatian border

Farmers market in Nevesinje

town—but ignore the large Serbian city of Trebinje just beyond.

And yet, Trebinje more than exists . . . it is bustling and prosperous. As I enter the city, police with ping-pong paddle stop signs pull me over. I learn that you must drive with your headlights on at all hours. My "dumb tourist" routine gets me off the hook. Parking the car, I head to an outdoor market to get cash at an ATM to buy some produce.

Drinks in Nevesinje

Bosnia-Herzegovina's money is called the "convertible mark." I don't know if they are thrilled that their money is "convertible" into other currencies—but I remember a time when it wasn't. I stow a few Bosnian coins as souvenirs. They have the charm of Indian head pennies and buffalo nickels back in the US. Some bills have Cyrillic lettering and Serbian historical figures, while others use the English alphabet and show Muslims or Croats. Like everything else in Bosnia-Herzegovina, the currency is a careful balancing act.

Later, after a two-hour drive on deserted roads through a rugged landscape, I arrive at the humble crossroads village of Nevesinje. Towns in this region all have a "café row," and Nevesinje is no exception. It's lunchtime, but as I walk through town, I don't see a soul with any food on their plate—just drinks. Apparently, locals eat economically at home, then enjoy an affordable coffee or drink at a café.

Studying graduation photos

A cluttered little grocery is my solution for a quick meal. The old man behind the counter seems happy to make me a sandwich. Salami, which looks like Spam, is the only option. I take my sandwich to an adjacent café and pay the equivalent of a US quarter for a cup of strong Turkish (or "Bosnian") coffee, with highly caffeinated mud at the bottom. Then I munch, drink, and watch the street scene. It's like seeing a play.

Big men drive by in little beater cars. High-school kids crowd around the window of the photography shop, which has just posted their class graduation photos. The flirtatious girls and boys on this cruising drag prove you don't need money to have style. Through a shop window, I see a young couple picking out a simple engagement ring. One moment I think that Nevesinje is very different from my hometown . . . but the next, it seems just the same.

Looking at the curiously overgrown ruined building across the street, I notice its bricked-up, pointed Islamic arches and realize it was once a mosque. Its backyard is a no-man's-land of bombed-out concrete and glass, where a single, turban-topped tombstone still manages to stand. The prayer niche inside, where no one prays anymore, faces east . . . to another empty restaurant.

After an hour's drive over a twisty mountain road, I leave the Republika Srpska and arrive at the city of Mostar. Pulling into town, I'm exhausted yet exhilarated with the experience I gained by taking the road much less traveled.

Mosque destroyed in the Yugoslav Wars in the early 1990s

Mending Bridges in Mostar

THE CITY OF Mostar lies at a crossroads of cultures: just inland from the Adriatic coast, in the southern part of Bosnia-Herzegovina. Mostar's inhabitants are a mix of Orthodox Serbs, Catholic Croats, and Muslim Bosniaks who lived in seeming harmony before the Yugoslav Wars of the 1990s, then suffered horribly when warring neighborhoods turned the city into a killing zone. The persistent reminders of the war make my visit emotionally draining, but I'm hopeful that connecting with the people here will also make it rewarding.

Before the war, Mostar was famous for its 400-year-old, Turkish-style stone bridge. Its elegant, single-pointed arch was a symbol of Muslim society here, and the town's status as the place where East met West in Europe. Then, during the 1990s, Mostar became a poster child for the war. First, the Croats and Bosniaks forced out the Serbs. Then they turned their guns on each other, staring each other down across a front line that ran through the middle of the city. Across the world, people wept when the pummeled Old Bridge—bombarded by Croat

Mostar and its famous bridge, rebuilt after the war

paramilitary artillery shells from the hilltop above—finally collapsed into the river.

Today, I walk over the rebuilt bridge in a city that is thriving. It happens to be prom night. The kids are out, their Bosnian hormones bursting with excitement. Feeling young and sexy is a great equalizer. As long as you have beer, loud music, twinkling stars—and no war—your country's GDP doesn't really matter.

And yet, as I stroll through teeming streets, it's chilling to think that these people—who make me a sandwich, stop for me when I cross the street, show off their paintings, and direct the church choir—were killing each other in a bloody war not so long ago.

Muslim tombstones of war victims

Walking past a small cemetery congested with a hundred white-marble Muslim tombstones, I notice the dates. Everyone died in 1993, 1994, or 1995. This was a park before 1993. When the war heated up, snipers were a constant concern—they'd pick off anyone they saw walking down the street. Bodies were left for weeks along the main boulevard, which had become the deadly front line. Mostar's cemeteries were too exposed, but this tree-filled park was relatively safe from snipers. People buried their loved ones here, under cover of darkness.

While pondering those tombstones, I meet Alen, a 30-something Muslim who emigrated to Florida during the war and is now back home in Mostar. "In those years, night was the time when we lived," he explains. "We didn't walk . . . we ran. And we dressed in black. There was no electricity. If the Croat fighters didn't kill us with their bullets, they drove us mad with their hateful pop music. It was constantly blasting from the Croat side of town."

Alen points to a tree growing out of a ruined building and says, "It's a strange thing in nature: Sweet figs can grow with almost no soil." He seems to be speaking as much about the difficult lot of Mostar's people as its vegetation. There are blackened ruins everywhere. When I ask why, after 15 years, the ruins still stand, Alen explains, "Confusion about who owns what. Surviving companies have no money. The Bank of Yugoslavia, which held the mortgages, is now gone. No one will invest until it's clear who owns the buildings."

Mostar's skyline is tense with symbols of religious conflict. Ten minarets pierce the sky like proud exclamation points. And, across the river, twice as tall as the tallest minaret, stands the Croats' new Catholic church spire. As we hike to the top of the stone bridge, Alen points to the hilltop high above the town marked by a single, bold, and floodlit cross. He says, "We Muslims believe that cross marks the spot from where they shelled this bridge . . . like a celebration."

The next morning, before I leave Mostar, I stop at a tiny grocery store to order a sandwich from a woman I befriended the day before. She's a gorgeous person, sad to be living in a frustrating economy, and unable to bend down because of a piece of shrapnel in her back that doctors decided was safer left in. As she slices the sandwich meat, I bend down to gather carrots and cherries to add to what will be a fine picnic meal on wheels.

On my way out of town, I drive over patched bomb craters in the pavement. In the capital city of Sarajevo, the bomb craters have been filled with red resin—which looks like splattered blood—to commemorate those who died. Here, the craters are patched in black to match the street . . . but because I know what they are, they appear red in my mind.

The High Life and Humble Devotion on Montenegro's Bay of Kotor

AFTER LEAVING Mostar, I drive south to yet another new nation that emerged newly independent from the ashes of Yugoslavia: Montenegro. During my travels through this region, my punch-drunk passport has been stamped, stamped, and stamped again. While the unification of Europe has made most border crossings feel archaic, here the breakup of Yugoslavia has kept them in vogue. Every time the country splintered, another border was drawn. The poorer the country, it seems, the more ornate the border formalities. By European standards, Montenegro is about as poor as it gets. They don't even have their own currency. With just 600,000 people, they decided, "Heck, let's just use euros."

For me, Montenegro, whose name means "Black Mountain," has always evoked the fratricidal chaos of a bygone age. I think of a time when fathers in the Balkans taught their sons that "your neighbor's neighbor is your friend" in anticipation of future sectarian struggles. Back then, for generation after generation, So-and-so-ovich was pound-

Montenegro's Bay of Kotor

ing on So-and-so-ovich, so a secure mountain stronghold like this was worth all of that misery.

A recent visit showed me that this image is now dated. The country is on an upward trajectory. Many expect to see Montenegro emerge as a sunny new hotspot on the Adriatic coastline. International investors (mostly from Russia and Saudi Arabia) are pouring money into what they hope will become their very own Riviera.

Unfortunately, when rich people paste a glitzy facade onto the crumbling infrastructure of a poor country that isn't ready for it, you get a lot of pizzazz with no substance. I stayed at a supposedly "designer" hotel that, at first glance, felt so elite and exclusive that I expected to see Idi Amin poolside. But the hotel, open just a month, was a comedy of horrible design. I felt like I was their first guest ever. My bathroom was far bigger than many European hotel rooms, but the toilet was jammed in the corner. I had to tuck up my knees to sit on it. A big hot tub for two dominated the bathroom, but there wasn't enough hot water available to fill it. I doubt it will ever be used—except as something to ponder as you sit crunched up on the toilet.

A huge thunderstorm hit with enough fury to keep the automatic glass doors opening and closing on their own. Nothing drained— a torrent cascaded down the stairs and through the front door. The rain also brought a backed-up sewage smell that drove me out of my room. And just as I sat down for a cup of coffee in the lounge, the lights went out. Peering past the candelabra on my table, the overwhelmed receptionist explained with a shrug, "When it rains, there is no electricity." The man who ran the place just looked at me and said, "Cows." (I think he meant "chaos.")

Visiting the island church by boat

Eventually the rain stopped, the clouds parted, and I went out to explore. My first stop was the Bay of Kotor, where the Adriatic cuts into steep mountains like a Norwegian fjord. At the humble waterfront town of Perast, young guys in swim trunks edged their boats near the dock, jockeying to motor tourists out to the island in the middle of the bay. According to legend, fishermen saw the Virgin Mary in the reef and began a ritual of dropping a stone on the spot each time they sailed by. Eventually the island we see today was created and upon that island, the people built a fine little church.

I hired a guy with a dinghy to ferry me out to the island where I was met by a young woman who gave me a tour of the church. In the sacristy hung a piece of embroidery—a 20-year-long labor of love made by a local parishioner 200 years ago. It was exquisite, lovingly made with the finest materials available: silk and the woman's own hair. I could trace her laborious progress through the line of cherubs that ornamented the border. As the years went by, the hair of the angels (like the hair of the devout artist) turned from dark brown to white. Humble and anonymous as she was, she had faith that her work was worthwhile—and two centuries later, it's appreciated by a steady parade of travelers from distant lands.

Silk and hair: a labor of love and devotion

I've been at my work for more than three decades now and my hair is also getting a little gray. I have a faith that it—my work, if not my hair—will be appreciated after I'm gone. That's perhaps less humble than the woman was, but her work reminds me that we can live on through our deeds. Her devotion to her creation (as well as to her creator) is an inspiration to do both good and lasting work. While traveling, I'm often struck by how people give meaning to their lives by contributing what they can.

I didn't take a photograph of the embroidery that day. For some reason, I didn't even take notes. At the time, I didn't realize I was experiencing the highlight of my trip. The impression of the woman's tenderly created embroidery needed time to breathe—like a good red wine. That was a lesson for me. I was already moving on to the next stop. When the power of the impression did open up in my mind, it was rich and full-bodied . . . but I was long gone.

If travel is going to have the impact on you that it should, you have to climb into those little dinghies to discover those experiences. The best encounters won't come to you. And you have to let them breathe.

Montenegro: A poor country rich in culture and natural beauty

Greece and Turkey

LET'S JOURNEY to the southeastern fringe of Europe: offbeat Greece, a celebration of Istanbul, and the distant east of Turkey.

In Greece, the Peloponnese Peninsula mixes ancient sights, a harsh and sparsely inhabited southern coast, and my favorite Greek city, Nafplio. The isle of Hydra, where roosters are alarm clocks and donkeys are taxis, is a car-free wonderland just a quick ferry ride from Athens.

Istanbul is striving to organize—adding lines on the mosque carpet and assigning seats in the minibus taxis. But the city's deep-seated organic chaos and rough edges persist, making it as enchanting as ever.

Farther east in Turkey is a world where commerce can be summed up in three words: "hay, dung, and ducks." Many villagers still think of electricity as new. Women wear scarves, shepherds play eagle-bone flutes, and every gathering comes alive with the promise of dancing.

Athens' Temple of Olympian Zeus

Greece's Underrated Peloponnese Peninsula

AT A BEACHSIDE restaurant, with my chair and table lodged in the sand, I hear a repetitive beat and feel a faint but refreshing spritzing. Looking around for the source, I see a tough young Greek man in a swimsuit the size of a rat's hammock. He's tenderizing an octopus by whipping it like a wet rag, over and over, on a big flat rock. That octopus will be featured soon for dinner . . . someone else's dinner.

Octopus drying in the sun

I order moussaka and—to be emphatically Greek—a glass of Greece's infamous, resin-flavored *retsina* wine. It makes me want to sling a patch over one eye and say, "Argh!" It's like drinking wood. A vintner once told me there's no such thing as a $50 bottle of fine Greek wine. I asked him, "What should I buy if I want to spend $30?" He paused, shrugged, and said, "Three bottles."

Taking another sip of *retsina*, I think that, like its wine, the Peloponnese is rough, but with a complex history. I'm pondering where to go next. Hordes of tourists flock to the Greek islands, unaware of the salty pleasures awaiting right here, on this peninsula—without requiring a ferry ride or flight. Stretching southwest from Athens and studded with antiquities, this ancient land offers plenty of fun in the eternal Greek sun, with pleasant fishing villages, sandy beaches, bathtub-warm water, and none of the tourist crowds.

I could go to the charming port town of Nafplio. It's small, cozy, and strollable, with great pensions, appealing restaurants, a thriving evening scene, and inviting beaches nearby. As the first capital of an independent Greece, it's historically important, and it's a handy base for touring the ancient sites at Mycenae and Epidavros.

Nafplio's harbor is guarded by a castle capping a tall cliff above the city. It's an old Venetian outpost, built in the days when Venice was the economic ruler of this end of the Mediterranean. On my last visit, I looked down from its highest ramparts, spying distant islands and peering deep into the mountainous interior of the Peloponnese. Looking down at the town, I noticed that the locals weren't climbing the castle steps; they were drinking tall iced coffees called frappés. Evidently, they had decided that the best-preserved castle of its kind in Greece is well-worth the thousand steps . . . once.

East of Nafplio, Epidavros has the most magnificent theater from the ancient world. It was built nearly 2,500 years ago to seat 15,000. Today, it's kept busy with tourists by day and reviving the greatest plays of antiquity at night. The theater's marvelous acoustics are best enjoyed in near solitude. On my last visit, I sat in the most distant seat as my partner stood on the stage. I could practically hear the *retsina* rumbling in her stomach.

Just north of Nafplio are the ruins of Mycenae. This was the capital of the Mycenaeans, who won the Trojan War and dominated Greece 1,000 years before its Golden Age. That means that for 3,000 years, people have stood before this stony citadel and gaped at its fabled Lion's Gate.

Mycenae's massive Lion's Gate, Cyclopean architecture circa 1250 BC

It was made with stones so huge that it was long believed that no man could have built it. It must have been the work of the Cyclopes—so it was called "Cyclopean architecture." Nearby, the *tholos* tomb, built in 1500 BC, stands like a giant stone igloo, with a smooth subterranean dome nearly 50 feet tall and wide. Standing alone under that dome, I realized that the people who built it were as ancient and mysterious to Socrates and Plato as Socrates and Plato are to us.

Another possibility is ancient Olympia. Modern tourists just can't resist lining up for photos on the original starting block from the first Olympic Games in 776 BC. The games were held as part of a religious festival, but also served a political purpose: to develop a Panhellenic ("cross-Greek") identity. Every four years, wars between bickering Greeks were halted for a sacred one-month truce, when leading citizens from all corners would assemble to watch the athletes compete. It was a hard-fought competition with strict rules. Drinking animal blood—the Red Bull of the day—was forbidden. Official urine drinkers tested for this ancient equivalent of steroids.

Further on, the Peloponnese boasts impressive remnants of Byzantine rule. Monemvasia, a colossal Gibraltar-like rock jutting up from the sea, has a romantic walled town at its base and ruins sprawling across

Inside a Mycenaean tomb—the greatest dome of its day

Ancient theater at Epidavros, renowned for its acoustics

its summit. In its 14th-century heyday, Monemvasia was one of the great commercial centers of the Byzantine Empire. The walled town is so well-preserved that, until I actually visited, I was convinced an aerial view I saw featured on a postcard was a computer-produced fantasy.

Wiping the salty spray from my glasses, I realize I haven't made much progress in deciding where to go next. I'm worried: The *retsina* is starting to taste good. I'm finishing my third glass, entering the danger zone. If I drink any more, I'll reek of it tomorrow . . . and never get around to tasting the other charms of the Peloponnese.

Monemvasia, rising from the sea

Cockcrow on Hydra

THE GREEK ISLAND of Hydra—just an hour by fast ferry from Athens—has one town, a quaint little harbor, isolated beaches, and some tavernas. There are no real roads, no cars, and not even any bikes. Other than zippy water taxis, donkeys are the only form of transportation. Slow and steady, these surefooted beasts of burden—laden with everything from sandbags and bathtubs to bottled water—climb the island's stepped lanes. On Hydra, a traffic jam is three donkeys and a fisherman.

In addition to the tired burros, this is a land of tiny cats and roosters with big egos. While it's generally quiet, dawn has taught me the exact meaning of "cockcrow." The end of night is marked by much more than a distant cock-a-doodle-doo: It's a dissonant chorus of cat fights, burro honks, and what sounds like roll call at an asylum for crazed roosters. After the animal population gets that out of its system, the island slumbers a little longer, as if hitting "snooze."

This afternoon, I've decided to head uphill, with no intention of anything more than a lazy stroll. One inviting lane after another draws me up, up, up . . . At the top of the town, shabby homes enjoy grand views, burros amble along untethered, and island life trudges on, oblivious to tourism.

Over the crest, I follow a paved riverbed (primed for the flash floods that fill village cisterns each winter) down to the remote harbor hamlet of Kaminia—where 20 tough little fishing boats jostle, corralled within a breakwater. Children jump fearlessly from rock to rock to the end of the jetty, ignoring an old man rhythmically casting his line.

A rickety woven-straw chair

Hydra has burros, not cars.

The port town of Hydra

and a tipsy little table at Kodylenia's Taverna are positioned just right, overlooking the harbor. The sun, as if promising a worthwhile finale to another fine day, commands, "Sit." I do, sipping ouzo and observing a sea busy with taxi boats, the "flying dolphin" hydrofoils that connect people here with Athens, freighters—like castles of rust—lumbering slowly along the horizon, and a cruise ship anchored as if threatening to attack.

This cloudy glass of ouzo, my anise-flavored drink of choice, and the plastic baggie of pistachios I purchased back in town are a perfect complement to the setting sun. An old man flips his worry beads, backlit by the golden glitter on the harbor. Blue and white fishing boats jive with the chop. I swear the cats—small, numerous, and oh so slinky—are watching the setting sun with me. My second glass of ouzo comes with a smudge of someone's big fat Greek lipstick. I decide not to worry about it before taking a sip that seems to connect me with the scene even more.

As twilight falls, my waiter brings a candle for my table. He lingers to tell me he returned here to his family's homeland after spending 20 years in New Jersey, where he "never took a nap." The soft Greek lounge music tumbling out of the kitchen mixes everything like an audio swizzle stick. Downing the last of my ouzo, I glance over my shoulder to the coastal lane that leads back to my hotel . . . thankfully, it's lamplit.

Walking back under a ridge lined with derelict windmills, I try to envision Hydra before electricity, when it was powered only by wind and burros. At the edge of town, I pass the Sunset Bar, filled with noisy cruise-ship tourists, which makes me thankful I took the uphill lane when I left my hotel. Resting on a ferry cleat the size of a stool, I scan the harbor. Big flat-screen TVs flicker on the bobbing yachts moored for the night.

Back in Hydra town, I observe the pleasant evening routine of strolling and socializing. Dice clatter on dozens of backgammon boards at tavernas, entrepreneurial dogs seek out scraps, ball-kicking children make a playground out of a back lane, and a tethered goat chews on something inedible. From the other end of town comes the happy music of a christening party. Dancing women fill the building, while their children mimic them in the street. Farther down, two elderly, black-clad women sit like tired dogs on the curb.

Succumbing to the lure of a pastry shop, I sit down for what has become my day-ending ritual: honey-soaked baklava. I tell the cook I'm American.

"Oh," he says, shaking his head with sadness and pity. "You work too hard."

I answer, "Right. But not today."

Sipping ouzo by the sea

Déjà Vu in Istanbul

WHEN I WAS in my twenties, I ended eight European trips in a row in Turkey. I didn't plan it that way—but it became the natural finale, the subconscious cherry on top of each year's travel adventures. Realizing I haven't set foot in Istanbul for nearly a decade, I have decided to return to the city where East meets West. Comparing today's Istanbul with the city that lives in my memories, will I find comforting similarities or jarring differences?

The moment I step off the plane, I remember how much I enjoy this country. Marveling at the efficiency of Istanbul's Atatürk Airport, I pop onto the street and into a yellow *taksi*. Seeing the welcoming grin of the unshaven driver, who greets me with a toothy *"Merhaba,"* I blurt out, *"Çok güzel!"* I'm surprised I remember the phrase. It just comes out of me—like a baby shouts for joy. I am back in Turkey, and it is "very beautiful" indeed.

As the *taksi* turns off the highway and into the tangled lanes of the tourist zone—just below the Blue Mosque—all the tourist-friendly businesses still line up, providing a backdrop for their chorus line of barkers shouting, "Yes, Mister!"

I look at the scruffy kids in the streets and remember a rougher time,

Hağia Sophia, in Istanbul—for centuries the grandest place of worship in all of Europe

when kids like these would earn small change by hanging out the passenger door of ramshackle minibuses. The name for these vehicles—a wild cross between a taxi and a bus—is *dolmuş,* literally and appropriately translated as "stuffed." The boys would yell out the name of the destination in a scramble to stuff in more passengers. I can still hear my favorite call, for the train-station neighborhood: "Sirkeci, Sirkeci, Sirkeci" (SEER-kay-jee). While Turkey's new affluence has nearly killed the *dolmuş,* the echoes of the boys hollering from the vans bounce happily in my memory: "Topkapi, Topkapi, Topkapi . . . Sultanahmet, Sultanahmet, Sultanahmet."

I pay my *taksi* driver and step out into the Sultanahmet neighborhood, stopping for a cup of tea to get my bearings. From my teahouse perch, I watch old men shuffle by, carrying nothing, but walking as if still bent under the towering loads they had carried all of their human-beast-of-burden lives. Istanbul, now with a population of more than 15 million, is thriving. The city is poignantly littered with both remnants of grand empires and living, breathing reminders of the harsh reality of life in the developing world.

And yet, this ancient city is striding into the future. Everyone is buzzing about the new tunnel under the Bosphorus, which gives a million commuters in the Asian suburbs of Istanbul an easy train link to their places of work in Europe. This tunnel is emblematic of modern Turkey's commitment to connecting East and West, just as Istanbul bridges Asia and Europe. I also see it as a concrete example of how parts of the developing world are emerging as economic dynamos.

Walking down to the Golden Horn inlet and Istanbul's churning waterfront, I cross the new Galata Bridge, which makes me wistful for the old bridge—now dismantled—which was crusty with life's struggles. I think of how all societies morph with the push and pull of the times. While the beloved old bridge is gone, the new one has been engulfed in the same vibrant street life—boys casting their lines, old men sucking on water pipes, and steaming sesame-seed bread rings fogging up the panes of their glass-windowed carts. It reminds me how stubborn cultural inertia can be.

On the sloppy harborfront, the venerable "fish and bread boats" are still rocking in the constant chop of the busy harbor. In a humbler day, they were 20-foot-long open dinghies—rough boats with battered car tires for fenders—with open fires for grilling fish . . . fish that's literally fresh off the boat. For a few coins, the fishermen would bury a big white fillet in a hunk of fluffy bread, wrap it in newsprint, and send me on my way. In recent years, the fish and bread boats were shut down because they had no license. After a popular uproar, they've returned—a bit more hygienic, no longer using newspaper for wrapping, but still rocking in the waves and slamming out fresh fish.

Inside the Blue Mosque

As the sun sets and evening prayer time approaches, I hike through teeming streets to the iconic Blue Mosque. The outer courtyard is crowded with families—worshipful parents and kids looking for entertainment. Two schoolboys high-five me and try out their only English phrase: "What is your name?" I answer, "Seven o'clock" and enjoy their quizzical look. I'm struggling to understand their society; they can deal with a little confusion as well.

Wandering under stiletto minarets, I listen as a hardworking loudspeaker—lashed to the minaret as if to a religious crow's nest—belts out a call to prayer. Noticing the twinkling lights strung up in honor of the holy month of Ramadan, I think, "Charming—they've draped Christmas lights between the minarets." (A Turk might come to my house and say, "Charming—he's draped Ramadan lights on his Christmas tree.")

The Blue Mosque offers a warm welcome. Stepping out of my shoes, I enter the vast space—more turquoise than blue—hoping for déjà vu that never comes. Something's missing. Gone is the smell of countless sweaty socks, knees, palms, and foreheads that had soaked into the ancient carpet from worshippers' energetic, physical prayer workouts. Sure enough, the Blue Mosque has a fresh new carpet—with a subtle design that keeps worshippers organized in the same way that lined notepaper tames written letters.

As the prayer service lets out, I'm caught up in a sea of Turks that surges toward the door. This is the kind of connecting-with-humanity moment that I seek out. It's the closest I'll ever come to experiencing the exhilaration of bodysurfing above a mosh pit. As I surf the flow of worshippers through the gate and out into the street, the only way to get any personal space is to look up into the sky. Doing that, I enjoy another prized memory . . . another Istanbul déjà vu: Hard-pumping seagulls flap their wings through the humid air in the dark sky before surging into the light, crossing and then circling the floodlit minarets.

The Hippodrome—a long, oblong plaza shaped like a chariot race-course, as was its purpose 18 centuries ago—is invigorated by the multi-generational conviviality of the Ramadan crowds emptying out of the mosque. While the crowd seems to be gaining energy, I'm running out of steam. But before heading back to my hotel, I look for a teahouse to follow my end-of-day ritual.

My rice-pudding ritual

I established this ritual in visits to Turkey as a backpacking student and I return to it now. I cap my day with a bowl of *sütlaç:* rice pudding with a sprinkle of cinnamon. It's still served in a square steel bowl with a small matching spoon. Another part of the ritual: I don't let a Turkish day go by without enjoying a teahouse game of backgammon with a stranger. Looking at the board tonight, I notice that it's cheap and mass-produced, almost disposable.

Today's dice—plastic and factory-perfect—make me miss the tiny handmade "bones" of the 20th century, with their disobedient dots. But some things never change. To test a fun cultural quirk, I toss my dice and pause. As I knew would happen, a bystander moves for me. When it comes to backgammon, there's one right way . . . and everybody knows it. And in Turkey, perhaps as a result of its ruthless history, when starting a new game, the winner of the last game goes first.

Playing backgammon—a great way to connect with the Turks

With each backgammon game, I think of one of my most precious possessions back home: an old-time, hand-hewn, inlaid backgammon board, with rusty little hinges held in place by hasty tacks, and soft, white wood worn deeper than the harder, dark wood. Twenty years after taking that backgammon board home, I open it and still smell the tobacco, tea, and soul of a traditional Turkish teahouse.

There's almost nothing in my world that is worn or has been enjoyed long enough to absorb the smells of my life and community. It's a reminder to me of the cost of modernity. At home, the feel and smell of my old backgammon board takes me back to Turkey. And when it does, I'm reminded how, in the face of all that modernity, the endangered though resilient charm of traditional cultures—anywhere in our world—is something to value.

Today in Turkey, the people—like those dots on the modern dice—line up better. The weave of a mosque carpet brings order. There's a seat for everyone on the *dolmuş*, which is no longer so stuffed. Fez sales to tourists are way down, but the use of scarves worn by local women (a symbol of traditional Muslim identity) is way up. As I get caught up in moments of déjà vu, I realize that Turkish society—like American society—is confronting powerful forces of change and progress while also wanting to stay the same.

Ducks, Dung, and Hay in Eastern Turkey

I'M IN KASTAMONU, five hours northeast of the Turkish capital of Ankara. It's a town that has yet to figure out the business of tourism. The business hotel where I'm staying is cheap and comfortable, but not slick. I hand a postcard to the boy at the desk, hoping he can mail it for me. He looks it over a couple of times on both sides, compliments me, and politely hands it back. As I leave, he raises his right hand and says, "Hello."

While changing money, I'm spotted by the bank manager, who invites me into his office for tea. I am his first American customer, so he wants to celebrate.

Outside, a gaggle of men wearing grays, blacks, and browns is shuffling quietly down the street in a funeral procession. A casket floats over them as each man jostles to the front to pay his respects by "giving it a shoulder." Turkey is a land of ceremonies. Everyday life here is punctuated with colorful, meaningful events. I'm always on the lookout, traveling with sharp eyes, hoping to add to my knowledge of the folk

They're as interesting to me as I am to them.

culture. Who knows, as the dust from the funeral procession clears, I may see a proud eight-year-old boy dressed like a prince or a sultan on a horse—riding to his ritual circumcision.

My plan is to continue driving inland, exploring further into Anatolia. While Istanbul and the western coast get the lion's share of Turkey's tourism, I'm looking for maximum cultural thrills, so I know I should head east.

Under 10,000-foot peaks, my guide and I drive up onto the burnt, barren, 5,000-foot-high Anatolian plateau to Erzurum, the main city of eastern Turkey. Life is hard here. Blood feuds, a holdover from justice under the Ottomans, are still a leading cause of imprisonment. Winters are below-zero killers. Villages spread out onto the plateau like brown weeds, each with the same economy: ducks, dung, and hay. But Allah has given this land some pleasant surprises. It's a harsh land, but gentle at the same time. The parched plain hides lush valleys where rooftops sport colorful patches of sun-dried apricots. You can crack open the sweet, thin-shelled hazelnuts with your teeth. Teenage boys prefer girls who dress modestly and shepherd children still play the eagle-bone flute.

Entering a village, we pass under a banner announcing, "No love is better than the love for your land and your nation." The town takes us warmly into its callused hands. A man with a donkey cart wheels us on an impromptu tour. Each house wears a tall hat of hay—food for the cattle and insulation for the winter. Mountains of cow pies are neatly stacked, promising warmth and cooking fuel for the six months of snowed-in winter on the way. Veiled mothers strain to look through my camera's viewfinder to see their children's mugging faces. The town's annually elected policeman brags that he keeps the place safe from terrorists. Children scamper around women who are busy beating raw wool with sticks—a rainbow of browns that will one day be woven into a carpet to soften a stone sofa, warm up a mud-brick wall, or serve as a daughter's dowry.

Driving east from Erzurum, we set our sights on the northeast corner of Turkey, marked by the 17,000-foot summit of Mount Ararat. Villages growing between ancient rivers of lava expertly milk the land

Making friends in Turkey as a teen

for subsistence living. After a quick reread of the flood story in Genesis, I think that this stark, sun-drenched, and windswept land has changed little since Noah docked.

On a ridge high above our car, I can make out the figure of a lone man silhouetted against a bright blue sky waving at us. The sight reminds me that this is a part of West Asia where mighty nations come together, denying the Kurds who live here a land of their own. The lone sentry is one of 10 million Kurdish Turks; many of them would like their own country. The turmoil in Iraq—and the prospect that those Kurds could form an autonomous nation—has reignited this prickly issue. One thing is for sure: Turkey does not want to share a border with an independent Kurdistan.

When I get up early the next morning to see the sun rise over Mount Ararat, I also see a long convoy of Turkish army vehicles. It reminds me that our world is a complicated place in which the daily news is just a shadow play of reality. What's so often missing is humanity. And to get that, you need to travel.

Enjoying the same hospitality now

Laz-pitality in Northeastern Turkey

I'M IN northeastern Turkey, the world's top hazelnut-producing region and home of the Laz people. It's located along the Black Sea coast, where it rains 320 days a year. And I'm enjoying an enthusiastic welcome, discovering that the locals ambush visitors with unforgettable warmth and a wide-eyed curiosity.

My tour group, which includes 22 American travelers and a Turkish co-guide, has been invited to spend an evening and a night with a Laz family—actually the families of three brothers, who all live in one large three-story house provided to them by their elderly parents. We are the first Americans that the 16 people who live there have ever seen in the flesh. They ask us to make ourselves comfortable. Adding our shoes to the pile by the door creates a thought-provoking commotion of high-tech American travel gear mixing it up with woven village footwear. Overlapping carpets are warm under our feet, giving the place a cozy bug-in-a-rug feel.

We are treated to a feast. As American visitors, we're elevated to a kind of royal status. Only the older men eat with us as women serve

Meeting a Laz family

and teens peek curiously from just outside the doors. Meanwhile, the little kids frolic freely, as if we were from just next door. The bread is fresh from the oven and hearty. The meat is dark and abundant—as if serving it is showing off wealth. And the salad puts me in that awkward space of not wanting to disappoint my hosts while not wanting to upset my stomach. As we praise the stuffed peppers, members of our group—in anticipation of tummy-troubles later—discreetly pass Pepto-Bismol tablets around under the table. The pouring tea doesn't quite mask the sound of ripping cellophane.

We enjoy some conversation as our meal digests. Having an interpreter helps with communication here, but it's not required. Somehow, communication happens. Many younger Turks speak English and many older Turks, having worked in Germany, speak German. Especially in small towns, their curiosity and eagerness to connect makes the language barrier fun to hurdle. If Turkish sounds tough, remember, it's the same in reverse. Certain sounds, like our "th," are tricky. (My friend Ruth is entertained by the tortured attempts Turks make at pronouncing her name: "Woooott.") Any English-speaking Turk can remember spending long hours looking into the mirror like a wide-mouth frog, slowly enunciating: "This and these are hard to say. I think about them every day. My mouth and my teeth, I think you see, help me say them easily."

After dinner, we pay our respects to the frail, bed-ridden grandma, looking like a veiled angel in white. She and her family know she will soon succumb to her cancer. But for now, she is overjoyed to see such a happy evening filling her family's home.

When we wonder about the wisdom of having an extended family under one roof, one of the sons says, "If a day goes by when we don't see each other, we are very sad." The three brothers married three sisters from a single family so that they would share the same in-laws—and assure harmony in the family. They also assure us that entertaining our group of 22 is no problem. If we weren't here, they'd invite just as many of their neighbors in for dinner.

No Turkish gathering is complete without dancing. Anyone who can snap fingers and swing a Hula-Hoop can be comfortable on the

Care to dance? Just snap your fingers and shake your shoulders.

living-room dance floor of new Turkish friends. Two aunts, deaf and mute from meningitis, bring the house down, with their shoulders fluttering like butterflies. We dance and talk with four generations until after midnight.

Stepping out into the late-night breeze, I notice that what had seemed to be just a forested hillside during the day is now a spangled banner of lights, each representing a Muslim home filled with as many family values as the one we joined this evening. So much for the stereotypical image of fanatical Muslim hordes embraced by my TV-addicted neighbors back home with no passports.

The next morning, before we leave, our friends toss a gunnysack of hazelnuts into our bus. Venturing on, we drive toward the far eastern edge of the country. For decades, this eastern end of Turkey's Black Sea coast was a dead end, butting up against the closed border of Soviet Georgia. But these days, rather than foreboding guard posts, the former USSR is ringed with sprawling "Russian markets."

We meet people, not stereotypes.

When tough times hit this region of the former USSR, boxy Lada automobiles, overloaded with the lowest class of garage-sale junk, careened toward the nearest border on a desperate mission to scrape together a little hard cash. We reach the Turkish coastal town of Trabzon, where 300 yards of motley tarps and blankets display

Turkish Laz-pitality

grandpa's tools, pink and yellow *champagnski,* comically tangled electrical gadgetry, battered samovars, fur hats, and Caspian caviar (the blue lid is best). A Georgian babushka with a linebacker's build, caked-on makeup, and bleached-blonde hair offers us a wide selection of Soviet pins, garish plastic flowers, and practically worthless ruble coins.

To satisfy my group's strange appetite for godforsaken border crossings, we continue out to the Georgian border. No one knows if we can cross or not. As far as the Turkish official is concerned, "Visa? No problem." We venture through the mud, past pushcarts bound for flea markets and huge trucks mired in red tape. In this strange economic no-man's-land, the relative prosperity of Muslim Turkey is clear. A sharp little Turkish mosque with an exclamation-point minaret seems to holler across the border to Georgia, "You sorry losers, we'll buy your junk." Young Georgian soldiers with hardly a button on their uniforms check identity cards and those who qualify for entry squeeze past the barbed wire and through the barely open gate. A soldier tells us we can't pass. In search of a second opinion, we fetch an officer who says, "Visa no, problem"— a negative that, earlier, we misinterpreted as a positive.

Kind of relieved that our silly mission failed, we turn around, confident we'll soon be enjoying more warm Turkish Laz-pitality.

Güzelyurt: Beautiful Land

EXPLORING Cappadocia's Ihlara Valley, famous for its poplar groves, soaring eagles, patient vultures, and early Christian churches, I've come to Güzelyurt. Known in Turkey as the town where historic enemies—Greeks and Turks—live in peace, it's a harmony of cultures, history, architecture, and religions. Strolling streets that have changed little over millennia, I overhear neighbors chatting convivially. A black bust of Atatürk, carved from the local volcanic stone, looms high over the small modern market square. Cafés are alive with the relaxed clicks of *tavla* (backgammon) pieces. Men on the street seem to be enjoying one eternal cigarette break, proudly making a point not to stare at the American visitors searching for postcards in this town with almost no tourism.

Leaving the center I hike steeply down into a ravine, winding through a community in the rough—where the chores of daily life seemed stuck in the Middle Ages. While rampaging Ottomans are a thing of the distant past, scowling sheepdogs, caged behind 10-foot-high troglodyte rockeries, add just enough tension to give my exploration a sense of adventure.

Climbing beyond the ravine to a little hilltop, I reach the end of town and a view of the snowy slopes of the Fuji-like volcano that rules the

Family transportation

horizon. From this perch, the vista extends back over the lush and densely populated gorge I have just explored. Retracing my steps visually back up that steep ravine, I notice how the gorge is stacked with building styles: Upon a 1,600-year-old church are those troglodyte caves, then Selçuk arches, and Ottoman facades. And atop everything, breaking the horizon, gleams the tin dome of a 20th-century mosque, with its twin minarets giving a constant visual call to prayer. The honey that holds this architectural baklava together is the community of people who live here, struggling to live well while honoring their past.

I put my camera away and sit silently to take in the sounds of the village. It's an ancient soundtrack—the timeless white noise of daily life: Children laugh, birds chirp, roosters crow, shepherds chase goats, and mothers cackle. (I ignore that distant motorbike.)

Below me, sleeping in the soft greens and wet browns of this tide pool of simple living, is the church of St. Gregorius. Built in 385, it's thought to be the birthplace of church music, specifically the Gregorian chant. Its single minaret indicates that it functions as a mosque today in a valley where people now call God "Allah."

Averse to change, small towns are cultural humidors—keeping fragile traditions moist and full of local flavor. The last time I was here, Güzelyurt was all decked out for everybody's favorite festival: a circumcision party. It's a wonderful celebration. Turks call it "a wedding without the in-laws." The little boy, dressed like a prince, rode tall on his decorated horse through a commotion of friends and relatives to the house where a doctor was sharpening his knife. Even with paper money pinned to his fancy outfit and loved ones chanting calming spiritual music, the boy looked frightened. But the ritual snipping went off without a hitch, and a good time was had by . . . well, at least, by everyone else.

A boy on his way to his (gulp) circumcision party

On a different trip, I was a special guest at a Güzelyurt wedding. The entire community gathered. Calling the party to order, the oldest couple looked happily at the young bride and groom and shared a local blessing: "May you grow old together on one pillow." At a wedding or at any family festival, village Turks turn on the music and dance. Everybody is swept onto their feet—including visiting tourists. It's easy: Just follow the locals as they hold out their arms, snap their fingers, and shimmy their shoulders.

During another party, the man of the house came over to me—the foreigner—and wanted to impress me. Waving me to a quiet corner, he said, "Here on my wall, the most sacred place in my home, is my Quran bag, where I keep my Quran. And in my Quran bag I also keep a copy of the Bible and a copy of the Torah—because I believe that we Muslims, Christians, and Jews are all 'people of the Book' . . . children of the same good God." While the dancing continued, I practiced my Turkish with a wide-eyed six-year-old girl. She showed me a handful of almonds and said what I first heard as "Buy dem." But she was selling nothing. *Badam* is Turkish for "almond," and this was her gift to me.

Enjoying her munchies, I reciprocated with a handful of Pop Rocks. As the tiny candies exploded in her mouth, her eyes widened with surprise.

Leaving those memories behind, I continue wandering. As I walk further along, the town becomes cluttered with ugly unfinished concrete buildings bristling with rusty reinforcement bars. The first time I saw them, I couldn't help but think, "Why can't these people get their act together and just finish these buildings?" That was before I learned that in Turkey, there's an ethic among parents—even poor ones—that you leave your children with a house. Historically, Turks have been reluctant to store money in the bank because it devalues with inflation. So instead, they invest bit by bit by constructing a building. Every time they get a hundred bucks together, they put it into that ever-growing house. They leave the rebar exposed until they have another hundred bucks, when they make another wall, put on a window, frame in another door . . . and add more rebar. Now, looking at that rusty rebar, I remember that Turks say, "Rebar holds the family together." It's no longer ugly to me.

Continuing on, after a short walk out of town, I come upon a little boy playing a flute as his mother cooks. It's carved out of an eagle bone, just like in biblical times. Listening, I hear another flute, out of sight,

Meeting with an imam in a mosque

coming from over the hill. Hiking farther, I see his dad tending the sheep. As boys like him have done for centuries, the son stays with the mom and plays the eagle-bone flute. The dad plays his flute, too, so the entire family knows that all is well.

From there, I climb the shepherd's hill to sit on my favorite bluff overlooking the town. On a higher hillside, just beyond that simple tin roof of its modern mosque, I see the letters G-Ü-Z-E-L-Y-U-R-T spelled out in white rocks. Güzelyurt means "beautiful land." While few visitors would consider it particularly beautiful, that's how the people who call it home see it. They'd live nowhere else. And for them, it truly is a *güzel yurt.*

I think about how there are countless Güzelyurts—including my hometown—proud communities scattered across every country on Earth. Each is humble, yet filled with rich traditions, hardworking people, loving families, and its own village-centric view of our world.

Rambling the ramparts
in Carcassonne, France

Across Europe

THE JOYS of travel are many-faceted, from eyewitness history to unusual cuisine and lovingly made handicrafts. And these joys transcend borders . . .

Knowing the history of a place gives you a context in which to better appreciate it. And a great way to learn that history is on location, from someone who lived it.

Some of the best cross-cultural experiences are edible. With affluence comes sophistication, but even as creativity in the kitchen has become trendy, the traditional, quirky cultural icons are still served. One thing offbeat food has in common across borders: It's *cucina povera*—the food of the poor. Tripe, tail, brain, and feet—wrap it in intestines, toss in some spice. Once fed to people who couldn't afford a decent meal, now it's served as a memorial to a generation that struggled to provide the foundation of today's affluence.

Throughout the Continent, I get inspired by artisans in action. While the shoemaker, the silversmith, and the engraver may no longer expect their children to follow them into their professions, Europeans still appreciate the one-of-a-kind crafts more than the mass-produced consumer goods. And masters still patiently apprentice craftspeople who take pride in making something with their own hands.

City walls have long been a part of the European story: walls to keep people out and walls to keep people in. But today, most Europeans aspire to build bridges rather than walls to help shape a more connected and peaceful future.

Wherever I venture, meeting people is key to good travels. If these slices of Europe sparkle, it's because of the people they feature.

Living History

ONE OF THE most rewarding aspects of my travels is connecting with people—old friends and guides who actually lived through the local history and make it real for me.

On one of my earliest trips to Europe when I was just 14 years old, a family friend in a dusty village on the border of Austria and Hungary introduced me to a sage old man. I remember thinking he was a caricature of a classic old Austrian, with a handlebar moustache, a wardrobe that looked like it was stolen from a museum, and an intricately-carved

As a boy (right), I met an eyewitness (left) to the start of World War I.

pipe. Spreading lard on rustic bread, he shared his eyewitness account of the assassination of Archduke Franz Ferdinand in 1914, which sparked the beginning of World War I. I leaned forward with awe as he described the motorcade, the archduke and his wife in an open car, the explosion of gunfire, and the hysteria that followed. That encounter, beside an onion-domed village church and in the shadow of the Iron Curtain, helped spark in me a lifelong interest in history.

Decades later in Prague, I walked with my Czech friend Honza down the path that he walked in 1989 with 100,000 of his countrymen, demanding liberation from their Soviet overlords. Stopping in front of a grand building, Honza said, "Night after night we assembled here, pulled out our keychains, and all jingled them at the President's window, saying, 'It's time to go home now.' Then one night we gathered . . . and he was gone. We had won our freedom." Hearing Honza tell this story as we walked that same route he did all those

My Czech friend Honza helped free his country.

years ago made me understand—and really feel—the jubilation of a small country winning its hard-fought independence.

As an advocate of freedom, I made a pilgrimage to the Gdańsk Shipyard where the Polish shipbuilders' union, Solidarity, was born, marking the beginning of the end of the USSR—and communist rule of half of Europe. Standing at the gate under a "Solidarity" banner hanging where the big letters "LENIN" once were, I met a retired worker who walked with us to the adjacent monument. As my guide translated, the man told us of the part he played in this pivotal fight for workers' rights. He explained that when Solidarity negotiated its way to victory in 1980, one of their conditions was that the Soviets let Poland erect a monument to workers killed a decade earlier while demonstrating for those same workers' rights. The government agreed, marking the first time a communist regime ever allowed a monument to be built to honor its own victims. Lech Wałęsa called it "a harpoon in the heart of the communists." The towering monument, with three crucified anchors on top, was completed just four months after the historic agreement was signed. It was designed, engineered, and built by shipyard workers—and our new friend was one of them. The trio of 140-foot-tall crosses still honors his martyred comrades today on Gdańsk's Solidarity Square. When you visit, there's a good chance that someone who helped build

This man at the Gdańsk Shipyard helped build this monument to martyred workers.

it—someone who stood up to tyranny and helped change history—will be there to tell the story.

In Northern Ireland, my guide Stephen made his country's struggles come alive for me when he took me to Belfast's Felons' Club. Stepping through a black metal security cage to reach the door, he whispered, "Membership here is limited to those who have spent at least a year and a day in a British prison for political crimes . . . but I think I can get you in." Once inside, I was spellbound, listening to heroic stories of Irish resistance while sharing a Guinness with a celebrity felon. His gift of gab gave me a deeper understanding of their struggles. The next day I walked along the green-trimmed gravesites of his prison-mates. Because of my time at the Felons' Club, I better understood what these people sacrificed—why they starved themselves to death for the cause of a united Ireland.

My uncle Thor lived through the Nazi occupation of Norway. He took me into Oslo's grand City Hall to show me the huge "Mural of the Occupation" and share his story of those dark days with the visual support of powerful art. Walking slowly, with a soft voice, he narrated the story scene by scene in the present tense—as if the mural told his personal experience as it was happening: "The German blitzkrieg

Oslo's *Mural of the Occupation* depicts Norway under Nazi control, then its joyful liberation.

overwhelms our country. Men head for the mountains to organize a resistance movement. Women huddle around the neighborhood well, traditionally where news is passed, while traitors listen in. While Germans bomb and occupy Norway, a family gathers in their living room. As a boy clenches his fist and a child holds our Norwegian flag—we love it so much—the Gestapo storms in. Columns lie on the ground, symbolizing how, by closing newspapers and the university, Germans did what they could to shut down our culture. Finally, years later, the war is over, prisoners are freed, and Norway celebrates its happiest day: May 17, 1945." Thor's voice cracked as he added, "Our first Constitution Day after five years under Nazi control." He finished by waving his arm wide and saying, "And today, each December, the Nobel Peace Prize is awarded in this grand hall."

We can go to places like Austria, the Czech Republic, Poland, Northern Ireland, or Norway to do some sightseeing yet learn nothing of their people's lives or their struggles. Or we can seek out opportunities to connect with people who can share eyewitness stories. Travel can—and should—change our perspectives and broaden our worldviews.

A Little Bone Envy

I WAS JUST 19, visiting Romania for the first time. A new friend took me inside his home, to the hearth, and introduced me to what was left of his great-grandfather. It was a skull . . . dry, hollow, and easy to hold in one hand. He told me it was a tradition in the mountains of Transylvania for families to remember long-dead loved ones with this honored spot above the fireplace. I remember feeling a little bone envy.

Saints' relics are often revered.

If you know where to look, you can find human bones on display in many corners of Europe. Later, on that same trip, I was in the Paris Catacombs. Deep under the city streets, I was all alone . . . surrounded by literally millions of bones—tibiae, fibulae, pelvises, and skulls, all stacked along miles of tunnels. I jumped at the opportunity to pick up what, once upon a time, was a human head. As what seemed like two centuries of dust tumbled off the skull, I looked at it . . . Hamlet-style. Just holding it was a thrill. I tried to get comfortable with it . . . to get to know it, in a way. I struggled with the temptation to stick it into my day bag. Imagine taking home a head dating back to Napoleonic times. What an incredible souvenir. But I just

Paris Catacombs

couldn't do it. The next year, I returned to those same catacombs, pumped up and determined this time to steal me a skull. It was a different scene. Skulls within easy reach of visitors were now wired together and signs warned that bags would be checked at the exit.

The Paris Catacombs show off the anonymous bones of six million permanent residents. In 1786, the French government decided to relieve congestion and improve sanitary conditions by emptying the city cemeteries, which had traditionally surrounded churches. They established an official ossuary in an abandoned limestone quarry. With miles of underground tunnels, it was the perfect location. For decades, the priests of Paris led ceremonial processions of black-veiled, bone-laden carts into the quarries, where the bones were stacked into piles five feet high and up to 80 feet deep, behind neat walls of skull-studded tibiae. Each transfer was completed with the placement of a plaque indicating the church and district from which that stack of bones came and the date they arrived.

Today, you can descend a long spiral staircase into this bony underworld (ignoring the sign that announces: "Halt, this is the empire of the dead") and follow a one-mile subterranean public walk. Along the way, plaques encourage you to reflect upon your destiny: "Happy is he who is forever faced with the hour of his death and prepares himself for the end every day." Emerging far from where you entered with white limestone-covered toes is a dead giveaway you've been underground, gawking at bones.

Capuchin Crypt in Rome

While I eventually outgrew my desire to steal a skull, in later years, as a tour guide, I've discovered I'm not the only one intrigued by human bones. If bones are on your bucket list, you've got plenty of options. Throughout Europe, Capuchin monks

Chapel in Kutná Hora, Czech Republic

offer a different bone-venture. The Capuchins made a habit of hanging their dead brothers up to dry and then opening their skeleton-filled crypts to the public. Their mission: to remind us that in a relatively short period of time, we'll be dead, too—so give some thought to mortality and how we might be spending eternity.

In the Capuchin Crypt in Rome, the bones of 4,000 monks who died between 1528 and 1870 are lined up for the delight—or disgust—of always wide-eyed visitors. A plaque shares their monastic message: "We were what you are . . . you will become what we are now."

The Capuchins of Palermo, Sicily, offer an experience skull and shoulders above the rest. Their crypt is a subterranean gallery filled with 8,000 "bodies without souls," howling silently at their mortality. For centuries, people would thoughtfully choose their niche before they died, and even linger there, getting to know their macabre neighborhood. After death, dressed in their Sunday best, their body (sans soul) would be hung up to dry.

In Kutná Hora, in the Czech Republic, monks take bone decor to an unrivaled extreme. Their ossuary is decorated with the bones of 40,000 people, many of them plague victims. The monks who stacked these bones 400 years ago wanted viewers to remember that the earthly church is a community of both the living and the dead. Later bone-stackers were more into design than theology—creating, for instance, a chandelier made with every bone in the human body.

In Europe, seekers of the macabre can get their fill of human skeletons. And in doing so, they learn that many of these bones—even long after death—still have something to say.

Europe's Quirky Taste Treats

MY PALATE has come a long way from my early "Europe through the gutter" days, back when my travel diet consisted of cheap baguettes spread with peanut butter and strawberry jam packed from home. Now one of my favorite parts of travel is sampling local specialties. And I do it with abandon. From pigs' ears in Spain to horsemeat in France and spicy sheep intestines in Turkey, I make it a point to try dishes that make a menu unique—no matter how unappetizing they sound. Think of it as sightseeing for your palate.

How much you enjoy the experience depends on your attitude. "Weird" is subjective. Countries with a seafaring heritage, like the Dutch, embrace herring as a vitamin-rich food. Pickled herring is considered a classic. Having tasted this delicacy, I can say it's something you won't soon forget (no matter how hard you try).

I still remember the first time I tried pickled herring in the town of Haarlem. It was on market day at a herring stand—the Dutch version of a hot-dog stand—with a big sign that advertised *"lecker en gezond"* (delicious and healthy). The fish looked more like bait than lunch. Sensing my hesitation, Jos, the friendly herring vendor, demonstrated how to eat it. "I give you the herring Rotterdam-style. You eat it like this," he said, miming swallowing a sword. "If I chop it up and give you these," he said, pointing to the toothpicks "this is Amsterdam-style." After my first bite, the only polite comment I could muster was, "It's salty." But the taste grew on me. As I wandered through the market, taking Amsterdam-style bites of my Rotterdam-style herring, I felt a

Herring, Amsterdam-style

fishy kinship with the Dutch. As I passed his herring stand again a few minutes later, Jos hollered, *"Lecker?"* I responded, *"En gezond!"*

Bull genitalia for sale

Most Scandinavian nations have one seafood dish that, while inedible to many people, is still cherished with a perverse but patriotic sentimentality. In Norway that's *lutefisk*—dried cod marinated for days in lye and water. My theory is that it's still served today to remind young Norwegians of their ancestors' suffering.

Local specialties often come from a challenging history and then become tradition. Roman cooking didn't originate in the kitchens of emperors or popes, but from the *cucina povera*—the home-cooking of the poor, common people. This may explain the Romans' fondness for meats the wealthy didn't bother eating. Known as the *quinto quarto* (fifth quarter), these were pieces like tripe, tails, brains, and pigs' feet.

Eating barnacles

Scotland's national dish, haggis, also began as peasant food. Unwilling to let any part of a sheep go to waste, cooks would create a hearty meal by boiling scraps of heart, liver, and lungs with herbs in stomach lining. The trick to appreciating such dishes is to think of how they taste, not what they're made of. Just like with caviar, hot dogs . . . or foie gras.

Foie gras is one of France's most expensive indulgences. Because it's made from fattening the livers of geese through force-feeding, it has attracted controversy. The dish is most popular in the Dordogne region, where ages ago, locals caught geese on their migration—and found the goose livers were enlarged for the long journey (like traveling with a topped-off gas tank). And you know those French: Mix those innards into the cuisine and create a new taste treat.

Fish with a smile in Portugal

Speaking of innards, Turks are serious about their *kokoreç:* chopped-up sheep intestines, often served on a sandwich as fast food. Several years ago, a rumor flew through the streets that stringent new European Union regulations would outlaw the beloved dish. Before the story was debunked, many Turks did some soul-searching and decided that if they had to choose, they'd gladly pass up EU membership for their *kokoreç.*

Wherever I go, I find the food that inspires such nationalism is worth a try. Eating these unusual dishes—from Iberia's *percebes* (barnacles) to Venice's *seppia* (squid served in its own ink) to Norway's *geitost* (goat cheese that resembles earwax)—not only helps me feel like a temporary local, but also gets me treated like one.

Haggis in Scotland

Artisan Europe

WHEN YOU'VE TRAVELED in Europe as long as I have, you experience changes big and small. And more and more, I notice traditional, local businesses making way for cookie-cutter chains and synthetic conformity. In historic city centers, as rents go up, longtime residents, families, and craftspeople are pushed out. Small hotels, one-of-a-kind shops, and individual craftspeople simply don't have the scale to compete with the big guys.

In Florence, the end of rent control made costs spike immediately, driving artisans and shops catering to locals out of business—to be replaced by upscale boutiques and trendy eateries. The same thing happened in Barcelona's Gothic Quarter. As landlords evicted long-term renters to make more money off short-term Airbnb rentals, mom-and-pop shops lost their traditional clientele and went out of business. In Istanbul, the city wants to move the iconic gold-and-silver workshops from the Grand Bazaar to a place outside the city center, while "Made in Taiwan" gift shops are able to pay higher rents and take their place, changing the character of the market.

Craftsmen lament that the next generation, drawn to the energy

Artist in Deruta, Italy

Craftsman at Corfe Castle, England

of big cities and lured by the opportunities of big corporations, won't be there to carry on the traditions. The artists who craft handmade guitars in Madrid, the family winemakers of Burgundy, the fishermen who sell shrimp on the Oslo harborfront . . . these have all been fixtures in my lifetime of European travel. What will become of these rich facets of local culture if the younger generation opts out? Of course, I can't blame the children of artisans for jumping into the modern rat race; I'm not an old-school piano technician like my father. But it's worth considering how the future will look when economic scale and efficiency trump artisan values.

It's a real joy when I stumble upon true artisans who are committed to doing things the traditional way, by hand—and communities that understand the importance of keeping them in business. I urge travelers to seek out and support artisan experiences while traveling—before it's too late.

Printmaker in Rothenburg

In Rothenburg, Germany, I visited with Peter Leyrer, a printmaker who proudly showed me his etchings. He makes his prints using the copper-plate technique, just as Albrecht Dürer did 500 years ago. Peter prints the black-and-white etchings, paints them with watercol-

Coppersmith in Montepulciano

ors, and sells them in his shop. Peter is getting older and will soon retire. He told me that with no one to take over for him, his 3,000 copper plates will likely end up in a museum. One of his etchings hangs in my office.

In the Tuscan hill town of Montepulciano, my friend Cesare is a proud coppersmith with a spirit as strong as the oak-tree root upon which his grandfather's anvil sits. For Cesare, every day is show-and-tell, as steady streams of travelers drop by to see him at work, fashioning special ornaments for the town cathedral and pounding out fine cookware.

In nearby Orvieto, Federico Badia is a young cobbler who's passionate about preserving the art of traditional shoemaking. After apprenticing at a leather shop in Rome, he set up his own studio, where he patiently crafts fine leather shoes for an appreciative clientele. Federico says that "Made in Italy" doesn't apply to mass-produced factory shoes—it's a label that rightly belongs only to the fine products handcrafted by artisans like him.

Back in Istanbul's

Silversmith in Istanbul

Potter in Kraków, Poland

Grand Bazaar, Dikran is a silversmith who uses hand tools to create finely designed, one-of-a-kind pieces. For a decade, he worked as an unpaid apprentice, studying under a master until he himself became one. In the past, a volunteer apprentice had to work hard to persuade a master to accept him. Today, it's a struggle to get young people to enter a field in which training takes years and incomes are limited.

Guiding a tour group through eastern Turkey, I once dropped in on a craftsman who was famous for his wood carving. We gathered around his table to watch him work, appreciating the pride he took in his art. Suddenly, he stopped, held his chisel high into the sky and declared, "A man and his chisel—the greatest factory on Earth!"

I don't have the answers on how to sustain Europe's age-old traditions, but I'm inspired whenever I meet the artisans who lovingly carry treasured and endangered crafts into the future. And it always feels right to buy a piece of their work.

Europe Tears Down Walls— and Builds Bridges

EUROPE HAS BUILT more than its share of walls. From Hadrian's Wall (constructed by the ancient Romans to defend the northern boundary of Britannia) to the Maginot Line (built by the French in the 1930s to keep out the Germans), these walls were symbols not of strength, but of mistrust and insecurity. They were necessary back then. But the promising news in our age has been a European society that is advancing—dismantling walls so that it can move forward. With the fall of the Iron Curtain and the rise of the European Union, walls and border checks have been replaced by free trade, free travel, and the Erasmus Program—a well-funded government initiative that subsidizes students and teachers working and learning in neighboring countries. Europe's key to a wall-free world: interdependent economies and lots of travel, which encourages empathy.

At one point or another, most of Europe's great cities—Paris, London, Rome, Florence, Milan, Barcelona, Vienna—were contained within walls, constructed during ancient and medieval times to defend against invaders. Many of these walls were torn down long ago as cities expanded beyond their historic centers and land was opened up for grand circular boulevards. Some intact walls have been preserved in places like Dubrovnik, Croatia; Rothenburg, Germany; York, England; Lucca, Italy; and Carcassonne, France. In each case, these walls have become people-friendly, park-like spaces where people stroll, gather, and enjoy the view.

Wall tower at Oberwesel, on the Rhine

Some walls seem to survive to take us back in time. One of my favorites, Hadrian's Wall, is the remains of the fortification the Romans built nearly 2,000 years ago in Britain. Now in ruins, this great stone wall once stretched 73 miles from coast to coast across the narrowest part of northern England, where Britannia ended and the barbarian land

Walled town of Carcassonne, France

that would someday be Scotland began. More than just a wall, it was a cleverly designed military rampart manned by 20,000 troops. At every mile there was a small fort guarding a gate. Imagine the bleakness of being a young Roman soldier stationed here 18 centuries ago. Today, two of these Hadrian Wall forts have been turned into museums, where visitors can see the ruins up close, view ancient artifacts, and get a sense of life in the distant past of a desolate corner of the Roman Empire.

Hadrian's Wall is much-loved by hikers, who follow the wall as it

Hadrian's Wall, the ancient Roman border of Britannia

meanders up and down the natural contours of the land. For years, I never ventured beyond the museums and car-park viewpoints. But finally, I grabbed a sunny late afternoon to actually hike the wall. Scrambling along Roman ruins, all alone with the wind and the sheep, I took a moment to simply absorb the setting. I surveyed vast expanses from a rocky crag that seemed to rip across the island like some horrific geological violence, frozen in mid-action.

Some walls have become museums and memorials, designed to inspire us to relate to our neighbors in ways that make them obsolete. The most poignant wall experiences focus on Europe's recent past. Thankfully, walls that once stood for fear and intolerance now symbolize peace and progress.

During the Troubles, the 30-year conflict that wracked Northern Ireland, so-called "peace walls" went up in Belfast to separate its sectarian communities: Catholics, in favor of a united Ireland, and Protestants, in favor of staying in the United Kingdom. Today, instead of separating its warring tribes, these walls are a tourist attraction. Visitors from around the world decorate the walls with colorful messages of hope and thanksgiving that the bombs and killing that came with the Troubles are no more.

Writing on the Peace Wall

Belfast Peace Wall mural

Europe's most famous wall is the Berlin Wall, designed not to defend against invaders but to keep residents from escaping. Built in 1961, this 96-mile-long barrier encircled West Berlin, making it an island of free-

Free speech at the Berlin Wall

dom in communist East Germany. When the wall fell on November 9, 1989, Europe enjoyed its happiest day since the end of World War II. In the euphoria that followed, "wall peckers" giddily chipped the Berlin Wall to smithereens. A surviving stretch of the wall has been preserved as a memorial to the victims of the Cold War. It's a long, narrow park stretching from a museum and viewing tower. What was once the notorious "death strip," with a deadly obstacle course of barbed wire and tire-spike strips, is now dotted with personal memorials and informational displays. That no-man's-land between East and West is now an everyman's land, famous for hosting the world's biggest karaoke party. And the long-hated wall has become a concrete canvas for graffiti artists— a people's gallery celebrating freedom.

Europe's walls were built for a reason. But, as travelers learn, the true success of a society lies in finding a way beyond walls. If you look at European currency, you notice that bills feature bridges, not walls. And so do the dreams of great leaders.

Conclusion

The Essence of Good Travel: Connecting with People

ON THE IRISH island of Inishmore, I stayed at a farmhouse B&B. At breakfast, I told the farmer of my plans to visit the island's main sight, Dun Aengus. It's an Iron Age fortress that hangs spectacularly on the edge of a cliff above the ocean. He nodded, saying, "The fort is so popular with visitors that we plan to build another 2,000-year-old fort next year."

He excused himself to do some farm chores and I asked to join him. Soon, we were working in tandem, putting out the hay. I asked about the weather and he said, "We wouldn't be putting out the hay if the weather wasn't going to be good." Pointing out that there were no gates on the stone fences that divided his land, he showed me how, when the sheep needed to pass, he'd simply unstack the rocks and then stack them back up. It worked for his father and it works for him.

The essence of good travel is connecting with people. If I'm leading a tour or writing a guidebook, the mark of a job well done is how well I connect people with people. If I'm making a TV show and it doesn't have a local voice, the show will be flat. When I'm enjoying a European vacation, my journal is more interesting when it includes stories of people I meet. And yes, in reading through this book, the essays I like the best are the ones enriched by connections with people.

Developing a knack for sparking such experiences is our challenge as good travelers. I like to take it a step further—to be a keen observer,

able to connect experiential dots that may seem random by putting them into cultural and historic context . . . and then to learn from them. As a travel writer, that's my challenge. And that's my mission, whether it's explaining the rationale behind the Dutch tolerance of marijuana, or celebrating the refreshing transparency of Berlin's glass dome over its parliament.

While memories of palaces toured and castles climbed fade into a jumble, it's the people, experiences, and cultural connections that stay vivid for decades . . .

In a pub in the Czech town of Olomouc, egged on by a local friend, I ordered the country's infamous stinky cheese, listed on the menu as the "Guttery Breath of the Knight of Lostice." It was served with a lid, mints, and the offer of a toothbrush. (The fun-loving menu noted they only have one toothbrush, so please leave it.)

At a bar in Brussels, I met Belgians who complained about their Lowland neighbors: "The Dutch have the worst beer, Heineken—but sell it all over the world. We Belgians make far better beer, and it is barely exported. Those Dutch are clever business people—they can sell anything."

In Italy, people from Siena hold a medieval grudge against the people of Florence, who defeated them centuries ago. Walking with my friend in Siena, I barely missed a dog mess. In a disgusted voice, he playfully showed his Sienese pride saying, "Those Florentines are everywhere these days."

One time in Austria, I lingered in a tiny village church. It was as quiet as a tomb. Suddenly the dozen or so visitors around me burst into a rich, Slavic hymn filling the sanctuary with life. They were a folk group from Slovakia whose director whispered to me, "We can't be in a church without singing."

Each of these encounters offers new insights into these places and the people who call them home. Gathering experiences like these into this collection of essays, I realize the most memorable travel connections aren't accidents. You create them consciously by being a free-spirited extrovert. Start conversations and then let serendipity lead you astray. (Who knows? You may find yourself drinking homemade *limoncello* with a Franciscan friar in his abbey overlooking the Italian Riviera.) Let surprises waylay your careful plans.

While some people count the countries they've visited, marking them off on a checklist, that number means nothing to me. Count instead the friends you've made while far from home. Making connections brings us closer together. Packing that attitude, you'll realize the world is a welcoming place . . . a place filled with joy, love, and wonderful people.

Filming on the Dalmatian Coast in Croatia

Rick Steves' TV Clips

Each essay listed below is featured in a short video clip, excerpted from my public television show, *Rick Steves' Europe*. To view the clips, go to my free Classroom Europe website (classroom.ricksteves.com), type the clip number (or keyword) into the search bar, then enjoy a little video clip about that particular slice of Europe. Each clip is excerpted from a 30-minute episode that you can stream for free any time via the video section at ricksteves.com, giving you hours of relevant video material and adding context and dimension to the essays in this book and to your travel dreams. Enjoy!

In the French Alps

Glencoe, Scotland

BRITAIN AND IRELAND

The Matterhorn, Switzerland   Hinterhornalm, Austria

GERMANY

MUNICH: WHERE THIRST IS WORSE THAN HOMESICKNESS 162

Clip: S109.9 (keyword: oktoberfest)
Title: Europe's Festivals: Munich's Oktoberfest

BATTLEGROUND BACHARACH 165

Clip: 212.1 (keyword: bacharach)
Title: Germany's Rhine River and Castles

THREE CASTLES: ELTZ, RHEINFELS, AND NEUSCHWANSTEIN 170

Clip: 212.2 (keyword: eltz)
Title: Germany's Mosel River, Burg Eltz, and Feudalism

ROTHENBURG'S NIGHT WATCHMAN 177

Clip: 212.3 (keyword: rothenburg)
Title: Germany's Medieval Walled Town of Rothenburg

GHOSTS IN BERLIN 184

Clip: 812.4 (keyword: berlin cold)
Title: Berlin and the Cold War: Divided, Then United

Ravenna, Italy   Vernazza, Italy

Agrigento, Sicily   Sognefjord, Norway

Scandinavia and the Baltics

Eastern Europe

Greece and Turkey

Start your trip at

Our website enhances this book and turns

Explore Europe

At ricksteves.com you can browse through thousands of articles, videos, photos and radio interviews, plus find a wealth of money-saving travel tips for planning your dream trip. And with our mobile-friendly website, you can easily access all this great travel information anywhere you go.

TV Shows

Preview the places you'll visit by watching entire half-hour episodes of *Rick Steves' Europe* (choose from all 100 shows) on-demand, for free.

ricksteves.com

your travel dreams into affordable reality

Radio Interviews

Enjoy ready access to Rick's vast library of radio interviews covering travel tips and cultural insights that relate specifically to your Europe travel plans.

Travel Forums

Learn, ask, share! Our online community of savvy travelers is a great resource for first-time travelers to Europe, as well as seasoned pros.

Travel News

Subscribe to our free Travel News e-newsletter, and get monthly updates from Rick on what's happening in Europe.

Classroom Europe

Check out our free resource for educators with 400+ short video clips from the *Rick Steves' Europe* TV show.

Audio Europe™

Rick's Free Travel App

Get your FREE Rick Steves Audio Europe™ app to enjoy...

- Dozens of self-guided tours of Europe's top museums, sights and historic walks
- Hundreds of tracks filled with cultural insights and sightseeing tips from Rick's radio interviews
- All organized into handy geographic playlists
- For Apple and Android

With Rick whispering in your ear, Europe gets even better.

Find out more at ricksteves.com

Pack Light and Right

Gear up for your next adventure at ricksteves.com

Light Luggage

Pack light and right with Rick Steves' affordable, custom-designed rolling carry-on bags, backpacks, day packs and shoulder bags.

Accessories

From packing cubes to moneybelts and beyond, Rick has personally selected the travel goodies that will help your trip go smoother.

Rick Steves has

Experience maximum Europe

Save time and energy

My guidebooks are toolkits for independent travelers. But for all they deliver, it's still up to you to devote the time and energy it takes to manage the preparation and logistics that are essential for a happy trip. If that's a hassle, there's a solution.

Rick Steves Tours

A Rick Steves tour takes you to Europe's most interesting places with great guides and

great tours, too!

with minimum stress

small groups of 28 or less. We follow Rick's favorite itineraries, ride in comfy buses, stay in family-run hotels, and bring you intimately close to the Europe you've traveled so far to see. Most importantly, we take away the logistical headaches so you can focus on the fun.

Join the fun

This year we'll take 33,000 free-spirited travelers—nearly half of them repeat customers—along with us on 50 different itineraries, from Athens to Istanbul. Is a Rick Steves tour the right fit for your travel dreams?

Find out at ricksteves.com, where you can also request Rick's latest tour catalog. Europe is best experienced with happy travel partners. We hope you can join us.

See our itineraries at ricksteves.com